% *THE ADVENTURES OF*
      THE WOMAN HOMESTEADER

WOMEN IN THE WEST
A Series

SUSANNE K. GEORGE

THE *Adventures of*
The Woman
Homesteader
The Life and Letters of
Elinore Pruitt Stewart

University of Nebraska Press

Lincoln and London

© 1992 by the University of Nebraska Press
Previously unpublished letters and manuscripts by Elinore
    Pruitt Stewart © 1992 by the Elinore Pruitt Stewart
    estate
Photographs © 1992 by the Elinore Pruitt Stewart estate
    unless otherwise credited
Manufactured in the United States of America
The paper in this book meets the minimum requirements of
    American National Standard for Information Sciences—
    Permanence of Paper for Printed Library Materials,
    ANSI Z39.48–1984.
Library of Congress Cataloging-in-Publication Data
    Stewart, Elinore Pruitt, 1878–
    The adventures of the woman homesteader: the life and
    letters of Elinore Pruitt Stewart / [edited by] Susanne K.
    George.
    p.   cm. — (Women in the West)
    Includes bibliographical references and index.
    ISBN 0-8032-2141-X
    1. Stewart, Elinore Pruitt, 1878–   —Correspondence.
    2. Women pioneers—Wyoming—Correspondence.
    3. Pioneers—Wyoming—Correspondence.
    4. Wyoming—Biography.   I. George, Susanne K.
    (Susanne Kathryn), 1947–   .   II. Title.   III. Series.
    F761.S77   1992
    987.7′03′092—dc20   92-1206
    CIP

To Fran Kaye,
my mentor, my friend
and for
the family of
Elinore Pruitt Stewart

❧ CONTENTS

❧ ILLUSTRATIONS

❧ PREFACE

From 1909 until 1933, Elinore Pruitt Stewart shared her daily life as a woman homesteader in Wyoming with her friends and the world through her letters. Although her writings describe the common events experienced by many women of her time, her personal window on the world commanded a universal view. Her published works, especially *Letters of a Woman Homesteader* (1914) and *Letters on an Elk Hunt by a Woman Homesteader* (1915), as well as her unpublished stories, letters, and journals, reveal historical perspectives on the settling of the West. They also present, with imaginative insight and vulnerability, a wider understanding of the feminine role in the homesteading experience and add to the American literary canon. Stewart's life, an odyssey northward through the plains from White Bead, Indian Territory, to Burntfork, Wyoming, symbolizes the independence, strength, and spirit of our pioneer foremothers.

I have compiled this collection of unpublished or little-known writings of Stewart from the personal collections of her children Clyde Stewart, Jr., and Jerrine Wire, from the original *Atlantic Monthly* articles, and from *Folk-Say IV: The Land Is Ours,* published by the University of Oklahoma Press. Although more letters and stories exist than those I have chosen to present in this work, this collection comprises about 90 percent of her known writings. Stewart mentioned other correspondents in her letters, but although I have queried archivists of historical societies, libraries, and universities in numerous states, I have discovered no more letters. However, I am certain that additional letters lie forgotten in boxes stored in attics and basements across America.

The editing of any author's unpublished works is an exciting and gratifying experience, yet problems particular to each writer generally arise. The first puzzle in my work with the unpublished letters and stories of Elinore Pruitt Stewart involved arranging the materials in chronological order. Although she religiously noted the month and day on her letters, Stewart seldom included the year. From postmarked envelopes, sometimes separated from the letter that should have been inside, from notations by Stewart's children on some of the letters themselves, and from references to national and personal events, I have, to the best of my ability, assigned a year to most of the letters.

Another problem concerned paragraphing, for Stewart seldom signaled breaks in her writing, and many letters and stories consist of one long paragraph. Always short of paper, she evidently did not want to waste space. When she did begin a new paragraph, she did not indent it but simply started a new line. If the last sentence of a paragraph happened to end in the middle of the line, that was the only clue that a new paragraph would follow. For ease of reading, I have broken the selections into paragraphs.

I have transcribed Stewart's previously unpublished writings as they appear in her existing manuscripts and typescripts, most in her large handwriting, some in her own careful typing. Errors in punctuation, characteristic misspellings, grammatical inconsistencies, and underlining for emphasis (rendered here as italics) are all intact except for about a half-dozen instances where I silently added a period or capital letter to assist the reader. (However, the use of italics for the greeting and signature in the letters is a design element introduced in this edition. Those features were not underlined in the original letters.) Although I rarely had trouble deciphering her neat script, I occasionally could not tell whether Stewart intended a punctuation mark to be a period, comma, or dash or a word to be capitalized or left in the lower case. Where I was uncertain about a word or phrase, I have added a question mark in brackets [?], and if I could not tell a comma from a period, I used my best judgment. A few of the letters, unfortunately, exist only in typed or handwritten transcriptions in which some editorial changes had already been made. All of the letters are printed in full, except those few from which pages are missing.

Next came the decision of how to arrange the primary and secondary materials. Although I did extensive archival research to discover and verify information about Stewart, most of my inquiries uncovered few details because of the lack of uniform record keeping in the Indian Territory and the newly organized states. Also, because Stewart was a very private person and lived in a remote corner of the West, no contemporary interviews or published biographical information exists except what she supplied to her editors. Discovering that Stewart—who adamantly believed that the past was past—occasionally led the public astray, I was faced with the task of sorting out the facts of her life from the image of "The Woman Homesteader" that she wished to present to the world. Thus, much of my biographical information necessarily came from my interviews with Stewart's three surviving children: Clyde Stewart, Jr., Robert Stewart, and Jerrine Wire. By comparing these three oral tape-recorded versions of their mother's life, by correlating these interviews with the written documents I did discover, and by reading, sometimes between the lines, Stewart's published and unpublished letters and stories, I was able to produce what I believe to be a consistent and accurate narrative. I do not quote my sources directly or document every date and activity, since that would necessitate documenting nearly every line and especially since the oral interviews, conducted separately, often supported one another. I have, however, provided a complete bibliography of my sources, both primary and secondary.

Although letters are traditionally considered historical documents, Stewart's writings blur the boundaries of history and fiction. As a literary critic, I have chosen to present Stewart's life and writings as "adventure," interweaving the biographical materials with Stewart's letters and stories in chronological order and enabling Stewart to tell as much of her life as possible, in the way that she told it in her two published collections of letters, rather than employing the traditional historical approach of separating the primary and secondary materials. How Stewart interpreted her life, what she chose to tell, and what the facts of her life reveal present an interesting contrast, for her unfaltering optimism concealed a life of poverty, illness, and hard work. I hope that the presentation of her life and writings in this book will lead to the discovery of more letters and encourage further interest in this important American pioneer.

Many people and institutions have supported me in my research and writing. During the initial stages of my research, Thomas Flack, my father, funded my travel to Washington, where I met Clyde Stewart, Jr., and first studied many of his mother's unpublished writings. Without my father's financial and emotional support, this book might have remained simply a paper for a plains literature course. In the following year, 1986, the University of Nebraska–Lincoln awarded me a Maude Hammond Fling Fellowship for research travel. This enabled me to interview Robert Stewart and Jerrine Wire, Elinore Pruitt Stewart's other surviving children, in their homes in New Jersey and Pennsylvania, thus increasing my knowledge of the Stewart family and expanding my holdings of copies of unpublished material. However, it was the Presidential Fellowship awarded me by the University of Nebraska–Lincoln for the 1987 term that gave the greatest impetus to my work, for I was able to take time off from my teaching position at Kearney State College (now the University of Nebraska at Kearney) and concentrate my energies on producing this book.

I am also indebted to many members of the English faculty at the University of Nebraska–Lincoln: Frederick Link, Barbara DiBernard, Robert Narveson, and Thomas Carr. Helen Stauffer, Don Welch, Harlan Hoffman, and Charles Peek, my colleagues at the University of Nebraska at Kearney, also supported and encouraged me. It is to Frances Kaye, though, my adviser and the chair of my graduate committee at the University of Nebraska–Lincoln, that I am most indebted. She introduced me to the published letters and stories of Elinore Pruitt Stewart, intelligently guided me in my research and writing, and watched over me with a wise and kindly eye.

I wrote literally hundreds of letters to historical and genealogical societies, county clerks, public and university libraries and archives, newspapers, and government agencies in Oklahoma, Missouri, Arkansas, Kansas, Colorado, Wyoming, Massachusetts, and Ohio to discover and verify information about Stewart's life and acquaintances. Although many were unable to find the requested information, all attempted and all responded, suggesting alternative sources and encouraging me in my labors. I appreciate their time and concern.

My family and friends too deserve recognition. My son, Chad Lindau, who accompanied me in my travel, and my daughter, Tami Lindau, who insisted I purchase a computer and who helped invaluably with typing, not only came to my aid but also understood why dinner sometimes was not ready. My aunt, Ruth Flack, kept in constant touch and was the first outside reader to heartily, though perhaps not without prejudice, endorse my manuscript. And special thanks go to my husband, Ken George, who gave me moral support, sound editing advice, and roses.

I owe my deepest gratitude to the children of Elinore Stewart, who opened their homes, their hearts, and their family treasures to me. I especially want to thank Clyde Stewart, Jr., whose wide-ranging experience, patient explanations, and careful copyreading have added accuracy and color to my text. I shared in their grief at the passing of Mrs. Clyde (Jeanette) Stewart, Jr., Jerrine Wire, and Robert Stewart, for when they made me a part of their lives, they became a part of mine.

❧ THE ADVENTURES OF
THE WOMAN HOMESTEADER

Childhood to Homesteading (1876–1916)

๙ According to Oklahoma folklore, a Caddo woman named White Bead
moved her family west of Pauls Valley in Indian Territory to escape a
smallpox epidemic, and the camp site became known as White Bead Hill.
At this settlement, in this legend-filled land of ruddy hills and lush valleys,
a child was born whose life would echo that of this courageous Native
American woman.[1]

Elinore Pruitt, the oldest of nine children of Josephine Elizabeth Courtney Pruitt, was born in White Bead Hill in the Chickasaw Nation, Indian
Territory, on June 3, 1876. Josephine was the daughter of Mary Ann and
Henry Courtney, who lived in the town of Davis, in the Arbuckle Mountains in what is now south-central Oklahoma. Some family accounts indi-
cate that Mary Ann had arrived in the region before 1840, and a Chickasaw
Nation census indicates that she may have been one-half Chickasaw.

Josephine had married a man by the name of Pruitt, whose first name is
unknown. He was the father of Elinore and was later killed on the Mexican
border while serving in the military. Then, in the late 1870s, Josephine
married her first husband's brother, Thomas Isaac Pruitt. At one time, Tom
Pruitt had procured horses, mules, and beef for Fort Arbuckle, nine miles
west of Davis, but the fort had been abandoned in 1870. After his marriage
to Josephine, Tom worked as a millwright. Elinore's mother bore eight
children to Tom Pruitt: Laura, Maggie, Lucius, Joseph, Eliza Josephine,
Thomas, Susie, and a baby who died shortly after birth.

1. This information was compiled from Brumley and Manning, "Whitebead
School Remembered," 1, 3A, and from Kathleen K. Smyers, granddaughter of W. G.
Kimberlin, cofounder of the Pierce Institute.

Little is known about Elinore's early years except that the family lived in poverty and she did not even have a pair of shoes until she was six years old. According to Elinore's version, her formal education was brief, ending abruptly when her teacher was hung from a sycamore tree outside the schoolhouse for stealing a horse. As a result, she had to teach herself to read and write from scraps of paper she found, questioning the local storekeeper about letters, words, and numbers.

Most likely, the school that Elinore had attended was Pierce Institute, located south of the White Bead cemetery, the only school in the Chickasaw Nation from 1879 to 1889. The institute was established by W. G. Kimberlin, a rancher, and Reverend John C. Powell, a circuit minister of Pauls Valley and superintendent of the school. Approximately five teachers taught classes ranging from elementary English and math to junior-college-level Greek, Latin, Hebrew, trigonometry, public speaking, and composition. The number of white and Native American students who attended the institute peaked at two hundred. By 1887, enrollment was rapidly decreasing because the Santa Fe railroad had bypassed the community. In that year, S. H. Davis built one of the first stores on the nearby shores of the Washita River. Perhaps Davis was the kindly storekeeper who helped Elinore with her reading.[2]

On January 10, 1893, soon after Josephine's ninth child was born, Elinore's mother died at the age of thirty-five from heart problems compounded by birth complications. She was buried in Maysville, a town some thirty miles from Davis. The baby girl, listed in the family Bible as Baby Bye, died one week later. The next year, Pruitt was killed in an accident at work, but not before he had found husbands for Laura, age thirteen, and Maggie, twelve. Maggie married a man whose children were older than she. Elinore became, at age eighteen, responsible for Lucius, ten, Joseph, eight, Josephine, six, Tom, four, and the baby, Susie, two. In *Letters of a Woman Homesteader,* Elinore explained to Mrs. Coney: "I don't know that I ever told you, but my parents died within a year of each other and left six of us to shift for ourselves. Our people offered to take one here and there among them until we should all have a place, but we refused to be raised on the halves and so arranged to stay at Grandmother's and keep together" (15–16).

---

2. Powell, *Whitebead Church History,* describes Pierce Institute, 5–7, and Brown, *Murray County,* discusses S. H. Davis, 67. The hanging of the schoolteacher has not been documented.

The children lived with their grandmother, the blind and twice-wid-owed Mary Ann Courtney, in Davis until at least 1900, according to the Chickasaw Nation census of that year. However, Elinore later noted that dissension among relatives forced her and her brothers and sisters to pack up and try to make it on their own.

Elinore, then about age twenty-five, and her brothers and sisters found jobs in Indian Territory working for the railroad, possibly the Santa Fe. The Gulf, Colorado, and Santa Fe Railroad had met the southbound Atchinson, Topeka, and Santa Fe division in Purcell in 1887. Beginning in 1900, the Frisco Railroad began laying 198 miles of tracks in future Murray County, and between 1901 and 1902, the Santa Fe Company initiated a great deal of new construction, building a bridge spanning the Washita River and extending branch lines west to Lindsay by way of White Bead.[3]

With Josephine's help, Elinore washed for the railroad crew while the boys drove the mules that pulled the scrapers used in building up the road-bed. Because the younger boys weren't big enough to harness the mules themselves, the corral boss would throw the heavy leather on the animals' backs, and the boys would buckle and hook up the equipment. At night, the children, exhausted after putting in a full day of adult manual labor, slept on the ground in an old commissary tent. Elinore tried to take care of Susie for about a year but could not adequately care for her. Since all Elinore had to feed the eight-year-old was coffee and bread, Susie had to be sent back to her grandmother's.

The story of Connie Willis in Elinore's second book, *Letters on an Elk Hunt,* seems much like Elinore's own story: "She said her name was Connie Willis, that she was the only one of her 'ma's first man's' children; but ma married again after pa died and there were a lot of the second batch. When the mother died she left a baby only a few hours old. As Connie was older than the older children she took charge of the household and of the tiny little baby" (3).

Connie Willis, as Elinore relates in the story, had been "saving up for a tombstone for ma for twelve years" (5). Unable to reach that goal, she had decided to spend all of her money to dress her youngest sister in beautiful finery. Perhaps Elinore experienced the same longing to mark her own mother's grave and saved for the same extravagances for Susie.

Where and for how long Elinore worked for the railroad is unknown.

3. From "One Hundred Years of History," 1, and Brown, *Murray County,* v.

Joseph, when he was fourteen, died from an accidental gunshot wound while at his grandmother's house. The other boys left, Lucius working as a farm laborer and Tom fleeing to the West because he thought he had killed a man in a fight.[4] Around 1902, Elinore married Harry Cramer Rupert, and they filed on a homestead in Indian Territory. Elinore would have been about twenty-six at the time of their marriage and Rupert about forty-eight. According to *Homesteader,* Elinore had met Harry at her Grandmother Courtney's home:

> Well, we had no money to hire men to do our work, so had to learn to do it ourselves. Consequently I learned to do many things which girls more fortunately situated don't even know have to be done. Among the things I learned to do was the way to run a mowing-machine. It cost me many bitter tears because I got sunburned, and my hands were hard, rough, and stained with machine oil, and I used to wonder how any Prince Charming could overlook all that in any girl he came to. For all I had ever read of the Prince had to do with his "reverently kissing her lily-white hand," or doing some other fool trick with a hand as white as a snowflake. Well, when my Prince showed up he didn't lose much time in letting me know that "Barkis was willing," [an allusion from *David Copperfield*] and I wrapped my hands in my old checked apron and took him up before he could catch his breath. (16)

Elinore evidently did not live long on the homestead. By 1906 she was living, probably with her sisters Josephine and Susie, in Oklahoma City,

---

4. According to Jerrine, Tom had a fight with another man while working at the railroad. Hitting him with a boot, Tom knocked him unconscious. Thinking he had killed the man, Tom ran away. Years later, after keeping on the move and never marrying, Tom contacted the family from Nevada and learned he hadn't committed a murder. During World War II, Jerrine received a letter informing her of his death and asking what should be done with the body. Living in a two-room flat, barely able to pay the rent and feed two small children with her husband away in the service, she had to write that she could do nothing, and he had to be buried in an unmarked grave in a potter's field somewhere in Nevada. Lucius left at about the same time that Tom ran away. Lucius educated himself, and he and Elinore remained close until he died in 1925. A few years after Elinore's death, Jerrine received a letter telling her that Lucius's wife too had died and that their son, Floyd Pruitt, about fifteen or sixteen, had no one to raise him. Jerrine sent him clothes and a railway ticket to Wyoming. The boy stayed several years and then went into the navy.

where she roomed and worked as a domestic at 322 West 12th Street.[5] Harry Rupert is not listed in the 1906 directory. On February 10, 1906, Elinore gave birth to Mary Jerrine at St. Anthony's Hospital in Oklahoma City.

During this period Elinore began submitting short articles to newspapers, mainly simple letters to the editor and "how-to-do-its," particularly advice on raising children. Some of these articles were published in the *Kansas City Star*. She later told her family that during her stay in Oklahoma City, a smallpox epidemic broke out and that she trained as a nurse for about six months at Bethany Hospital, west of the city.

Then, about ten months after Jerrine's birth, Elinore left by train with her daughter for Colorado, taking along Susie and Josephine. She planned to visit the Mesa Verde cliff dwellings, established as a national park in 1906, and write an article on them for the *Kansas City Star*. Unfortunately, on her arrival at La Junta, Colorado, she became seriously ill with erysipelas and could not finish the journey. When she had recovered enough to travel, she, Jerrine, and her sisters continued to Denver to find work.

According to Elinore's account, Rupert's death prompted her move. He was killed when a bridge he was inspecting on the Canadian River collapsed. After Harry died and was buried in Grand, Oklahoma, as the story goes, Elinore continued working at the hospital in Oklahoma City until a friend, a police matron, warned Elinore that Rupert's relatives from Ohio wanted to raise Jerrine and that officials had begun proceedings to take her daughter away from her. The police matron gave Elinore money for travel, urging her to leave immediately and asking not to be told the destination.

In reality, Harry Rupert was not buried in Grand, for only one grave, not his, has been recorded at the cemetery. And although Oklahoma did not keep accurate records until granted statehood in 1907, no record of his death exists for that time period.[6] Additional evidence that Harry survived his alleged early demise is found in a patent application receipt from the General Land Office in Guthrie, Oklahoma, dated November 16, 1908.[7] Seven and a half years later, Harry C. Rupert and Bertha Rupert, husband

---

5. This address was found on a letter sent to Elinore and postmarked July 1906; the address was also listed in the Oklahoma City directory for that same year.

6. Rhea Nine of the Ellis County Historical Society, Oklahoma, provided this information on Grand, from Speer, *Our Ellis County Heritage* 2:315.

7. Homestead entry number 25273.

and wife, conveyed the homestead by warranty deed, subject to an existing mortgage of six hundred dollars plus interest and taxes, for fifty dollars to the Preacher's Aid Society of the St. Louis German Annual Conference of the Methodist Episcopal Church. Bertha signed the deed with an x.[8] As was common in most small communities on the plains, residents knew little about others' backgrounds, but Rupert's circumstances paralleled the story of hundreds of others who arrived in that area with a team of horses, a wagon, and a plow; they homesteaded, stayed a few years, and moved on, their destination unknown.[9]

The facts of Elinore's marriage to and divorce from Harry Rupert cannot be confirmed because of the lack of uniform record-keeping in Indian Territory and the frequent loss of records in courthouse fires. However, it is assumed that both took place, since Elinore and Jerrine both used the name Rupert and both Elinore and Harry remarried.

Once in Denver, with no job, little money, and no friends, Elinore rented one-room cold-water flats at two locations, 2046 and 2130 Delaganey Street. Leaving Jerrine at a nursery while she worked, Elinore found employment at the only jobs an uneducated woman at that time could obtain: cooking, cleaning, ironing, scrubbing floors, and stoking coal furnaces.[10] On good terms with the people in the nursery, she may have done

8. This patent application receipt was discovered by Gail Sides, Roger Mills Deputy County Clerk.

9. A few months before her death, Jerrine revealed a postcard she had found beneath the lining of her mother's old trunk, a mystery that had haunted Jerrine throughout her later years. Postmarked December 24, 1908, from Grand, Oklahoma, and addressed to Mrs. H. C. Rupert, 2046 Delaganey, Denver, Colorado, the card simply states: "Well, Nora. I wish you a Happy Christmas. H.C.R." Furthermore, a former resident of Grand, Bess Bullard of Cheyenne, Oklahoma, attended the Rupert school and knew "Aunt Bertha" and "Uncle Harry" well. She recalls Harry Rupert as a short, slender, dark-haired farmer, a description that matched the image in a small photograph Jerrine had found with the 1908 Christmas postcard. Bullard remembers the day a mall-order bride, a plump, blond Dutch woman later known as "Aunt Bertha," arrived by train. Harry, who had always been considered a bachelor, and Bertha were married by a justice of the peace.

10. Her life was typical for a single woman in Denver at the beginning of the twentieth century. Most women met only exploitation and discrimination in the employment market, and "by 1905 women earned much less than men (sometimes only half the wage of men) for doing identical work," according to Dorsett and

extra work there to help pay for the child care as well as working as a housekeeper for a while at the "institution for nurses in Denver" (*LWH,* 189).[11] Her sisters eventually left for California.[12]

One time, taking Jerrine home and laden with groceries, Elinore wheeled her daughter across the elevated street walkover and went back for the groceries, only to meet Jerrine bouncing down the steps in the carriage. She returned to her room, soothed the child, and, exhausted from the day's work, blew out the candle and went to bed. The next morning, in the sunlight, she found blood all over the bedding from a large cut on the back of Jerrine's head. Medical help, of course, was impossible for her to afford. Instead, for problems like this, she wrote for instructions to a physician friend, a Dr. Theresa Fantz, who boarded at the Oxford Hotel. Elinore then performed the doctoring by herself. This note from her friend, in the guise of a letter to the baby, shows the doctor's concern for Elinore's plight:

December 26, 1907
Denver, Colorado
Dear Little Jerrine,
    Your little hint is very much appreciated by me.
                                             Your Doctor Fantz.
Mrs. Rupert, why do you not come see me?

McCarty in *The Queen City,* 107. The following classified ad in the *Denver Post* on March 25, 1909, exemplifies the difficulty most women faced: "A German woman wants to do anything by day. 4940 46th Ave."

11. It is not certain whether Stewart's comments about the nursery refer to the institution for nurses in Denver, which she mentions, or to the child-care services of the Sunshine Rescue Mission, which she also frequented. Hereafter in the text references, *Letters of a Woman Homesteader* will be abbreviated *LWH.*

12. Jerrine related that in California, Susie married, and she and her husband trained dogs for the movies. She never had any children and died at thirty-five of a kidney problem. Josephine disappeared, and the family thought she had been killed in a flood during a Texas coastal hurricane. Suddenly, one Easter about 1930, she began corresponding with Elinore and later visited the ranch in Wyoming, arriving with her family at Burntfork in a big, new car. Josephine's second husband, Jim Moore, a well-to-do Osage Indian, had acquired much wealth in the oil fields. A beautiful, tiny woman, Josephine had married and had a child, divorced, remarried, and had more children.

Elinore also found it difficult to afford clothing for her baby. She remembered when a neighbor's daughter, about Jerrine's age, proudly showed her a pair of shiny new shoes. Terribly discouraged by work that day, Elinore could not bring herself to admire the shoes she knew she could not afford to buy for her own daughter, shoes she herself did not have as a child. Crushed, the little girl turned away, and Elinore remembered the incident all her life, regretting that she had not risen above her own troubles to make the small child happy.

In "As It Happened," a short story about a poor southern laundress in Denver, Elinore perhaps adds some insight into details of her own life there.[13] Aunty Smith, an old black woman, was so poor that she could not even afford a ticket for the circus. The story begins:

> "I can't go to de circus, praise Gawd; I done loant Pearly Ann all de money I had, but praise Gawd!" The early morning sunlight lay in long, golden bars across Aunty Smith's clean kitchen floor. One stray beam was playing tag on the ironing board with Aunty's toil worn hands as she busily pushed the irons over snowy clothes. She had been working since long before light and already there was a noticeable cavity in the big basket of damp clothes. Like many of the old time darkies, Aunty sang her thoughts aloud when thinking deeply, unaware that she did so. And she was deeply thinking this morning.

Aunty, who had lost her entire family during the Civil War, had followed her mistress, Miss Sally Selwyn, to Denver, faithfully supporting Miss Sally with her laundry work and nursing her until Miss Sally too died, leaving the old woman alone. Aunty took in ironing from Miss Mildred, the "Nursery Lady," another southerner who worked among the city's poor, caring for the children while their mothers worked: "The years had not brought peace nor had her streneous work among Denver's poor. To her days were added many worries. So many to find work for, so little work to find." Unexpectedly, Miss Mildred's old beau, "Marse George," arrived and accompanied Aunty to the circus; he promised to take them all back to their beloved South again, as soon as Aunty was well enough.

Since the story differs from Elinore's later works in its Denver setting and its transplanted southern characters, as well as in its less polished

13. "As It Happened" is reprinted in full in Lindau [George], "My Blue and Gold Wyoming."

grammar, this could possibly be one of her first fiction attempts.[14] Although parts of the story are missing, it provides clues to Elinore's life-style and friends during this obscure period in her history. Elinore considered herself a southerner, worked for the nursery, and knew the hardships of poverty. Perhaps she too couldn't afford a twenty-five-cent circus ticket.

Eventually, Elinore obtained employment with the genteel Juliet Coney, who resided at room 10, 1010 17th Avenue. She labored seven days a week as a nurse and housekeeper for the long-widowed schoolteacher from Boston. Part of her wages of two dollars per week went to pay for Jerrine's day school.

Life did not seem to be working out for Elinore as she had dreamed. Years later, in a letter to Mrs. Coney, she confessed the adventures she had once coveted:

> I had not thought I should ever marry again. Jerrine was always such a dear little pal, and I wanted to just knock about foot-loose and free to see life as a gypsy sees it. I had planned to see the Cliff-Dwellers' home; to live right there until I caught the spirit of the surroundings enough to live over their lives in imagination anyway. I had planned to see the old missions and to go to Alaska; to hunt in Canada. I even dreamed of Honolulu. Life stretched out before me one long, happy jaunt. I aimed to see all the world I could, but to travel unknown bypaths to do it. (*LWH*, 188)

Again, an illness precipitated a major change in Elinore's life. She recounted to Mrs. Coney, in a letter from the *Homesteader* collection, the events leading up to her move to Wyoming:

> But for my having the grippe, I should never have come to Wyoming. Mrs. Seroise, who was a nurse at the institution for nurses in Denver while I was housekeeper there, had worked one summer at Saratoga, Wyoming. It

14. Although the date Elinore wrote this tale, in manuscript form in the Jerrine Wire private letters, is unknown, perhaps Elinore penned it in response to two advertisements in the *Denver Post*. The first, a classified ad in the January 3, 1909, edition, promised "Cash for Good Stories" and announced that the editors would accept anything of merit as long as it was "sunny and cheerful." Two months later, in its Sunday morning edition on March 7, the *Post* heralded the Shrine Circus, which would begin a week of performances on Monday, March 29. Large headlines declared, "Get tickets NOW!" Ranging in price from twenty-five cents to one dollar and fifty cents for box seats, such tickets admitted patrons to "The Big Sells-Floto

was she who told me of the pine forests. I had never seen a pine until I came to Colorado; so the idea of a home among the pines fascinated me. At that time I was hoping to pass the Civil-Service examination, with no very definite idea as to what I would do, but just to be improving my time and opportunity. I never went to a public school a day in my life. In my childhood days there was no such thing in the Indian Territory part of Oklahoma where we lived, so I have had to try hard to keep learning. Before the time came for the examination I was so discouraged because of the grippe that nothing but the mountains, the pines, and the clean, fresh air seemed worth while; so it all came about just as I have written you. (189)

Meanwhile, Elinore took advantage of the services at the Sunshine Rescue Mission, 1822 Larimer Street, founded by James Goodheart and several Social Gospel ministers. The mission offered a helping hand to "men, women, and children derelicts" while seeing to their spiritual needs.[15] The Reverend Father Corrigan, a Catholic priest, offered to tutor Elinore for the civil service test. When she went to visit the kindly priest, she confided in him her fears and dreams:

> Rev. Father Corrigan had been preparing me to take the Civil-Service examination, and that afternoon a lesson was due, so I went over to let him see how little I knew. I was in pain and was so blue that I could hardly speak without weeping, so I told the Reverend Father how tired I was of the rattle and bang, of the glare and the soot, the smells and the hurry. I told him what I longed for was the sweet, free open, and that I would like to homestead. (LWH, 226)

He counseled her to obtain a position as a housekeeper for some rancher who could advise her about land, water rights, and homesteading.

About this time, Clyde Stewart, a Wyoming homesteader, decided that he needed a housekeeper. Every January, after cleaning and repairing harnesses, he traveled to Boulder to visit his mother for a month or two, until the beginning of spring ranch work necessitated his return to the Wyoming ranch.

Clyde had grown up on a farm near Boulder. His father, James Cordon

---

Shows" with its "Menagerie-Museum and Circus," "Mammoth Zoo," and "World Famous Armour Grays: The Prize-Winning Six-Horse Team."

15. Dorsett and McCarty, *The Queen City*, 145.

Stewart, a mine supervisor from Terre Haute, Indiana, and a Civil War veteran who had been wounded at Fredericksburg, had moved to Colorado for his health. While farming with his father, Clyde also began apprenticing in the Boulder construction business, later building a home for his widowed mother, some houses on Bluff Street, and a church.

In 1895, Clyde married Cynthia Hurst, "Sis," a French-Canadian housekeeper and secretary to the president of the University of Colorado in Boulder. The newlyweds moved to Jensen, Utah, where Clyde began farming, but he was persuaded by developers of a new irrigation project in the Lucerne Valley to file on the Burntfork homestead on the west branch of Birch Creek in Sweetwater County, Wyoming. Clyde took 160 acres bordering the Wyoming-Utah line under the Homestead Act, plus an additional 80 acres under a desert claim. Together, Clyde and Sis cut enough wild hay with a scythe, cradle, and rake to winter their horses and cattle. They also built the original section of the cabin and the barn, and by 1905 they had received their patent. The couple had no children, and in 1907, at the age of thirty-five, Cynthia died of cancer.

Alone now, Clyde needed help on his ranch. Although Elinore states in *Homesteader* that she placed an ad in the *Denver Post* on Sunday and that Clyde came for an interview the following Wednesday, it was actually Clyde who placed the ad between January and March of 1909. Perhaps this ad from the classified section of the March 7, 1909, Sunday morning edition of the *Denver Post* was the one that brought the two together: "WANTED—Young or middle-aged lady as companion and to assist with housework on Wyoming ranch; a good permanent home for right party. Box 3, W117-Post."

Family members give different versions of this initial meeting. According to Jerrine, after Elinore saw Clyde's ad for a housekeeper, she went to Father Corrigan and asked if he would interview Clyde at the rectory and help her decide whether to take the job. The priest approved of Clyde, and Elinore accepted the position. However, Clyde, Jr., recalled his mother telling him that before the priest gave his approval, Elinore visited for nearly a week at the home of Clyde's mother in Boulder, also for an approving vote. Elinore herself described the meeting differently in *Homesteader*. After crediting herself with the writing of the advertisement, perhaps to solidify her role as the seeker of her own fortune, Elinore recounted that she took Jerrine uptown and rented a room where they might rest quietly and wait a response to her inquiry. She explained:

On the following Wednesday I received a letter from Clyde, who was in Boulder visiting his mother. He was leaving for Wyoming the following Saturday and wanted an interview, if his proposition suited me. I was so glad of his offer, but at the same time I couldn't know what kind of person he was; so, to lessen any risk, I asked him to come to the Sunshine Mission, where Miss Ryan was going to help me "size him up." He did n't know that part of it, of course, but he stood inspection admirably. I was under the impression he had a son, but he had n't, and he and his mother were the very last of their race. (227)

Regardless of the circumstances of the first meeting, the position was offered and accepted, and soon Clyde, Elinore, and Jerrine took the twenty-four-hour train ride together from Boulder to Carter, Wyoming. The three continued their journey by what Elinore termed a "stage coach," really just a spring wagon that carried the mail from Carter to Burntfork, fifty miles southwest of Rock Springs. Elinore wrapped Jerrine up in a quilt against the cold Wyoming winter, and the squeak of the wagon wheels in the snow announced their arrival in Burntfork the first week of March.[16]

When Elinore arrived at Burntfork, the town consisted of a log school-house and a big two-story hall that the Odd-Fellows had first built in Bridger and then moved to the tiny settlement. The post office occupied the first floor, with a dance hall above. George "Dutchy" Stoll had a saloon there for a time, and the postmaster sometimes kept gum and candy for the children to buy. The Stolls were among the earliest settlers in the valley, and Dutchy's wife, Mary Anne ("Grandma Stoll"), became the Mrs. Louderer of Elinore's stories. Later, Burntfork erected a separate post office building. For supplies, the ranchers had to travel north over sixty miles of sagebrush-covered badlands to Green River.

The Stewart ranch was two and one half miles southeast of Burntfork in

16. According to Frost, *Notes on General Ashley,* an expedition headed by William Henry Ashley explored the area in 1825 for trading purposes. Ashley and his partner, Andrew Henry, an experienced fur trapper, mapped the Platte, the South Platte, and the Green River valleys, initiating the first trappers' rendezvous, or temporary wilderness market, near where Henry's Fork flows into the Green River (46). Local sources say that the expedition, coming up Henry's Fork, saw a large streak that had been burned up the side of a mountain by a forest fire. Because the burn made a conspicuous landmark, this portion of the tributary became the Burnt Fork of Henry's Fork.

the fertile valley watered by Henry's Fork and Burnt Fork creeks. At its height, the ranch contained eleven hundred acres, including Grandmother Stewart's claim near the ranch house and another at Cedar Crest, a part of the Bald Range, about four miles away. Clyde usually ran about one hundred head of cattle, a medium-sized operation for that time.

In May 1909, Elinore, accompanied by a neighbor and his daughter, realized her dream by traveling to Green River and filling on 160 acres adjoining Clyde's homestead. The journey to the county seat and the newly built courthouse took "a whole week to go and come," and "in the whole sixty miles there was but one house, and going in that direction there is not a tree to be seen, nothing but sage, sand, and sheep" (*LWH*, 8). Although she could have homesteaded more acres, all of the nearby land had already been claimed. She had wanted to live in the forest but found the valley land much more practical. She related to Mrs. Coney:

> Well, I have filed on my land and am now a bloated landowner. I waited a long time to even *see* land in the reserve, and the snow is yet too deep, so I thought that as they have but three months of summer and spring together and as I wanted the land for a ranch anyway, perhaps I had better stay in the valley. So I have filed adjoining Mr. Stewart and I am well pleased. I have a grove of twelve swamp pines on my place, and I am going to build my house there. I thought it would be very romantic to live in the peaks amid the whispering pines, but I reckon it would be powerfully uncomfortable also, and I guess my twelve can whisper enough for me; and a dandy thing is, I have all the nice snow-water I want; a small stream runs right through the center of my land and I am quite near wood.   (*LWH*, 7–8)

Federal regulations required homesteaders to build and occupy a residence on their claim, so Elinore compromised: "My house joins on to Mr. Stewart's house. It was built that way so that I could 'hold down' my land and my job at the same time. I see the wisdom of it now, though at first I did not want it that way. My boundary line runs within two feet of Mr. Stewart's house, so it was quite easy to build on" (*LWH*, 77).

On May 5, 1909, eight weeks after Elinore's arrival at Burntfork, she and Clyde were married. Had it been just a matter of the heart, said Clyde, Jr., his mother and father would have gotten married in Boulder before going to the ranch. Jerrine, however, believed that what began as a strictly business affair blossomed into love at Burntfork because of mutual attraction and the need each had for the other. Elinore herself interpreted the event in *Homesteader,* when she felt the need to "confess and get it done with" to Mrs. Coney. "The thing I have done," she admitted, "is to marry Mr. Stewart. It was such an inconsistent thing to do that I was ashamed to tell you" (*LWH,* 79–80).

Clyde was forty-one and Elinore was thirty-three. William Pearson, the justice of the peace, performed the marriage, and his wife, Addie, and daughter, Lucy, witnessed the ceremony. The wedding itself, held in the Stewart home, closely followed the events as related in *Homesteader:*

> Well, there was no time to make wedding clothes, so I had to "do up" what I did have. . . . Well, I had most of the dinner cooked, but it kept me hustling to get the house into anything like decent order before the old dog barked, and I knew my moments of liberty were limited. It was blowing a perfect hurricane and snowing like midwinter. I had bought a beautiful pair of shoes to wear on that day, but my vanity had squeezed my feet a little, so while I was so busy at work I had kept on a worn old pair, intending to put on the new ones later; but when the Pearsons drove up all I thought about was getting them into the house where there was fire, so I forgot all about the old shoes and the apron I wore.
>
> . . . As soon as the newcomers were warm, Mr. Stewart told me I had better come over by him and stand up. It was a large room I had to cross, and how I did it before all those strange eyes I never knew. All I can remember very distinctly is hearing Mr. Stewart saying, "I will," and myself chiming in that I would, too. Happening to glance down, I saw that I had forgotten to take off my apron or my old shoes, but just then Mr. Pearson pronounced us man and wife, and as I had dinner to serve right away I had no time to worry over my odd toilet. Anyway the shoes were comfortable and the apron white, so I suppose it could have been worse.   (*LWH,* 186–88)

Over three years later, she commented on the marriage, now solidly successful, in a letter to Mrs. Coney:

> I have often wished I might tell you all about my Clyde, but have not because of two things. One is I could not even begin without telling you what a good man he is, and I didn't want you to think I could do nothing but brag. The other reason is the haste I married in. I am ashamed of that. I am afraid you will think me a Becky Sharp of a person. But although I married in haste, I have no cause to repent. That is very fortunate because I have never had one bit of leisure to repent in. So I am lucky all around.   (*LWH,* 184–85)

Clyde had built the ranch house on the southern half of the valley and into a small hillside, facing the east. It looked out on a fertile, grass-covered valley bounded by Phillipeco Mountain to the east and the Bald Range of the Uintas to the south and west. On the north, across the valley and Henry's Fork creek, rose the imposing badlands.

The original cabin, sixteen by twenty feet with a cellar beneath it, occupied the north end of the house and served as the kitchen. To this, Clyde built on a large living and sleeping room, approximately twenty-four feet long and twelve feet wide, which became the center of much family activity. The addition of Elinore's cabin, twelve by sixteen feet, made the log house even more spacious. The connecting room, approximately eighteen feet long by sixteen feet wide, later housed the boys' bedroom, and Elinore's cabin became the couple's room. When Grandmother Stewart came to live with them, Clyde partitioned off the west end of the large living room for her private quarters. Sturdy and sunny, protected from the winds by the hillside, with the front yard watered by the west branch of Birch Creek (which Clyde called Aggie Creek, "Aggie" being his affectionate name for Elinore), the ranch house was comfortable and picturesque:

> My house faces east and is built up against a side-hill, or should I say hillside? Anyway, they had to excavate quite a lot. I had them dump the dirt right before the house and terrace it smoothly. . . . Every log in my house is as straight as a pine can grow. . . . The logs are unhewed outside because I like the rough finish, but inside the walls are perfectly square and smooth. The cracks in the wall are snugly filled with "daubing" and then the walls are covered with heavy gray building-paper, which makes the room very warm, and I really like the appearance. I had two rolls of wall-paper with a bold rose pattern. By being very careful I was able to cut out enough of the roses, which are divided in their choice of color as to whether they should be red, yellow, or pink, to make a border about eighteen inches from the ceiling. They brighten up the wall and the gray paper is fine to hang pictures upon.   (*LWH,* 137–39)

Pride in her first real home glows in her description of the cabin she built, yet two years after her marriage, Elinore became concerned that she might not be able to hold on to her homestead. She remained optimistic, however, in an October 14, 1911, letter to Mrs. Coney:

> No I shall not lose my land, although it will be over two years before I can get a deed to it. The five years in which I am required to "prove up" will have

passed by then. I could n't have held my homestead if Clyde had also been proving up, but he had accomplished that years ago and has his deed, so I am allowed my homestead. Also I have not yet used my desert right, so I am still entitled to one hundred and sixty acres more. I shall file on that much some day when I have sufficient money of my own earning. The law requires a cash payment of twenty-five cents per acre at the filing, and one dollar more per acre when final proof is made. I should not have married if Clyde had not promised I should meet all my land difficulties unaided. I wanted the fun and the experience. For that reason I want to earn every cent that goes into my own land and improvements myself. Sometimes I almost have a brain-storm wondering how I am going to do it, but I know I shall succeed; other women have succeeded. I know of several who are now where they can laugh at past trials.   (*LWH*, 133–34)

Although U.S. laws established that a single woman filing on a homestead could keep her land if she married and if her husband had proved up on a homestead, as Clyde had done, it stipulated that she must fulfill cultivation and residency requirements. The Department of Interior declared it illegal for a couple to share a residence while homesteading neighboring properties. Since Elinore had not built a separate cabin but had simply added on to Clyde's, she decided to relinquish her rights to Clyde's mother, Ruth Caroline Stewart, in 1912. Grandmother Stewart then proved up on the homestead by living there during the summers under the more lenient 1912 residency requirements, which permitted homesteaders a yearly absence of five months' duration. She received a patent to the land in 1915 and five years later sold the land to her son for one hundred dollars.[17]

Raising children soon became Elinore's chief priority. Three of her five children born on the ranch, all within four years, survived: Henry Clyde, Jr. (July 25, 1911); Calvin Emery (July 22, 1912); and Robert Clinton (December 3, 1913). Elinore joked that she had her babies so fast they practically came out holding on to each other's ankles. Grandma Stoll helped with the deliveries of the Stewart children in the southwest corner of the kitchen by the warm stove.

Elinore and Clyde's first son, James Wilber, was born during a winter

17. Sherry Smith amplifies the issue of the legality and implications of Stewart's homesteading decisions in "Single Women Homesteaders."

blizzard in February 1910. He died of erysipelas, two days after Christmas of the same year. Jerrine, four, recalls her father and mother sitting up against the stove, with Elinore bathing little Jamie. Elinore was crying, and Clyde, on his knees in front of his wife with his arms around the infant's body, shook with silent sobs. Although Jerrine did not understand what death was all about, she broke into tears too. They washed him, laid him out on a table in the cold middle room, and covered him with a sheet.

The death devastated Clyde and Elinore. Clyde, an accomplished carpenter, built a coffin while Elinore took some curtains down and washed them white and clean to use as lining for the coffin. She added a row of little rosebuds, the kind that came on a tape for sewing, all the way around the casket under the lid, and made a little satin cushion. Clyde built a fire and let it burn for hours on the frozen ground in the Burntfork cemetery, several miles away, so that he could dig a grave. There were no ministers to call on for assistance, so Elinore read a chapter from the Gospel of John. Friends and neighbors from as far away as thirty miles attended the funeral.

Elinore later described these events to Mrs. Coney:

> A dear little child has joined the angels. I dressed him and helped to make his casket. There is no minister in this whole country and I could not bear the little broken lily-bud to be just carted away and buried, so I arranged the funeral and conducted the services. I know I am unworthy and in no way fitted for such a mission, but I did my poor best, and if no one else is comforted, I am. I know the message of God's love and care has been told once, anyway, to people who have learned to believe more strongly in hell than in heaven. (*LWH*, 98–99)

The date on this letter in the published collection reads August 15, 1910, although the child did not die until December 27, 1910. Elinore neglected to include the year in the dates on most of her letters, and the *Atlantic Monthly*, arranging them as best it could, presumably made a mistake. The letter should probably have been dated August 15, 1911. Or, since she wishes Mrs. Coney joy in "this New Year" (*LWH*, 99), the month could have been wrong too, and the letter could have been written on January 15, 1911. The death haunted Elinore, for on December 2, 1912, nearing the second anniversary of the loss of her son, she again wrote Mrs. Coney of the tragedy, describing once more the death, the preparation for burial, and the funeral service itself, as if putting the grief on paper would erase it from her mind. Toward the end of the letter, she alluded to her marriage as well as her grief: "So you see, our union is sealed by love and welded by a great sorrow. Little Jamie was the first little Stewart. God has given me two more precious little sons. The old sorrow is not so keen now. I can bear to tell you about it, but I never could before" (*LWH*, 191).

Elinore had lost another child in 1910, a premature daughter they named Helen. They buried her under a tree by the house, the same tree that Clyde and Cynthia had first camped under when they had arrived to homestead the ranch.

The night the last child, Robert, was born, the hired girl who was to have assisted with the birth eloped, and Clyde had to help with the delivery. Elinore, who was in labor all night, didn't call Clyde from his slumbers until shortly before the birth. Born under a caul, Robert was blue from lack of oxygen, so Elinore instructed Clyde to slap the baby to start his breathing. Clyde was too tenderhearted, however, and Elinore had to take matters into her own hands. Afterward, Clyde told Elinore he couldn't help wash and dress the baby; he felt weak and needed to make himself a sandwich.

Elinore recorded the events of these first years in Wyoming in letters to her friends. What began as personal letters to her beloved former employer in Denver, Juliet Coney, became the text of her first book. In the beginning, Elinore simply intended the letters as a private correspondence to a crippled and housebound friend who could not get out to enjoy the beauty of nature. Elinore attempted to bring something of interest into her life, embroidering everyday incidents to add interest. However, at some point in the correspondence, Mrs. Coney, on a visit back to her home in Boston, took the letters to her friend Ellery Sedgwick, the editor of the *Atlantic Monthly*, saying she believed that they should be shared with others. He agreed and published the letters in a series from October 1913 through April 1914.

At that time Sedgwick, according to his autobiography, *The Happy Profession*, was looking for a "fringe of informality" that would build his magazine subscription list, and he found it in the world of the familiar letter, "the warmest and friendliest among the satellites of Literature." In his search for "an unpremeditated record of interesting happenings by an interesting person," he discovered Elinore Pruitt Stewart (197). He warmly described their relationship in his autobiography:

> One such delightful and persistent comradeship I formed with a Woman Homesteader who in the face of every conceivable obstacle had taken up a

quarter section in a remote corner of Wyoming. Elinore Rupert was a young woman, vigorous in body and mind, but Destiny seemed determined to test her out before showing her the way. Her husband had been killed in a train wreck and she was left with a two-year-old daughter, Jerrine. She had not a friend, nor was she trained to make a living. In instant need of support, she had turned laundress to a kind mistress, one Mrs. Coney of Denver. This helped her over the blank wall right ahead and a larger future beckoned. She determined to turn homesteader and stake out a claim of her own in the world. After an adventurous year she wrote an account of it to the lady who had befriended her. By happy chance Mrs. Coney was a devotee of the *Atlantic*. She sent the correspondence to me and we were off.

It really mattered very little what life Elinore Rupert had been born into. She could have made a go of anything. She might have become the perfect servant; as mistress of a great household she would have kept everybody happy, and if the dance of her genes had revolved in high circles, she would have made a very respectable Duchess.   (198)

Even the famed F. N. Doubleday personally sent her a note on October 3, 1913, inviting her to publish with his company:

> I have read with tremendous interest your letters in the current number
> of "The Atlantic Monthly." Have you ever thought of writing a book, per-
> haps a novel picturing life as you have done in these letters? We publish a
> book called "The Wind Before Dawn," which is somewhat on this line,
> and of which I should be glad to send you a copy if you will give me your
> address. If the matter interests you at all, it will be a great pleasure to hear
> from you at your convenience."[18]

Elinore nearly panicked when she discovered how many people would read her writing, but Sedgwick's patronly advice and encouragement reassured her, and a lifelong friendship developed between them. Sedgwick's letter of January 10, 1914, was the first of many such letters received at Burntfork:

> I dare say you have been getting many letters from Atlantic readers.
> The enclosed postal will, perhaps, give you particular pleasure. It may
> also serve to show you how glad we shall be if you have been able to find

---

18. Permission to publish this excerpt from F. N. Doubleday's letter was granted by Doubleday, a division of Bantam, Doubleday, Dell Publishing Group, Inc.

time to chronicle that other episode in your adventurous life. The series of letters ends in our February issue. We should like to pause for a month and then begin with two or three more. The one I have I shall be glad to use if it can be followed (as I wrote you before) by a paper which has the story interest a little more strongly marked.[19]

With the publication of her articles in the *Atlantic Monthly* came nation-wide fame, and Elinore received many postcards and letters from all across the United States. One arrived from a Miss Maria Wood of Lexington, Missouri. Elinore responded on January 21, 1914, initiating a lifelong correspondence:

Dear Miss Wood

I am plumb glad you like the letters and I hope to be able to send lots of this big breezy West to those who could not enjoy it otherwise.

The only difficulty now is to get help to do my housework. I have four children, three of them not yet three years old. That is rather a staggering statement but it is true. A mother is always ready to talk about her children and I am almost in the same plight as the old woman who lived in the shoe.

Jerrine is my oldest. She will be eight years old next month   I could hardly keep house with out her she is so helpful. I had a dear little one join the angels three years ago and now we have Clyde, Jr. Calvin Emery, and my baby boy just six weeks old whose name is Robert Clinton—You see how difficult it is for me to knock about among the delightful people among whom my lot is cast. I have tried so hard to get help but have failed so far.

I must thank you for the lovely card, it makes me mighty proud to have you write me such delightful things, and it is so nice and friendly. I wish I had a pretty card for you but haven't. I should like powerfully well to claim you as my friend. May I? If so, then beleive me

Sincerely your friend
Elinore Pruitt Stewart

19. All excerpts from Ellery Sedgwick's letters to Elinore are from the Houghton Mifflin Papers, Houghton Library, Harvard University. Used by permission of Houghton Mifflin Company and the Houghton Library.

What was it about Miss Wood that prompted Elinore to undertake what would become a nineteen-year, long-distance friendship? Perhaps Elinore saw in the elderly woman, lame and alone, similarities to her own beloved Mrs. Coney.

A cultured and gentle lady, well-educated and always carefully dressed, Miss Wood was known by everyone in the small town of Lexington as Miss Maria (pronounced "Muh-ri'-uh" with a long "i"). The daughter of William T. Wood, an attorney and circuit judge, she came from a highly respected family in the community. She had been educated in a local private seminary, never married, and did not have to work. Dressed elegantly in black in the winter and in white in the summer, when she carried a parasol, she faithfully attended the Presbyterian church services and "circle." Her friends Anne Chalkley and Laura Ireland Frazer, sisters who lived in the other half of her duplex on South Street, often accompanied her on her outings.[20]

According to references in Elinore's letters, many of Miss Maria's friends also corresponded with Elinore, among them William Chamberlain, who lived across the street from Miss Maria. Knowledgeable and refined, he was probably the uncle of Mary Celeste Henry, the "Miss Henry" mentioned in the letters. Miss Maria's other friends included Miss Locke (pronounced "Lock-ie") Arnold, another refined spinster, who was slightly younger than Miss Maria and who lived with her elderly aunt Mrs. McCausland. Mrs. McCausland was quite a legend in Lexington. As a young woman, high-spirited and a true southern patriot, she had stood on the front porch of her home in 1864 and waved a Confederate flag as the Union troops marched by. Her impertinence caused the imprisonment of her husband and much hardship for her father. Elinore referred to another correspondent, Lelia Tidball, who was also related to Mrs. McCausland, perhaps a sister.

Miss Maria was nearly eighty when she died in the late 1930s, making her close to sixty when she began her correspondence with Elinore. In

---

20. Information on Miss Wood and her acquaintances was provided by Buddy Samuels, of the Lafayette County Historical Society, Elizabeth Ray, a Missouri genealogist, and John Ryland Wallace, a noted Lexington historian. Because a fire destroyed the pertinent records, no exact dates for Miss Maria's birth or death exist and since she was the last of her family, no tombstone marks her grave. However, Wallace, on the basis of his records, estimates that Miss Maria was nearly eighty when she died in the late 1930s.

1936 she returned to the family all of her letters from Elinore. A note written at the top of the first letter from Elinore declared, "Do you wonder I loved, and miss her so!" By the date, she had noted, "We were just getting acquainted."

Miss Maria's reply to Elinore's offer of friendship occasioned a second letter from Elinore on February 19, 1914:

Dear Miss Wood

Your charming letter to hand today and I am so delighted with it that I am plumb eager to answer. In order that you may not think me insincere or just "spouting" I ought to explain to you that I get a great many letters from people who just write it seems, to be writing, so when there is a *real* chance to make a friend I am mighty glad to find the good grain among so much chaf. I can't write to every one of course so I am rejoicing that I found you for you are exactly what I want for a friend so if you are of the same mind let us say Dear Friend from now on. I dont think friend-ship is always a matter of years. I wonder if you would mind if I sent your letter to Mrs. Coney? She would be plumb "happyfied" over it. She is a dear old soul, she will be seventy six next month. Mr. Stewart's mother will be seventy three in July. She is coming out in May. She lives in Boulder Colo.

The grandmother I loved so fondly was eighty four when she died more than three years ago. All my life I have loved old people best and Jerrine is the same way. I feel that I don't deserve all the nice things you say about the "Letters". Publication was no part of my thoughts when I was writing them, I was just trying to enterest Mrs. Coney. Her family consists of herself and two daughters, one daughter is the principal of a Denver school and the other is a teacher so she is alone all day. No one could know her and not love her and I used to think she was lonely so that is how the "Letters" came to be.

I beleive you are trying to give me the "big-head" but you will never succeed and the reason why is that size settled on me quite early in life, haven't you heard of kinds of sickness that went down on folks? Well, if you could see my feet you would know that I can never have the big head with the kind of feet that I have. The 'letters' are to be published in book form in the early summer. If you will accept a copy I should be right proud to send you one.

If you like children I should like to have you near me but you would

have to have a great deal of love for them to put up with my noisy boys
and scarcely less noisy girl. Calvin will be two years old in July but he
can't walk yet. he goes where he chooses though, if the doors are not
latched. he does what Jerrine calls "scrooging." That is a pretty good
word for it. he just hitches along using one foot and one hand. I don't
think there is any weakness of any kind; I think it is just because he is so
heavy that he is afraid to walk. He is very fat. He has gray eyes and is
very fair. Junior and Jerrine are complexioned exactly alike, both have
brown eyes and hair. The look very much alike. Jerrine was eight years
old Feb. 10. She is tall for her age. She takes her brothers very seriously
and is a real little mother to them.

The baby is always a mother's pride. Mine is no exception. He was
born Dec. 3rd. He is the only one of my babies that I ever nursed. He has
a whole mop of dark brown hair, the only baby I've had that had hair
and he is blue eyed. I just love blue eyes. My own are brown, perhaps
that's the reason. Junior will be three years old in July so you see my
boys are all in a bunch; there is three days lacking of being a year between Junior and Calvin. Jerrine has given us all a place in Mother
Goose. I am the Old woman who lived in a shoe and had so many children she didn't know what to do.

I am afraid you people will get in bad by writing to Jerrine. She will
overwhelm you with poorly spelled and badly written letters. Once she
compelled me to promise I would leave her "spondence" alone and I
have kept my word to her although she sometimes lets me advise her a
little by that means I can kind of regulate her "spondence."

I think it a most beautiful thing that you were there with your friends
when their sister went Home. Your mutual sorrow will bind more closely
together and you will in a way seem a sister to them. I am so glad you
have each other and I am glad you told me of them. It isn't hard for me
to imagine I know you all and that you are all my friends.

Jerrine was powerful tickled with the manicure set. You will be getting
a bulky letter soon. I feel that I ought to appologize for her poor writing
and spelling. She has never been to school. They only have school in the
winter and the snow is too deep for her to go. We are seven thousand and
three hundred feet above sea level. We have lots of snow and when the
wind blows the drifts are terrible. Please let me say with much love

Your friend

Elinore Pruitt Stewart

Soon letters sped between Miss Wood and Elinore, almost on a monthly basis. On March 28, 1914, Elinore continued:

My Dear Friend

This is one of those dark, misty days that make us feel so comfy and confidential. You'd think that so high up on the mountains as we are there would never be any thing like a fog but we have all kind of cloud effects. I've seen the valley below us full of vapory, white cloud and the sun shining brightly here on the mountain at other times the clouds will completely hide the mountains above us but today we are right in the heart of the storm. This is such powerfully poor ink I can hardly write. It is impossible to get good ink in the winter as it has to be freighted so far that it freezes on the road.

Do you smell my bread baking? Shall I send you a piece of my coffee cake? We like it with cinnamon, raisins and sugar in and it is raising fine it will soon be ready for the oven. I've had a neighbor from higher up in the mountains here with me for a week helping me sew. She has the dearest little girl, Edith that Jerrine writes of. They've only lately moved onto their ranch which they call Blue-bird Ranch, from Idaho and their little Edith has had kindergarten training so she knows many pretty little songs and games. I am mighty glad to have her visit Jerrine. The snow is falling so fast that I can't see the barn yet I have another visitor, an old lady sixty years old who has home-steaded on a mountain side across the creek north of us. It is seven or eight miles over there but I can see their lamp light from our back porch. She has come all that way to teach me to make ginger drop cakes. I just love people. She is the dearest little dumpy thing, perhaps that is why I love her. for I am not little nor dumpy either. I should like to be small and graceful but I'm five feet six inches tall and weigh almost two hundred pounds. I have heavy black hair and brown eyes. Jerrine is tall for her age and slender, she has light brown hair and dark brown eyes. She is the best thing to help me but she really dont like housework. She would like to sew, she is just beginning to try I must get her a thimble but I dont know how the numbers run for sizes.

She and Edith made themselves a doll quilt. Jerrine loves dolls but some misfortune has happened to evry one she has ever had. Santa Claus brought her a beauty but one day Calvin got it and broke the head all to bits before we knew it. She has another but we can't keep its hair on. I thought once I would get her some soft oil calico and cut her some doll clothes so that she could learn to sew while she plays but I have not done so yet. I never could cut doll clothes very well. Mrs. Coney sent her a bunch of ribbons off candy boxes and Christmas packages. She set up what she calls a military store and she was very happy until she tore up Junior's straw hat to get braid to make her hats, then we had a disagreement.

We raise a heap of flowers but they never finish blooming before the frost gets them. What we raise are beautiful. We have poppies, zinnias, pansies lark-spur, cosmos, nasturtiums sweet peas, sweet alyssum ragged robin, holly-hocks dahlias, morning glorys—and wild cucumber vines; At the east window of the dining room we have a hop vine that climbs to the top of the house. We all love roses but have never succeeded in getting them started. I think they would grow here, there are lots of wild ones but they are always dried out and brittle before they get here. Now that we have parcel post I should think they could pack them with enough moisture to bring them safely. There [are] acres of beautiful iris here and we have columbine and wind-flowers wild. At this altitude there are no wild vines. I miss them so, the woods at home, in Oklahoma were a tangle of vines.

The parcel post is the most wonderful benefit we have ever had for people situated as we are: We have just received three cases of canned goods by mail. After our present suppy is gone we shall get our flour and sugar by mail. Jerrine says tell "dear Mary Celeste that she has not forgotted her." Will you forgive me for this *long* letter?

With much love
Elinore Stewart

June 12, [ca. 1914]
My dear friend

I really don't think you've done anything to merit such punishment as having another letter flung at you but that is one of the afflictions that goes with my friendship. Any way I feel like visiting with you this morning—so I am going to tell you a little "happy" that you helped to make. four years ago I became acquainted with a young tenderfoot. He was very reticent and we didn't even know his name. Evry one gets a nick-name when they come West and this boy was called Big Medicine. Why, I don't know. He is very fair and just back of his ear is a long *black* scar—it is very noticeable and was made black by some one sprinkling soot from a chimney on the new wound—when it healed some of the soot remained and was grown over. That is an old remedy that I have seen used when I was a child so I knew that some one who had cared for him was an old fashioned some-body.

The majority of the men in the West drink and swear and are as rough as they can be. They are good men, too, but it just seems their way. It is a part of good manners in the West not to be curious as to ones past—therefore no one questioned Big Medicine as to whence, why or where. It was his contribution to ride wild, bucking horses. So one day some fellows got him onto a bad horse that bucked so hard the boy was almost jerked to pieces and then thrown across a fence. It almost killed him. They carried his limp body to the shade and began pouring whiskey down him trying to help him. Although he had tried to practice Western-ways, he would never drink, so the whiskey made him drunk and I really thought he would die.

A search through his clothes revealed nothing that told a thing about him. Ofcourse it was evident that he wanted no one to know his name or where he was from. They had laid him on a cot and I was working with him. When the men had gone out I questioned him—but he wouldn't tell me so I waited a while then I handed him a pencil and told him he was too drunk to write his name and address. Poor fellow, he had been dared so much that he thought of nothing else so he took the pencil and feebly wrote Edwin Carson Galesburg, Ill. The effort was too much. The bucking of the horse had caused a hemoraghe and he began to vomit clots of blood. He was *very* sick for a few days and when he was better I saw he didn't know he had given me his name, but in the meantime I had written to a friend of my in Gales-burg and she had found all about him. You see I was afraid he would die and I felt his people should know. Well, it seems that his mother is a widow and he is her only son, he has one sister, younger than he. They own a small farm, once it was larger but since the death of the father they have had to sell off some of it in order to educate the children—even then they have had to mortgage some of it from time to time until at last the entire home was covered. The man who bought some of the land also held the mortgage—he had a son who made improper advances to the sister—he repeated the insults so often that at last Edwin shot him. It happen at almost sundown—before it was dark Edwin had "skipped out."

He thought he had killed the fellow and so he lost himself in the great West where he has worked and saved to raise money to pay off the mortgage, he entended to send it to his mother when he had enough. On the other hand Mother and sister had been straining evry nerve to keep the enterest paid up enough to defend Edwin should he ever be caught for although he failed to kill the fellow he crippled him for life and it seemed that the penitentiary would claim another victim.

Take courage, that is all the bad there is, all the rest of the tale is good—here is where *you* come in, that big ink blot is not intended to represent you, that came there by accident. You remember those pretty postcards you sent at Easter? Two of them were of the Old Oaken bucket series. They were so beautiful that I felt they would rake up old memories. I wrote a little message on one and sent it to my friend, inclosed with a letter. She in turn inclosed it in an envelope addressed to the Boy with a Black Scar Burnt Fork. You see neither mother nor sister would talk about him, neither knew where he was and they were afraid they would make it worse for him. My friend learned the story from outsiders. We hardly knew how to proceed. Just as soon as he was able to know any thing I gave him the card, but he knew it was not from his mother or sister and he didn't know how much I knew and I was afraid to tell him so I hurried the other card off in order to get it back before he would be able to "skip out." The night the last card came it happened a lawyer friend was stopping over night with us. We were at supper when the mail came. The post cards were the first word he had had from home since he left. he was too over-come by the second one to pretend that he was not he as he had done at first. he left the table and went to his room. Afterwards we had a general "fessing" up and we took counsel with our lawyer friend who advised Edwin to go back and face the music.

Edwin had almost a thousand dollars saved. The lawyer advised him to use that if necessary to defend him-self and to attend to the mortgage later. This week I had a long letter from the boy. There is no case against him, his mother and sister had saved almost as much money as he, there was enough to pay off the mortgage and to pay for a course of electrical engineering for Edwin. Now the very best part of it is this. This family would never amounted to anything if it had not been for this trouble— they are good people but they were shiftless and careless. They had no business training and until this happened they just drifted along. When they needed money they sold something. None of them were prepared to meet the days problems. Had they kept on as they were they would soon have been homeless, in need and there's no telling what would have happened. They are much better off than they would other-wise have been and so I'm glad it happened. I am not at all sorry for the man that got shot. he only got what was coming to him. It was your pretty cards that made Edwin so homesick he couldn't stay away and I love you a heap.

At last we got Pollyanna. My eyes are not strong this summer so we have not read it but shall soon. Jerrine is about to have a caniption fit because she has "lost Mary Celeste." We don't know where to send a letter. Will you forgive me this long blotchy letter if I promise never to do it again?

With much love,
Elinore Stewart

In 1914, Houghton Mifflin compiled Elinore's first series of letters into the book *Letters of a Woman Homesteader*. A letter of April 25, 1914, from the editors reveals authorial and editorial concerns:

> We have your letters of the 8th and the 15th. We see that no one would be liable to a suit for libel from the publication of the Mormon story in full, but nevertheless it seems better to omit the passage in question in the interests of verisimilitude. We are pretty sure that it would raise questions in the reader's mind which, considering the faithfulness of your story as a whole, it would be better not to raise.
>
> As to the passage which you wish omitted from your letter of last autumn to Mrs. Coney, we can assure you that it will not appear in the book—in fact we do not find any such passage in any of the manuscripts, and think Mrs. Coney probably took it out before sending the letter to us.
>
> The question has come up as to whether the facetious synonym for eggs which you give in your horse-thief story is really "cockle-berries" as the *Atlantic* printed it, or "cackle-berries." The latter would seem, perhaps, to be the more natural name, and an "o" for an "a" would be an easy mistake in reading handwriting. Please let us know whether "cockle-berries" is the form preferred in Wyoming or not, in order that we may have it correct in the book.

Letters of a Woman Homesteader, illustrated by the renowned N. C. Wyeth, sold for $1.25. Elinore received five hundred dollars for the book, insisting that Mrs. Coney take part of the money, and continued to receive royalty checks every six months. She was proud of her contribution to the family finances, for money was scarce in Wyoming, and most ranch families lived on credit. Her first purchase with the money was a gasoline lamp to light the dark corners of the log house for her late nights of writing. The lamp was so bright, it seemed almost like electricity.

Newspapers and magazines across the United States, even in Canada and England, enthusiastically reviewed the work. The *New York Times Book Review,* in its June 7, 1914, edition, praised Stewart's writing:

> One closes her little volume with the conviction that she missed her vocation. She ought to have been a war and travel correspondent and journeyed into far lands and strange scenes, out of which she would have plucked their inmost hearts and set them, still warm and beating, before a hundred thousand readers. Some other correspondent might contradict her and say the hearts didn't beat that way at all, but her readers would believe her. (259)

Ironically, Elinore had once wanted fervently to be a travel writer. Other periodicals agreed with the *Times. The Dial,* a journal of literary criticism and discussion, also wrote a long and favorable review on July 1, 1914:

> [The letters] give promise of attaining no inconsiderable fame in the literary world. They are, indeed, an example of that variety of the unexpected which make it worthwhile to be an editor. Mrs. Stewart's enthusiasm for homesteading is infectious, as are also the high spirits and jollity of her admirable letters. Her neighbors are made to live and breathe before our eyes as she hits off their various peculiarities and amiabilities; to their faults and foibles, if they have any, she makes no allusion. It is a hearty and wholesome book. Six good drawings accompany the reading matter. (22)

Delighted with the success of her first letters, the *Atlantic Monthly* commissioned another series, to be published from February through May of 1915. So, in August 1914, leaving Clyde, Jr., then age three, at the ranch with his grandmother, Elinore and Clyde left on the adventure that would form the basis for the second series, *Letters on an Elk Hunt.* The party took two wagons, one for the Stewart family, including Jerrine, eight, Calvin, two, and Robert, eight months, and the other for the Stevenson brothers and their friends. Elinore, the only woman on the trip, wrote the letters as the hunt progressed, forwarding them to Sedgwick. On August 27, 1914, he responded to her queries about them:

Your hunt is four days old today. I wonder how many elk-skins you are sleeping on at night.

It is easy enough to answer your question. An Atlantic article ought to be five or six thousand words. The letter which you sent me the other day amounted perhaps to three. My notion is that each installment of The Atlantic should be made up of two or three letters of yours, but I had just as lief have it made up of one, provided a single episode gives you enough to write about. The whole idea of having more than one letter is simply to avoid the temptation of working a single theme threadbare. You need not try to write regularly, for I have an idea that you are one of the geniuses who write best when the spirit moves them; so when the blind madness of writing (as my old Latin book used to say) comes over you, give way to it whether an elk is sighted or not.

On the other hand, do not feel obliged to spin out a letter if you are tired or have not anything to say. I am announcing a new series by you just to show my confidence, and there need be no hurry about sending the copy.

A week or two ago I had the nicest card from Jerrine. I shall write to thank her when I have time. If she is with you, tell her how pleased I was with her message.

Even while on the elk hunt, Elinore found time for Miss Maria. In camp, on September 27, 1914, she wrote:

My Dear, dear friend

I wonder what you are doing this snowy afternoon, picking out the good of the sermon you have listened to this morning I suspect. As for me, I am thinking of kind little you—wondering whether you would like it in camp. I beleive you would like it here. There is so much that is grandly beautiful, such a sweep of beauty, miles and miles of it, but dear Miss Wood I am going to confess to you that as a huntress I am a rank fraud. I *hate* guns. When I first came to Wyoming I tried to make my self beleive I liked to shoot. I used a shot gun and hunted for sage chickens but I have seen the dying agony of two that I have shot and I think there can be no happy satisfaction where there must be so much remorse. Ofcourse the publishers suppose me to have a little courage and valor and I suppose most of the readers of the coming series of letters will suppose so too but to you I must confess I am a trembly kneed coward when it comes to shooting the wild creatures just for the name of doing so. The mountains are full of hunters, each one hoping to kill a bull elk in order to get it's antlers. They each have a right to kill a cow elk too. Many of them shoot on sight without trying to see if their shot is going to leave a calf without a mother.

I was out with a woman from a neighboring camp. We were up on a ledge of rock enjoying the sun and the beautiful view—below us ran a small stream. A trembling golden leaved grove of quaking aspen grew on the opposite hillside and while we were quietly sitting on the rock a doe and two fawns came out and came down toward the stream. The woman raised her rifle and fired—instantly the poor mother went down but it was a poor shot and she struggled up again and used evry instinct of her mother-hood to save her young. She was shot through the shoulder but she threw her poor wounded body between the fawns and danger and ran, guiding them along the easiest slope of the hill toward timber. The woman was already scrambling down to get a second shot but from my high vantage I saw the whole procedure. As soon as the mother deer reached timber, she turned and ran along the edge while the fawns disappeared among the big trees.

I wondered why and followed the woman: a trail of blood marked the course of the mother. We followed that and soon overtook the poor tortured thing. The second shot more merciful than the first ended the suffering and the babes were saved. Then I saw why she had left them. That woman's name figures frequently . . . [pages missing] . . . of the outing. There is so much to enjoy. The huge forests. The snow peaks the lakes, streams and waterfalls the great cliffs and mountains and the people to be met. They *all* have a charm for me. I love the glorious sunrises, the frosty mornings and the silent fall of the snow. All that I love most and beleive you would like I am trying to put truthfully in the new series soon to appear in the Atlantic but if in any letters it seems as if I enjoyed *hunting* you will know that is humbug.

I am so short of paper. We are two hundred and fifty miles from home have been here a month. Will start back soon. With much love to you.

> Elinore Pruitt Stewart
> Burnt Fork Wyoming

The elk hunt was a success, for Elinore not only bagged a new series of letters, but she forwarded to Sedgwick some valuable elk teeth as well. He replied on January 7, 1915:

Many thanks for all your letters. I seem to have become a silent partner in this pleasant correspondence.

As I write, a delightful little note of good wishes comes from Jerrine,
but she does not speak of a book which I sent her and which I hope duly
found itself in one of your Burnt Fork saddle-bags. Then, I have to thank
you for the "ivories" which happily arrived to form a permanent memento
of the pleasures I have lost in not becoming one of your party. Very many
thanks.

Now for the letters. You speak of others, and I certainly want to read
them. My idea is to make a series of at least four, and, possibly, five papers. For this you shall receive certainly $400, and, possibly, more. As
an . . . [?] . . . of this, I have sent you the first check for $100 and will
send you another next month.

Later that year, Houghton Mifflin compiled these letters into a second
book, *Letters on an Elk Hunt,* which sold for one dollar. Elinore continued
to use her advances and royalties to purchase supplies for the ranch:
horses, seed, and equipment. She bought two push rakes for haying, an
overshot stacker (the only one of its kind in the area), a Milwaukee grain
binder (the first in the Henry's Fork area), and two Milwaukee mowers.

Letters on an Elk Hunt, like its predecessor, was favorably received. The
Boston Transcript echoed other reviewers' opinions when it wrote on October 13, 1915:

In this new collection of letters, the author of "The Letters of a Woman
Homesteader" has given us another glimpse of Western life. Simply, humbly,
Mrs. Stewart relates the little daily occurrences which make up her trip to
the hunting grounds and back. There is no assumption of finished style, no
attempt at fine language, no unified plot development, simply the natural
recital of incident to the friend at home. She relates the experiences of an
ordinary woman who loves her children and her fellows and the open
country. But these experiences compass the tragedy and romance of every
soul whom she meets on the way. Their struggles against poverty and
discouragement, their pitiful romances, their glad self-sacrifices, their eternal good fellowship, all these she makes her own, to give again in her letters.
Arrived at the hunting grounds, we feel with her the zest and the pathos of
the chase.

The freedom of the open, the calm and peace which persists in spite of
cold and hunger and even death, is what Mrs. Stewart has described in these

plain little unadorned letters. Yet it is the people, more than the country itself, which appeal to the author. "I had not expected," she writes on the last page, "to encounter so many people or to get the little inside glimpses that I've had, but wherever there are human beings there are the little histories." Not everyone discovers them, but Mrs. Stewart did. And it is the loveable human quality which counts.

During this same period Elinore also wrote a series of stories for the *Youth's Companion,* which, along with the prestigious *St. Nicholas,* dominated magazine publishing for young people. Stewart kept good company, for the contributors to the *Youth's Companion* included Mark Twain, Jack London, Oliver Wendell Holmes, Theodore Roosevelt, Rudyard Kipling, H. G. Wells, Sarah Orne Jewett, Alfred Lord Tennyson, and Henry Longfellow.[21]

Faithful to her editor Ellery Sedgwick, Elinore at first felt concerned that her loyalty to the *Atlantic Monthly* might be questioned, so she wrote to Mrs. Coney for advice. Her old friend replied on March 10, 1914:

Dear, dear Mrs. Stewart—

I don't see how you remembered that I had a birthday yesterday. And how did you think with all your cares to make it known to me in such a lovely manner. I hope you realise how lovely I think it was in you and that I thoroughly appreciate your kind thoughtfulness and generosity. When the flowers came I was much surprised and couldn't imagine who had sent them. But when Mrs. Allen came after having been to the florist's the mystery was explained. The plant was a pot of beautiful tulips in bloom—14 plants in all—bright and lovely, yellow with stripes of red—very handsome. I would send you one, only it would not look so pretty pressed. I have been ill and housed up the last three weeks—but not sick in bed—I am improving now and if we have some nice weather shall go out any day now.

Thanks for sending me the letters. They show how much you are ap-

21. Meigs, in *A Critical History of Children's Literature,* adds that the *Youth's Companion*—a weekly with self-imposed restrictions on the depiction of tobacco and alcohol use, love relationships, and death—was the longest-lived youth's magazine and had subscribers in households across the United States and abroad (261–62).

preciated from one end of the United States to the other and I am very proud of my acquaintance with you inasmuch as I know what a level head you have and good sense so that you wont let whatever any body and every body may say turn it a bit from your husband children or home—or *me*. Dont you think I am conceited? But don't you get a lot of superannuated old parties on your hands—for they will depend on you and you have duties enough of your own.

Wasn't it nice that the Youth's Companion sent you such a nice letter and in such an honorable way too—through the Atlantic. Quite different from some other publishers wasn't it? But the others didn't get ahead of your time did they—I'll risk you. As what the Y.C. asked of you is so different from what you are doing for the Atlantic it seems to me it would be all right for you to write for both. You will know. I dont see how you get time to write at all—but you know you are a "wonder"—so perhaps you can accomplish both—and grind out an occasional story for the Y.C. But I don't believe you will ever give up our first love the Atlantic.

I am hoping for a letter from you soon for I am sure I look for yours as eagerly as you do for mine. Do you know when the book of "letters" is going to be published? I did not receive any magazines from you so I hope you did not send them as you intended for I should feel very sorry to have deprived you or your friends of them. You have no idea how much I enjoy reading "the letters" over and over again. Hardly a day passes but I read some of them. Just think how many people they have amused and interested and entertained.

I hope Jerrine has received the last beads I sent her and has turned the others over to you.

We have been looking over our books and I am going to send some to Jerrine—they are not new, but I hope she won't mind that, for the reading is just as good. And I am going to put in one or two for you. Did you receive "The Wind Before the Dawn"? I sent it a week or more ago—didn't care very much for it.

Do please excuse blots—I don't know what is the matter with me.

> Good-bye with much love,
> J. S. *Coney*

Thanks for the little poem which I shall not return, but keep.

The *Companion* works, in story form rather than Elinore's usual letter form, centered on an imaginary family, the Culbersons, and reflected her own philosophy of "making do" with courage, optimism, and generosity. Although the magazine paid for approximately seven to twelve stories that Elinore submitted, it published only four during 1914 and 1915, returning to her the unpublished manuscripts. She modeled the Culberson children after her own, and the staunch Ma Culberson may have personified Elinore herself. The Culbersons—like Ella, Johnny, and Mrs. Sanders, the family of Eden Valley from the *Elk Hunt* collection and, perhaps, the genesis of her *Companion* series—lived in desperate poverty and struggled to survive in the harsh environment. In "A Burnt Fork Santa Claus," Elinore introduced the family:

> "Pa" Culberson was one of those Micawberlike persons who are always expecting something to turn up. In more prosperous days, when the Culbersons had lived farther east, they had owned a good team of horses and a cow; but Pa's waiting propensities had encouraged the man with the mortgage to "turn up," and the family had been left without their horses and their cow.
>
> Mrs. Culberson had urged her husband to sell their little plot of land and to use the proceeds to begin anew in another place. Pa had a "swapping" streak in him, and so it was not long before they had traded their land for a rickety wagon and a pair of small beasts that Mrs. Culberson called "dunkeys." Then, with all they owned piled into the wagon, they set forth to make a fresh start in the world. . . . One night they had camped by a stream in a fertile little valley. Mrs. Culberson liked the water and the view, and refused to go on. Weeks of wandering had worn out the children's shoes, and winter would soon be upon them; so they unloaded their scanty belongings and set about building their cabin. . . . as soon as he had finished the tiny stable, Pa went off to get work with the sheepmen.

As story continues, a lonely neighbor, Jack Nevin, journeys to Burntfork for provisions and, on a whim, decides to buy Christmas gifts for his own imaginary family. On the trip home, as he wonders what to do with his purchases, he passes the Culbersons' empty shack (the family have gone to bring Grandma back to share their Christmas supper), enters to warm himself, and notices the family's poverty:

> For an hour, Jack worked busily and happily. All that he had bought for his "family" he carried into the cabin; then, opening cases of his own supplies, he carried in canned goods, dried fruit, a ham, some sugar, coffee, and a package of tea. When he had finished, he gazed about the little room and smiled.

When the family returns, they find the packages and a note signed, "Yours Truly, Santa Claus."

The *Youth's Companion* enthusiastically accepted this first story for their 1914 Christmas issue, and in a March 25, 1914, letter, Arthur S. Pier, the editor, solicited more:

> The Christmas story is just the sort of story we want, and the sort that I felt sure you would give us. We are delighted to have it, and are confident that it will appeal strongly to our readers. I think, however, that they would like to have a glimpse of the Culberson family after their return to the shack, and their discovery of the visit that Santa Claus has made. Could you not supply a paragraph or two which would finish off the story in such a manner? A cheque in payment will be sent to you at once. I hope that we may have many more stories from you, and I thank you for sending us this manuscript, and also for your gratifying words about the *Companion*.

The other three stories, published in January and February 1915, continue the adventures of the Culbersons. In "When Culberson Lost the Sheep," Pa is to drive a herd of thoroughbred sheep to Crawford, but a blizzard and wolves scatter the sheep, and the company fires Pa. However, Ma and the children find them, exert great effort to feed them and keep them from danger, and are rewarded when the manager discovers his sheep and notes the family's diligence. "Bread upon Waters" continues the theme that "no one is so poor they have nothing to give." The children, in their efforts to befriend "Grandma," an elderly neighbor, reunite her with a long-lost nephew, the president of the sheep company. The Culbersons, because of their unselfishness and hard work, are more prosperous in "How the 'Young Uns' Got Their Chance," yet Ma knows that her children will not have a chance in life without an education. However, Grandma, lonely now that she is living in Denver with her nephew, writes the Culbersons and asks Lizzie Isabel to come and stay with her and go to school. Henry Clay's chance comes when he nearly dies after saving a rich sportsman from a forest fire. The hunter, who had lost his son and wife, plans to take Henry Clay to St. Louis and educate him as an engineer, fulfilling Henry Clay's dream. Since Elinore's *Atlantic* letters had been published in book form, she hoped to compile the Culberson children's stories also, but the book never progressed beyond the planning stages.

Elinore did most of her writing on the kitchen table at night by her gasoline lamp, for during the day she had household and garden chores to

complete. Clyde, although proud and supportive of her work, also needed
her help on the ranch. Elinore completed her household chores in the
morning, worked beside the men on the ranch during the day as needed,
and wrote late into the night. Yet, no matter how exhausted Elinore was,
her need to write, to chronicle the events of her life and to share her
thoughts with others, compelled her to fill page after page with her expan-
sive script.

July 27, [1915]
Burntfork Wyo.
Miss Maria Wood, Lexington, Mo-
My Dear Friend.
   Both your good letters received. How glad I always am to hear from
you. How I wish you were here with me. I think you'd like it. The kiddies
and I are camping alone away up on the mountain where we found little
Star Crosby. We find it a lovely spot in summer, only one cabin remains,
the one we are camped in. Huge mountains rise on every side. Our cabin
is in a canon, a cool little stream murmurs past between flowered bor-
dered banks, over mossy stones   Wild roses, Columbines and a dozen
other kinds of flowers whose names I do not know grow profusely. great
pines and trembling quaking asp murmur "Be of good cheer, peace, quiet,
rest, the great, clean airy out-doors. These are *yours*." Evry day I take
long walks and climb mountains, evry day I think of my dear Miss Wood.
A dozen times I see something I know you would like. The flowers, a
beautiful tree a deer, a fine view, a bed of fern, *all* bring to mind my unseen friend with whom I'd like to share it all. Should you like to sleep on
a bed of pine boughs? I just rejoice that I can. The very thought is health
inspiring to me. I cannot understand why people go to resorts for their
outings when a whole beautiful world is theirs for the taking.
   We are nine thousand five hundred and seventy feet above sea level.
In the purple and amber dawn of each new day a pair of deer come to
drink at our spring. We see them out of the cracks of our cabin. Evry day
a mother grouse walks proudly past with her seven little ones. Rabbits
eat the scraps from our step. Chipmunks are entirely to neighborly. They
come into the cabin and help themselves. Squirrels bark at us and then
scamper up the tallest tree in a frenzy of fright if we go toward them.
Some times we see a great eagle soaring high above us. I had no idea I
was tired but I must have been for I find the idea very soothing. I love

the smell of the pines. I love their stately confidence. They inspire me with the thought, 'All is well. *Why* worry, life *can't* go wrong.'

How I wish I could pass that message on just as fresh and restful as I received it to all tired, worried humanity. It's so good to let go, to relax, to trust. How I wish I could bring evry sick, half-cared for little baby out of the sweltering east and south and keep them up in this cool fragrant air. And the *dear* old folks, how I love them. If I only had some way of lifting them from their cares and seating them under these pines without the fatigue of climbing, let them rest their eyes on the beauty that lays evry where around. I dont care a *thing* about golden crowns, stars in my crown, harps, robes or mansions—If God will only let me help, let me minister to old folks and babies I shall be content. Crowns and wings can go to those who want them. I want to help. Am I boring poor dear you? Well, I wont preach any more. My heart is so full that I *had* to let it out some-way.

Perhaps you dont know how much you have helped Jerrine. She has always been a very enthusiastic child at first beggining, but she loses enterest. Two things however hold, nature study and patch work. The little thimble you sent her is a fine excuse—evry day she says, "I must member Miss Wood and sew a little." She has forty blocks of nine patch pieced. she never tires of patch work. She has a great collection of rock and petrified wood. It is a poor day when she dont add a specimen. She knows nothing about classifying them but she does know an enteresting or unusual piece when she sees it and she is *always* looking for them—It seems I have bushels I want to tell you but I am sure you must be tired. Wont you please remember me to Miss Henry and Mr. Chamberlain? With much love to you I am very

Sincerely your friend
Elinore Pruitt Stewart

I find that after all, I have not told you how came the "Letter."

My Beloved was very much alone, her only children, two daughters, were teachers in the Denver schools. So Mrs. Coney was alone in her apartments so much. She was always so interested in evry thing that it was a pleasure to share adventures with her. She was so very "Bostony" that I used to try to shock her mildly and at the same time give her as nearly as I could a true picture of the West. She was so very conventional that some one who was not so had the best chance of being enteresting and entertaining. So, I wrote her those things that . . . [remainder of letter missing].

Aug. 2, 1915
My Dear Miss Wood.

Are you ready for another letter from long winded me? I thought you would appreciate a rest along with your vacation. I have been very busy weeding my garden and doing dozens of other things, among others entertaining a couple of "high brows" from Pennsylvania and one from Soux City Iowa. Picture me trying to come up to their learned level. I didn't. I knew I couldn't so I let my visitors "run off at the neck" to each other while I *tried* to keep the boys clean.

One day, after their afternoon nap I dressed them so clean and sweet in their little white suits. One of the Pennsylvania ladies, a graduate of Welsley and of the John Hopkins was ill nearly the whole time. That afternoon I was trying to help with her. We were *all* busy. In the mean time Calvin and Rob had gone down to the stock yard and had smeared themselves all over with machine grease off the mower. They were *sights*. Because she was ill Miss Wykoff prefered her eggs raw. Calvin fell in love with her so he undertook to supply her with eggs. He put seven into his blouse and then fell down on them. One of the ladies had a garter with a rabbit foot on. Robert saw it one day, he thought it powerfully nice so he kept trying evry chance to get the rabbit foot. He has the croup often so when he begins to hoarse up we give him medicine that we keep for him. He don't like it so to please him Miss Murray pretended to like it. After that he thought "Murr" should take it evry time.

Jerrine says she is going to be a proffessor of Bugs when she grows up. She has on hand at all times all kinds of bugs, worms and evry obnoxious thing she can get. When she is hunting specimans she takes a baking powder can, drives nails into it to make air holes. She puts her specimens into the can and puts the lid on and is able to bring home a great many more captives than I like to have around. One night I had taken great pains with the table. It was beautiful. In the center was a tall dish of Rocky mountain columbines lavender and white and some ferns that grow 'way up in the mountains at an altitude of ten thousand feet. I had that perfectly satisfied feeling that always precedes disaster.

We were at supper. I heard a soft little thud and a horned toad raced across the snowy cloth. Jerrine is always catching them so I thought she had had it in her pocket and it had escaped. By the time ice cream was served bugs, spiders, worms, beetles and evry thing that creeps or crawls it seemed to me was creeping and wrigling in evry direction. The guests shreiked in terror, the children in glee—as for poor me, I would have gotten down under the table and wept only I was afraid the things would get down my back. Evry one took up their ice cream and I took off the table cloth. Then the source of supply was discovered to be Jerrine's specimen can which the cook had set under the ferns to prop them. Some way the lid had come off so the prisoners escaped. You see, I am all the time guessing. I am glad I do not wear a wig. I would never know where to expect to find it.

Some one killed our dog last winter, he was such a good *friend* that we grieved over him for months. His name was Keno; he was such a fine big fellow and so gentle and kind. The babies used to ride him. I used to let him come in to play with the boys. When he got tired of being a "horse" he would scratch on the door to be let out. I do hope that you are not worrying and I most earnestly hope you are feeling well. I have no picture of myself. Too homely. I don't think I will write any more for the Atlantic for a year.

Sincerely yours

E.P.S.

Nursing the sick, delivering babies, and caring for the elderly concerned Elinore throughout her life. Even in her choice of correspondents she favored the elderly and the confined, for example the widowed Mrs. Coney, the lame Miss Wood, and later the blind Mr. Zaiss. However, her poverty, her lack of education, her support of her brothers and sisters, and then her responsibilities of homestead and children did not allow her the luxury of realizing her dream of becoming a doctor. Although she had little formal education in medicine, having picked up bits of information from her brief training as a nurse at Bethany Hospital, from her own household experience, and from friends and neighbors, the Burntfork community considered Elinore their "doctor." Compassionate and dedicated, she did what she could with her home remedies and limited medicines. Elinore's cure-all for ill health combined fresh mountain air with wholesome homegrown food and the renewing physical labor she herself found in gardening. Most often, however, her nursing abilities helped alleviate the sickness and suffering of her own husband and children.

Burnt Fork
Dec. 10, [1915]
Dear Miss Wood.

   I am sure I cannot resist the temptation to write you   I have to steal
time to do it so reckon I should be called Procrastination, being the thief
of time. The doctor says Mr. Stewart is not in danger if he takes care if
himself, says it is just a break down owing to too hard work in days gone
by. We are still on the ranch but the renter releieves Clyde of all the worry
and all the work but feeding the beef. Two more months will see that all
done then he will be a liberty. The renter has homesteaded land joining
the ranch so must live on his homestead, he can do so and yet run this
place with ease so I can live on here as I very much prefer to do. The am-
bition of my life has been to be thoroughly helpful and useful. Some
times I think I am going to see my dream realized, but I can do more
here than in town so here I want to stay.

   Some day when I am sure you wont think me a bragadocio I am going
to tell you some of the efforts that enterest me. 'Spect you'll laugh when I
tell you but I wont care for that, I like to laugh. I can't wait to tell you
one of my "do's". Being without those necessary evils, physicians we are
obliged to rely upon one another. In earlier years one of my fleeting
dreams was to become a trained nurse. Accordingly I worked for six
months in Bethany hospital and since have read evry thing I could get
hold of about nursing. Result, I have a smattering of knoledge that is
sometimes called upon here. Mrs. Lamb was the first case of the kind I
had ever attempted alone, evry thing went well and now she has gone
home with a fine boy to her credit, that being successfully over with,
three more prospective mothers have asked me to help them.

   See what I am coming to? No? Let me draw the picture. Behold! A wob-
bly old buggy that creaks and groans and seems undecided whether to stay
on the road or to wobble out and fall over, drawn by a decreptit old flea-
bitten white horse who seems afraid and to be feeling his way. Behind, in
the buggy clucking to, admonishing and encouraging the horse sits an ex-
pansive old lady with four chins and not much lap. In the buggy is a rusty
old black bag that has a great capacity and possibilities. Inside the bag are
rolls of antiseptic gause, cotton, tweezers, clinical thermometer trocars
umbical cord and sweet oil, carbolic acid boric acid, horehound drops,
catnip, some linen, some mint sticks for good children and—lots of things
I hope. Guess who the old lady is and where she is going.

I wonder do I "dast" write a letter to the poor, sick Miss Arnold? I feel a real enterest in her. Miss Locke Arnold was so good to Jerrine and Mrs. Tidball sent me a real Pangora's box only evry thing in it was a blessing. All the poems she sent I kept for myself. I have three of them on my *own* door and catch an inspiring word evry time I open the door. I wish I could spare some of my abundant health to Miss Arnold. How gladly I would do it, as I cannot I wish I could give her *some* thing. There are a great many funny "sick room" experiences in this country. I wonder if it would amuse her or make the time a little less tedious for her if I wrote them to her? Perhaps she would be disgusted.

Are you tired of this long letter? I reckon you think I have been powerfully good but I "aint". I am getting to be plumb trifling about work. I can easily count a dozen things I should do right now but I had rather write to you. Wont you send me *your* picture. I'd like to know what you are like. I may not get to write you any more before Christmas, if I do not I am wishing you a very happy day, a tranquil, *peaceful* day and I hope Santa Claus puts evry thing into your stocking that I would like to put there.

With much love,—
Elinore Stewart

May 17, [1916]
Dear Miss Wood

I meant to answer you right away but was plumb out of paper. Living so far from town is considerable of a handicap and we have to take any thing we can get so this paper is not meant as a personal insult at all. I just have to use this until I can get better.

It seems so hard to give up our friends I think. None of us have a single one to spare but when they suffer so long it seems to me we should rejoice at their release. Our dear old Mr. Pearson who died a year ago was so long going that this entire neighborhood was completely worn out with the care and our hearts were crushed with seeing him suffer. I had not entended to tell you but my beloved Mrs. Coney has been with God since in September. Her's was a long road to the goal but she went smiling serenely. She went bravely—absolutely secure in her faith and trust. She did much toward teaching me how to live and more toward teaching me how to die. Oh! I love her. I think your Miss Arnold and my beloved might well have inspired this little inset.

THE VALUED DEAD

Thanks be to God that such have been,

Although they are no more.

John Chadwick

I shall write to Mrs. Tidball. I dont want to lose her and I know that she has been too worried to think of outsiders. Do you enjoy a laugh? there is much that is funny in a nurse's experience as well as much that is sad. In this community we have to depend so much upon one another that we all know the little ins and outs of each other's lives. If you should ever come to see me I will take you to see dear old Grandma Stoll. You'd love her at once, evry one does. She can neither read or write but she is the only physician or nurse that the majority of Burnt Forkers ever knew and she has had many amusing experiences.

One of the funniest happened to Lige. Now Lige is an old sinner, he must be a hundred. At one time he was very wealthy but no one ever accused him of being good. He has no family and when he was younger he rode bronchos and so ruptured himself   his rupture is abdominal and some times causes him great trouble. All the young men about are devoted to Lige for no other reason that I can see than that he keeps plenty of whiskey and can yet play an enteresting game of poker. His cabin is about a mile and a half from us and about a half a mile from Grandma Stoll's. Well, one day word went out that Lige was about to die. Loud groans issued from his cabin and a breathless young man burst in upon Grandma who was hurriedly preparing to go to a sick woman.

"Oh! Come, come quick, grandma, Lige is having a rupture." gasped the boy.

"Well—I don't care if he is" calmly replied grandma as she tied on a clean apron. "Doll Hickey is having a baby which is more use than a rupture so I am going to her."

She was up all night and all day with the mother so when she got home she crept into bed hoping for a night's rest but no sooner did Rob, her baby boy 22 years old find that she was home than he asked her to do something for Lige. Now grandma had helped him many times. Her method was to use a thick fold of woolen rung out of hot milk. This stoupe she put upon the rupture until the skin was soft and the pain reduced then she gently worked the rupture back into place. She thought evry one knew how so she gave Rob a bucket of sweet milk and a pair of old drawers telling him to wring them out of the milk and put on. Away dashed Rob but in the gray of early morning he was back wildly pounding his mother's door. So grandma hurried to her patient. She found him suffering terribly but still able to speak.

"They're killin' me gran'ma. they're killin pore old Lige. Them young galoots has been puttin them drawers on and pullin' em off my *legs* all night long." That is the way they had interpreted grandma's directions and the poor old reprobate could not see that wearing wet drawers helped his rupture any.

You may think by this long letter that I've been good but I "ain't." It is so good and dear of you to say that I have cheered you even a little bit. That makes me happy but I am afraid it is just that you are very appreciative. I seem unable to write without an objective point and since my beloved has gone there seems no one to have good times for or to tell them to. Oh! I miss her. The mail seems so incomplete since I do not see her dear letters but I know she is happy some where and as long as I live I shall do all I can to justify her faith in me.

With much love,
Elinore P. Stewart

Often during the summer, Elinore, usually with Jerrine, would escape to the mountains or to a deserted sawmill on Phillipeco Mountain southeast of the ranch to write, sometimes for an afternoon, other times for several days. Occasionally, the whole family accompanied her on her outings. Next to personalities, nature inspired her writing most of all, and she never missed an opportunity to observe it in detail.

Burntfork
July 12, [1916]
My Dear little Woodsy-person.

Guess who this is that is writing. Some one who loves you? Ofcourse! But what name; you have forgotten? You well may say that so let us call this penpusher Mrs. Dally Diliatory. Well, after our more than forty days of being in a deluge of work, loss and anxiety I emerge and send this, dove of a letter to see if it will bring me back a green leaf of remembrance. See what a poet I be. First thing you know you will be receiving an impassioned Ode to a Shoe-string or some "sich." But I feel so much better than I did. I had such a case of "ruination, Despair and dreadful Ivy [?]" (that is from my friend Ed) that I felt like a morgue reporter. But

I *had* to work. Moping won't grow peas or lettuce, so I planted garden. It came up, so did the cut worms. Then I j'ined the cut worm campaign and took fiendish satisfaction in killing the things. Then I replanted and by that time the Stewart had a brief lull in his work so we took the Clan to the mountains for a brief outing on Independence Day.

The Stock Growers Association of which My Stewart is a member gave a great time at Lone Tree and you would have thought we would have gone there. But two things restrained us. First and *finest* Mr. Stewart disapproves of bucking contests. It hurts him and makes him angry to see a horse tortured and abused til it bucks in its' efforts to free its'self of its' tormentor. So he didn't want to go or have the Clan go on that account. And *I* didn't want to go because we would have to have so many new things. New hats, new shoes, new dresses and evrything so we asked the children if they would like to camp out in the mountains. They most joyously would.

So we took a great roll of bedding and our mess-box and all clambered into the wagon and were off. We went for miles up Burnt Fork Canon to a deserted cabin we own but found when we arrived that cattle had been in so we prefered to camp out side. The Columbines and choke-cherries were in bloom, just a riot of bloom so it was more beautiful than I can tell you. Here Burnt Fork is a madly rushing mountain stream roaring and cascading over great boulders. Just back of us rose the crags and cliffs of the "hog-back" all beautifully etched against the sunset sky. The canon widened a little here so we had a tiny valley in which to camp. The man who built the cabin had thought to find coal and had tunneled back into the hogback but all he ever brought out was white sandstone. There was a huge dump of it and as our teeth were chattering I hurriedly made a fireplace and soon had a blaze. Such skurrying around! such hunting for coats and sweaters for, although the great pines bowed politely and murmured kind welcomes yet a breeze down the canon directly off the snow banks above gave us a cold welcome. But very soon the odor of frying potatoes, bacon and coffee added to the sweet fragrance of the forest. Then we ate by the light of our fire and after that unrolled our beds.

Perhaps it was the coffee which we never use at night but up there it was so cold we felt the need of a hot drink. Any way we couldn't sleep. We lay watching the moon come up slowly, as if reluctant to look down upon our scant privacy. Little voices from the boys' bed repeating "Lady

Moon, lady moon, Where are you Roving." I looked over at Jerrine, she sat in her nest hugging her knees, looking at Lady Moon and softly singing "When in thy dreaming, moons like these shall shine again." I guess we were moon-struck. I thought Clyde asleep, he had a sheep-skin coat over his head, he's bald, you know, but I saw his eyes glisten.

"It was a night just like this when poor Tod Herron was killed. We were night herding together just out from Ogalalah. I was only a kid then, had run away from home"—and my silent Scot told me a touching little story, he who has so *few* words. And I—I had had moon-light nights, too. My mother's last night on earth was a glorious moon light night and we children sat huddled together, knowing ourselves motherless wondered how the moon *could* shine when the end of our world had come. so I lay thinking. Over-head the quaking aspens were wrestling with the wind all night long, just as Jacob of old wrestled with the angel. I had much to tell you of our trip but this letter is already too long   I have'nt told you half I meant to. You wont get a bit of my outing but you will get all my love. Are you well? Has your trouble left you? May be a stay with me in our clean, cool air would help. Your little nook in our home is always here for you.

Yours,
Elinore Stewart

TWO

Settling In (1917–1925)

World War I exploded, unsettling lives even in the remote sagebrush-filled corners of Wyoming. Elinore's burdens doubled when Ernest Eubanks, the Stewarts' hired man, enlisted. In addition, her war garden consumed many of her hours. An avid gardener, Elinore loved experimenting with plants most people said could not grow in Wyoming, and her stack of pamphlets from the Department of Agriculture piled higher and higher each year on her library shelf in the kitchen. She even raised sugar beets and attempted to make sugar. Since she had no way to separate the molasses from the sugar—to crystallize out the white sugar—the sugar was black. Yet the family had sugar when others were going without. In addition, she raised much more than was needed by her own family, giving the surplus to others less fortunate. Elinore also worked actively in civilian support of the war, assisting with Red Cross work and selling war bonds. President Wilson even honored her for her efforts.

Meantime, the success of her writing prompted visits from people from all across the United States: admiring readers and fellow writers, scholars, politicians, schoolteachers, theologians, doctors, and dentists. Sometimes these guests would hazard the arduous journey to Wyoming and across the sage-covered badlands for a day or two of conversation with the famous homesteader. Because of the Stewarts' hospitality, the visitors often remained for weeks or even months. One such woman, Mary Antin, a Jewish-Russian immigrant and author from Boston who was also published by *Atlantic Monthly* and Houghton Mifflin, visited the Stewarts several times.[1]

1. At the age of eleven, Mary Antin made her debut in literature with her account, written in Yiddish, of her journey to America. At thirteen she translated the

At first strangers, all those who undertook the long pilgrimage to the homestead soon became friends.

Burnt Fork
Oct. 9, [1917]
My dear friend,
    I was so glad to get your letter and meant to write at once but I have been so busy. I have hardly had time to think this summer. First my war garden and my flowers took up my time and cooking for hay men kept me busy. Then the two little boys came down with bloody flux and I did have my hands full. As soon as they were better the two oldest kids had to go off to school. I had to rush around to get them off and next day after they left I had a telephone message saying that Dr. Grace Meigs of the childrens welfare bureau of Washington D.C. Mrs. Bartlett a nurse taking a survey of this country in the enterest of the bureau, Mrs. Morton, secretary of the House Defense league of Wyoming and Mrs. Taliaferro, chairman of the League would be at my home that day. I had been under such a strain that I had been resting that day and the house was topsy-turvy. But I got busy. Well, I spent some anxious time at the telephone and got up a meeting for that night. We had some good talks. Next day, two of the ladies went home but Dr. Meigs and the nurse stayed on. They went to all the homes.
    One evening while we were at supper the phone rang; a very cultured masculine voice on the wire informed me that he, the Rev. Mr. Kagey of St. Pauls Episcopal Church in Evanston was coming with his good wife to visit me. I had never seen the Rev. Mr. or Mrs. either and I looked forward to their visit with rather a doubtful joy. Fortunately the Dr. and the nurse were about ready to go so I "shooed" them out with the broom I swept their room with. The whirr of their auto had hardly died away before the honk-honk of another Ford announced the arrival of my Rev. visitors. I hurriedly adjusted my company smile which was kind of sagging at the corners—and ran out to meet them. I said de-lighted with all

story into English, and it was published in 1899 as *From Plotzk to Boston* (Boston: W. B. Clark, 1899). She further clarified her vision of the accessibility of the American Dream in her second work, *The Promised Land,* which was serialized in the *Atlantic Monthly* and later brought out in hard-cover by Houghton Mifflin in 1912.

the abandon and emphasis of a Roosevelt on a campaign. Oh! I lied
cheerfully, but very soon it ceased to be a lie, for Mrs. Kagey is from
North Carolina and we were at home with each other in two minutes.
And Mr. Kagey is a very earnest young man. Clyde of course, took to
him. That night we had a little service at the school house. They left after dinner next day. Their visit did us both a world of good. I feel so
rested and relaxed since they were here.

The draft has made us so short of men that I find myself in my element again, on the mowing machine. Oh, I'm glad I can mow and rake
and even stack hay. I have been having a perfectly lovely time helping.
And we have had a perfectly glorious fall. There has been no snow or
rain and the frost has been so light that my flowers are not harmed. My
beautiful blue and gold Wyoming! You would love it. My poor, dear you.
How I wish I could bring you right here now, while my curtains are fresh
and my company room clean and while the quaking aspens are so
golden. From the window of what would be your room you could look
out upon Phillipeco, a big mountain near. High upon its' side is a perfect
cross, now flaming gold, where the quaking aspens are. It rest me to look
at it and it would you. How many sorrows have come to you, my poor
dear, and I so dumb to comfort you. But I love you dear heart, I do indeed. You might not love me if you saw me but I would love you for I
know how precious you are. We are all well.

> With very affectionate regard
> *Elinore Stewart*

The children spent the winters of 1917 and 1918 in Boulder in order to
attend the better schools offered by a larger city, for Elinore was determined
that her children should receive a good education. Between 1911 and 1917,
the children had attended school haphazardly. Clyde, Jr., the oldest boy,
had been sent to live with his grandmother so that he could attend first
grade in Boulder, and Jerrine had spent a few years in a convent school.
However, for the most part, Elinore had attempted to educate all of her
children at home. As the children grew older, though, she realized that they
needed a more formal education and believed that Colorado offered better
opportunities than those available in the small Wyoming towns. The family
ties to Boulder strengthened the choice.

At first the family lived in Clyde's parents' former home in Boulder.
Then, sometime in 1923–24, Elinore and Clyde purchased a house near

Grandmother Stewart's. Elinore usually arrived after the fall haying and ranch work was completed and left in early spring, before school dismissed, to help Clyde with the calving and planting. The children, often with Grandmother Stewart, returned to the ranch during the summers. During these years, Elinore wrote more stories, both in Boulder and at the ranch. Finally, after years of rejections, the *Atlantic Monthly* again published one of her letters. "The Return of the Woman Homesteader" appeared in the May 1919 issue.[2] In this letter, "written to a friend in the South," The Woman Homesteader and Mrs. Louderer travel the countryside, selling war bonds.

Burnt Fork, Wyoming, October 26
My Dear Friends—
I have neglected you for so long that I do not expect either of you to recognize me again. Still, when I sent you the note, I promised to tell you of my adventures in bond-selling. I thought I had done pretty well, and was planning to send in my final report a whole week before the drive was over. I was filling in the blanks when a heavy tread and a well-known voice announced Mrs. Louderer.

To you I can confess that my feelings were a little mixed, because I have not been quite certain how she felt about the war. Somehow, our old careless ways have slipped from us, and every day is so full of pressing work that we no longer have those good house-to-house visits that once were such joys.

But my dear Mrs. Louderer came in with her great knitting-bag, from which she took some candy for the little boys. "You have not been to see me, so I have came," she calmly announced as she seated herself and began to "toe off" a khaki sock!

I never supposed a sock could produce thrills of relief, but that one did. But I was ashamed to tell the truth, or may be I feared to hurt her. Anyway, I plunged into telling about my efforts to sell bonds.

Mrs. Louderer is never very talkative, and so I rattled on, immensely pleased with myself, until she remarked, "If all made so poor do as you, the Wyoming will not go over the top. For why does the government ask for money? Because it is needed. For who is it needed? For those who

2. "The Return of the Woman Homesteader" was published in the *Atlantic Monthly* of May 1919. Reprinted by permission of the *Atlantic*.

leave their homes, give their time, their money, their very life; and yet
you think you do well when you have hardly begun. Have you seen
Lund? Have you spoken to Herman? No! that would mean some work;
that would take your time from monkeying with your own little jobs.
Yah!" She finished so scornfully that I was perfectly dumfounded. Before
I could say a word, she began to tell me how to make rye-bread, "so as
you can eat." Indignation flared up, but her words had struck my self-
conceit such a blow, that I could think of nothing to say.

Then Clyde came in, and they began a discussion about cattle, and I
was glad to slip away to prepare supper and try to collect my scattered
thoughts and a little self-respect. But what she said was true, and it was a
humbled woman who presently called them to supper. "The gude mon"
and Mrs. Louderer did indeed "talk of many things," but beef and the
Kaiser had a greater place in their discussion than "cabbages and kings."

Mrs. Louderer left me to do up the kitchen work, while she and Clyde
went out to look at some mule colts that are a new addition to our
ranch. I was glad she did so, for never before was the giftie gie me to see
myself as others see me. I did n't like the picture at all, and I am afraid
that conversation would have been a little difficult.

While I was busy putting the little Highlanders to bed, she came in
and told them a story. When the boys were asleep, she said,—

"To-morrow we will go after Lund and some more, and make them
dig up the price required to teach some of their brothers and odder kin
the folly of being *anything* but Americans."

"I can't go so far from home," I told her. "I've set sponge to try out
your rye-bread recipe, and the children are so troublesome on a long trip
as that will be."

"Now you see?" she interrupted me; "you can't let go your own affairs.
But you are going. Already have I said so to Clyde, and to-morrow we
will hitch Chub and Kronprinz to the little wagon. We will be gone some
days, may be, so you can get ready for that."

That night Clyde told me that he would take care of my work, and
that he really thought I should go. "And," he added, "have the very pleas-
antest time you can, for I know what she said to you."

So it was with a perfectly clear conscience that I seated myself beside
Mrs. Louderer next morning, and left undone many waiting tasks. Many
times I wished for you. The blue-and-gold charm of October Wyoming
would have charmed you. It did me the first time I saw it, and I have

remained under its spell ever since. I wish I had words to paint it for you, but you will have to picture the lonely buttes, with the shifting lights of blue, gold, and rose; the suggestive reach of the desert; and perhaps the next turn of the road would present the crags and clifts of the hog-back. Back of that, the forest reserve, and back of that again, the shining snow-peaks.

The air seemed golden, and everywhere the quaking aspens had been touched by Midas.

I could not talk while such beauty lay spread before me. Mrs. Louderer thought I was sulking. "You should not pout because I said to you as I did. You do not know, as I do, what will happen if we should lose."

"I am just enjoying the beauty," I told her.

"That is well," she replied. "Folks in Belgium will not see much beauty in the ruins that are left. If heaven itself had been in Belgium, it would have been bombed and gassed. St. Peter was not German, and he would have been gassed or worse. I have no time to look at yellow trees and blue mountains. I have in me only a wish to see green bills."

She gave Kronprinz such a spiteful cut with her switch, that he sprang forward and almost spilled us both.

"Why do you call you horse the name you do?" I asked.

"Because he should be killed almost, he is so hateful; only I would be glad if only I had by me the Kronprinz, so as I could beat his back as it should."

So she urged the horses on, our wagon jolting and creaking protestingly. She seemed unable to win me away from my pleasant contemplations, and I was just as unable to keep her from her unpleasant ones.

We were miles from home when we saw a figure some distance ahead of us in the road. It was Herman. He was trudging along on his way to a sheep-camp where he was to work. After a pleasant exchange of greetings, he produced his pipe.

"Herman," began Mrs. Louderer, "you have no one dependent upon you and you have wasted all your life—"

Herman interrupted her with something in German.

"I will not so speak. I will say my words only in United States, if you please," she informed him with severe dignity.

I could n't keep up with them for the next few minutes. They both talked at once, and talked in German and United States, though each denied the German.

Mrs. Louderer won out, for when Herman stopped for breath, she kept on. "We have come that you should buy bonds. We were going to Lund's to see you there, and here you meet us on the road and insult us, so," she finished indignantly.

Herman calmly knocked the ashes out of his pipe, lighted it, took a few puffs, then very deliberately said, "I will buy no bonds. I have no money."

Then war *did* prevail.

"Loafer, Schweinehund, for why do you live? What haf you done with the seven hundert dollar which I paid you six year ago? Why shall young men go fight, die, to protect you and your old pipe, while you wander the road by insulting me?"

Herman contemplated the distant skyline. Presently he took his pipe from his mouth, and gravely remarked, "Louderer, you make too much noise wit' your mouth. The money what you paid me I put with four hundert more. With it I bought the Symes sheep when he enlisted. It's few they is, yet a living they will be for Callie Archer while her two boys, Joe and Eddie, herds them. Besides the money what you ask so much about, I had yet twenty-three hundert dollars; with that I bought bonds by all the drives. I have yet by me the receipts. See?" He took a small book from his pocket and showed us the receipts.

Mrs. Louderer again belabored Kronprinz, and we drove on. I looked back. Herman was trudging on. I wanted to giggle, but did n't dare. Soon we came in sight of Lund's. The small valley in which they live seemed a blaze of gold. The road here is a dug-way and hugs the red crags of the hog-back. Along the top gray-green cedars cling, distorted by years of buffeting wind. Far below us was the low cabin of logs, the sheep-pens and outbuildings of the ranch.

The dug-way was a perilous road, and we crept down slowly; but at last we drew up at the cabin. Mrs. Lund was washing, but she came out and welcomed us cordially, her bright blue eyes beaming and her tanned, weatherbeaten face all smiles.

"For twenty years I have lived by this ranch Frau Louderer, and now is it the first time you have come by me. Lund is gone with the sheep to market. If only he was here! Before this war always Carl went off with the sheep; but he has gone. In training he is, at Camp Lewis, so Lund goes by the sheep."

All the while she was busy spreading the table, and her little daughters were hanging up the clothes on the line outside. For dinner we had mutton and "war-bread," which Mrs. Lund declared was enough to make anyone want to fight if they ate it. We had delicious cheese, and pickles made of young squash. Mrs. Lund told us about her boy in training. "I am calling him Charlie now, Carl is too German," she told us. "Why do you suppose Germans in the Fatherland is so bad? Why so butchers do you think, Louderer?"

"It is because they have been lied to and deceived."

"Then they are fools. Why do they not come to Wyoming once and see how is?"

So the talk went on. Mrs. Louderer told of the Red Cross needs, the Y.M.C.A., and the Liberty loans.

"We have come to let you buy some bonds once. For the kinder it will be good. By them they can prove they are not Germans. Five children you have. We will sell you a bond for each."

"Oh, oh! how can I?" wailed Mrs. Lund. "Lund always does the business; he it is that pays all the bills; I *never* did it. He is gone by the sheep to Omaha. Yesterday he started, and if he was here I could not ask him for so much, because I made him promise to put two whole sheep on my head, four are to go on my back, and some on each of the children."

"But," Mrs. Louderer interrupted, "these are war-times. Why choose now to spend sheep-money?"

"Twenty-five years it is since Lund and I get married. I had a new hat then; since then I have had none. All these years I have worked and saved. We both thought it foolish to spend money, but now Ca—Charlie is a man and Bertha a woman, and I want that they shall not be ashamed of me, so I told Lund to buy me a fine hat and some other things to go with it."

"I suppose you will wear it to the funeral of the boys who are sent home in their wooden overcoats," remarked Mrs. Louderer.

I remembered my own recent lashing and escaped with Bertha. She is to be married when Gideon Prescott comes home. She showed me her "trousseau." It consists of six big puffy pillows, a lot of wool-filled quilts, some bright, homemade rugs, and a box of dishes.

In a lull in our conversation, we heard Mrs. Louderer ask, "Who signs Lund's checks? He cannot write, I know."

"Me, I do," Mrs. Lund replied, promptly and proudly.

Presently I went back to the kitchen. Mrs. Lund was writing a check.

"This a wedding present will be for Bertha. She is to marry an American soon yet."

"That is as is right. An American girl *should* marry an American," Mrs. Louderer agreed. She was *very* pleasant and exerted herself to show it. She held four checks in her hand.

"Now," she smiled at Mrs. Lund, "you see how it is to be an American wife. You can help your country when you *want* to. You are free to write a check when the time is."

"That is not new," Mrs. Lund protested; "already we are naturalized, long since, and I always wrote Lund's checks."

"As he said, yes," Mrs. Louderer said, as she gathered her belongings; "but to-day you have wrote them as is best for all, and Lund will put the sheep on your head yet. I am glad. I hope your hat has the finest plume and the largest roses that can be had in Omaha."

After the most pleasant of farewells, we again set forth. This time we did n't try the dug-way: we kept down the valley. We had many gates to open, but Mrs. Louderer said that was my job. I did n't mind. No one could mind opening gates when each gate led from one enchanted spot into another.

"Now you see what an injustice would be done the Lunds if so we had not gone there. Fife hundert dollars it is, and for the first time in her life she is free. Never before did she spend a dollar without Lund says so."

"Mr. Lund may have bought bonds in town," I reminded her.

"Well, and if he has! What then? She has bought bonds on the ranch, and they have money enough yet, even with sheeps on the head and back and on the children. There is few, very few Germans on any poor farm. Germans hate failure same as we do the Kaiser."

Again she pounded the Kronprinz, and again we slowly mounted to the ridge-road.

I must stop this letter but I cannot send it until I write you of our last stopping-place in this drive. I will do that to-morrow.

E.R.S.

It was quite late, almost dark, when we got to the Bird ranch that night. Our horses were very tired, and I was glad enough to stop. The Birds are French and Indian. Their large, comfortable log-house is beautifully situated up against a granite bluff, in a bend of Green River. Great pines form a splendid wind-break on the north, and add greatly to the beauty of the place. The river flows southward here, and through its granite cañons glimpses of forests and snow-peaks can be had.

It is a very beautiful spot, yet to me it seemed a tragic one. I don't know why, unless it was the constant low murmur of the river or the sighing of the pines. We were warmly welcomed. Mr. Bird is one of the most courteous of men, and Mrs. Bird made us feel that our welcome was genuine. They have a large family of grown children, most of them married and gone, and two sons in France. Some of the children were visiting their parents, and all was a pleasant bustle in the kitchen, where we were seated by the fire, for the gathering shadows had been chill.

In the large room adjoining, Mr. Bird and the "baby-boy," a handsome, dark-eyed youth, were taking the ashes from a huge fireplace and preparing a fire for our enjoyment after supper. There are not many fireplaces in Wyoming, and the prospect of an open fire made me very happy.

Supper was served on a long table, and every face around was glad.

While we were still at the table, the dogs outside set up a terrible barking and a horseman rode up to the door. Mr. Bird went out, and there followed a subdued conversation.

"I will stay with you to-night, if you want, Jacques. Others are coming to-morrow," we heard the newcomer say.

"Oui, oui—I want you, yes. Put up your horse and come in. I'm—all undone, friend."

The face that had left the table with a happy smile was haggard and drawn. Mrs. Bird asked something in French. Mr. Bird leaned heavily on his chair. Never was a face more eloquent of sorrow.

"It is Lonnie, Marda. Our Lonnie is dead in France—killed in action."

I can never forget that scene. There was no outcry. I could hear the pines grieving, the river murmuring its sorrow. One by one the family slipped away. The man who brought the news came in. I laid him a plate. Mrs. Louderer brought a cup of coffee. The lamp sputtered a little, and I could hear the newly made fire crackling, but there was no talking, no weeping.

Presently someone crept into the sitting-room, and in passing the door I saw it was Mrs. Bird, sitting, bowed and stricken, before the fire. Two of the girls came in and assisted us with the dishes. They moved about quietly, and only their big black eyes told of sorrow. After a while another daughter told us that we were to sleep in the little bedroom off the sitting-room.

Mr. Bird and the man who brought the news were outside, talking in low tones. Sometimes we caught a word.

"Yes, the postmistress at Burnt Fork saw the name in to-night's casualty list. She 'phoned to me at Manila, and I came at once, only stopping at Linwood for your mail, and the telegram from the War Department was there for you. There is no mistake, Jacques. I wish there was. Lonnie is gone."

"It is hard, hard," the father said; "more bitter because both his mother and me opposed his going. He enlisted against our wishes, and we did n't get to say good-bye. We had only one letter, and have not answered it, so he will never know how proud we were of him. And—we'll never see the reckless boy again. He could find no horse too wild to ride. He would ride into Green River when it was out of its bank in flood-time. Oh!—"

I heard no more of their talk, and soon Mrs. Louderer and I retired to our bed. There was no door to close between the sitting-room and ourselves. There had been a curtain; the rod was still up, but it had been taken down in the house-cleaning and not put back. We heard the others going to bed. The neighbor and Baby-boy were to share the same bed, but the boy rode away in the velvety night, and we heard the man when he turned in.

I could not sleep. Mr. Bird came in with some wood for the fire. From where I lay I could see the two sitting silently by the fire. A clock struck twelve. Mrs. Bird went outside. We heard her step off the porch. Soon Mr. Bird went out and brought her in. They spoke a few words in French, and Mr. Bird said, "Stay away from the river, Marda. You *might* fall in. That would not help. It is hard, I know, but we got to bear it."

But Mrs. Bird seemed not to hear. She moved over to the window and stood staring out into the night. I could see her hands clench and unclench themselves, and at times a shudder passed over her. Again she went out. This time Mrs. Louderer rose and went out for her. She brought Mrs. Bird in, and going into another room, brought a rocking-chair.

"Sit in this chair, Marda—the chair that Lonnie brought you for a birthday present. You did n't think when he took such pains to bring this back that in it you should sit to think of him being dead. I remember him when he was a baby, Marda. Such fat legs he had, and such a mop of black hair. You remember the little red socks I knit for him? And the little moccasins you beaded? And he loved you so, Marda. Always was he a mamma-boy."

On and on she talked, and for once I was thoroughly angry with my friend. It seemed brutal to keep adding sorrow to sorrow; but she would not heed the signs I tried to make.

At last, I could stand it no longer. I rose and went into the kitchen to make some coffee. I hoped that Mrs. Louderer would come out and help me. When the coffee was made, I took a cup to Mrs. Bird. She took a swallow of the scalding liquid. Her eyes were hard and dry; she sat holding the cup and staring into the fire.

"And you remember the time when you ran the sewing-machine needle into your finger, how he cried and cried for you; his heart was melted for you, and now he lies dead, may be mangled, in France, with not a tear for his going."

Mr. Bird was sobbing, but Mrs. Bird only looked at him curiously. It was a long night. How Mrs. Louderer ever held up, I do not know. Once Mr. Bird asked her out to the kitchen, where I had laid him a lunch which he would not taste.

"I can stand no more," he said. "Will you not stop talking of Lonnie? See, my heart is broken, I am crushed; you have brought back the little boy of years ago."

"Jacques, you are safe; but Marda, she should weep. It is to save you a greater trouble, a darker sorrow, that I talk so."

And nothing we could do could prevent her raking up every little incident of the past.

At last, the east lightened reluctantly, a little breeze came whispering along. Mrs. Bird went out on the porch, and we followed. A new note had crept into the river's crooning.

"Even the river and the trees miss him. Listen, how they mourn," said Mrs. Louderer.

Mrs. Bird's lips quivered and she turned her face away.

Just then a horse came up to the gate, hung his head over, and whinnied. Mrs. Bird left us. She went up to the horse and patted him, parted his mane and stroked his neck. Next she was sobbing and clinging to the horse, who seemed human in his intelligence. Great tears rolled down her face, and there seemed no depth too deep for her sorrow. I wanted to go to her, but Mrs. Louderer restrained me.

"That is Lonnie's horse, and it will do her more good to weep it out with him. We will start breakfast and see what we can do."

Mr. Bird took a shawl and went out to his wife. The girls came out, and together we prepared the meal. After a while Mr. Bird and Marda came back. There were signs of tears, but both were relaxed. We expected to stay until more neighbors came. After breakfast Mr. Bird said—

"I have bought no bonds; to tell the truth I did n't think I would, for I felt hard about Lonnie going. But he's gone. Marda and I have talked it over out under the pine where he played. If he cared enough to give his life for what he was fighting for, it should for us be a gracious gift. We will not grudge the price. Both life and the cause he died for are priceless. We are not so poor, and if Lonnie had lived, there would have been a share for him. That share we will use to buy bonds. We will decide afterwards what we shall do with the bonds, but it will be something in memory of our boy."

So I filled out the blanks. Mrs. Bird and Mrs. Louderer were rocking and talking quietly.

"Sorrow is so hard to bear," said Mrs. Bird. "Last night, when I stood by the river, it seemed to say, 'Come on, come on, join your boy. Plunge in, forget, forget.'"

"Yes," said Mrs. Louderer, "sorrow is hard. I know. My Bennie is gone, and he could n't die for his country like Lonnie. We are like Mary at the Cross. Let us be glad that our own dear boys brought us there."

Soon other friends came, and as our drive home was a long one, we started at once. We did n't say much. I felt a new love for my kind, gruff, precious old neighbor.

"Dear, *dear* Mrs. Louderer," I said, "how do you do it? How can you know just what to do every time?"

"Maybe I don't," she said; "but I should. I have lived a long time. Many sorrows have lain on my heart, and this war—We must all do all we can. You see what Mrs. Lund has got by the war—freedom once. You see what Mrs. Bird gave. But she has gained too. You must gain and give. I must, too."

Only the creaking of our protesting wagon broke the silence. I was glad when the roof of my dear cabin home came in sight; happier still, when shrill childish voices shouted, "Mamma, mamma, we have been good boys and papa made funny biscuits. The cat scratched Robert, and Calvin rode on the red pig."

And now, my dear friend, you see a little of why I have not written oftener, and why I have to write at such great length. I really don't get any more work done than anyone else, but it takes more work to accomplish results. I *must* stop now.

Most truly your friend,
Elinore R. Stewart.

The winter of 1919–20 proved difficult. In the fall of 1919, the Stewarts had built up a fine crop of steers and a herd of good horses. If they had been able to sell the livestock, the ranch would have been entirely free of debt. However, prices were low, and they decided to winter the cattle, hoping for a better return in the spring. To add to the strain, Elinore needed medical care and had to travel to Boulder, where the boys again were attending school, leaving Clyde unaided with the chores. That winter the whole family in Boulder, including Grandmother Stewart, contracted the flu. Jerrine had joined the family because a coal strike had forced the closing of the Cheyenne convent school, the Academy of the Holy Child Jesus, which she had been attending. Elinore, struck especially hard, sent for Clyde at the ranch to come to Boulder to help out.

2144 Bluff Street, Boulder, Colo
[December 30, 1919]
My Dear little Woodsy person,
I should n't mind being in the hospital at all if you were in with me so I could "holler" out to you. Maybe you would n't want me to if you are so uncomfortable but I could scratch your back for you. As for me, you wont think I am ill or deserving of sympathy when I tell you what I did. But I had a lot of fun. The very learned physician who has charge of me warned Clyde and myself that as the valves of my body had given out I must not walk or work. Violent exercise would mean my death. So he sent down a wheel-chair where-in I dole fully perched my self. I felt so weak, helpless worthless and blue. My family seemed to enjoy having an invalid. They took too good care of me and got along quite well with out my priceless assistance. It takes an idea a long time to get through my dense head but at last I saw that I am not nearly so important as I had believed my self to be. People get along *very* well with out me, and yet I was unhappy. Christmas preparations went on just the same and evry one who came in was joyfully *full* of Christmas. But there I sat, unhappy, dully resentful like a last year's Christmas gift, kept for sentimental reasons, not for use or beauty.

So one afternoon Mother and the children went to a Christmas exercise and I resolved to run off. I got out and onto the porch with ease but went bouncing down the two steps at an alarming rate, hurt my fingers, too, trying to hold the chair back. The side walk was clear so I rolled out and down to the next street. I progressed beautifully but my wrists and hands became tired so I turned on to a cement walk that led up to some one's back-door. Then, I saw a little old lady walking about in an uncertain way on the lawn. After a few moments I saw that she was blind so I called to her. She came across to me and confessed that she had run away and from no one! "I have no one to run away from but this Christmas feeling is hard to bear so I came out." Her steps are higher than ours so after she had pushed me along the walk we had the steps to consider for she had envited me in to have tea with her. So I tried my weight upon my feet quite successfully I mounted the steps. I didn't fall dead.

Miss Lewis is eighty-five years old. She has cataracts so is unable to see well but she still goes to church, the Presbyterian. She had been a school-teacher for many years so she laid by enough to keep her for her life-time if she is careful and she is very, very careful but Christmas is a trial because she would like to give to little ones for the sake of the poor little ones her mother heart has longed for and never had but as she has lived longer than she expected to she had not dared to buy and she can't see well enough to make. All this came out over our toast and tea.

Well, I *walked* home only a block and a half. I pushed my chair. I carefully brushed the wheels and was seated as if nothing had ever happened when Mother returned with my noisy hoodlums. My own hateful feelings left me and I caught the Christmas spirit. I took my sober little Jerrine into my secret. She called upon Miss Lewis and from the talk they had learned what was wanted and needed for the small folks the dear old soul wanted to remember. Jerrine went to a bazaar and bought a little pink cap and a pair of booties for a little baby and friends had remembered my children generously so Jerrine and I opened the packages and filched a little. When we had got together all we could Jerrine took the basket to Miss Lewis and she sorted the little offerings to suit her self and with Jerrine to see the way for her set out to deliver her gifts just as happy as she could be. With Jerrine to guide her she went to the Christmas tree and heard the carols. When they got home that night the Rotarians had left a big basket for Miss Lewis. It was the happiest

Christmas ever for Jerrine. she helped. And happy for all of us because I shall not be all together useless. I send you my love my Dear friend and may the New Year bring you happiness and peace.

> Your
> *Elinore Stewart*

However, the return to Burntfork the following spring proved to be a less than joyous homecoming. The winter had been especially hard, and Clyde had had to borrow money to buy feed for the cattle. Still the animals had simply lain down on the hay and died. Only about eight or ten head of cattle and five or six horses had survived.

Burntfork
May 22, [1920]
My Dear, Dear Maria Wood
Do you think I have gone back on dear little you? Well, "I aint." Witness my hand and seal. But I have had a streneous time was snowed in for almost a month and have been muddied in for as long. We left Boulder April 6th and my trunks have not come yet owing to the impassable roads. The mail came on pack-horses for a month. My paper and ink are in my trunk and I kept waiting to get that before I wrote. But a dear little friend sent me this and as the mail can now bring me small parcels I can write and tell you and my dear Mrs. Tidball that I love you dearly.

And added to my many troubles, Jerrine, who came home with me to see me through with my tasks fell from a horse and dislocated her shoulder, so there! And then, the cattle died in piles and horses in other piles and I didn't want to write to any one.

But I can tell you my dear, that it is a releif when things get to their worst. You know what the worst *is* then and can begin to plan for better things. That's what I have done. I have planted flowers evry where and am glad that I have a picture of Poop o' Rome—and Jerrine is better too. She can use her arm a little, can comb her own hair, Thank Goodness. I know that you will not love me any more when you see how homely I am but here's some snaps for you if you want them, if not, throw them away. Will you please give Mrs. Tidball my love? And yourself. Will you please say to your-self; "That big, funny woman *loves* me."

> For I *do.*
> *Your Elinore Stewart*

Part of Elinore's plan for better things included a long-delayed wedding journey. She persuaded her bridegroom of eleven years to escape the frustrations of health and finances and climb to the mountains, her eternal spiritual retreat. The whole family, including the hired man, joined in the celebration.

Burntfork, Oct. 24, [1920]
Miss Maria Wood. Lexington
My Dear, my dear

It seems a long time since I had a line from you. Dont you love me any more? I *have* neglected you I know and with no better excuse than my usual one—work. I had a young lady visit me this summer and when I found that I would probably be too tired to write inteligently I asked her to write you so that you would know I was thinking of dear you. But I dont want to wait fourteen months for an answer so wont you please seat your self, take your pen in hand and drop me a few lines?

Since I last wrote you I have done a great many things but perhaps what would enterest you most would be my wedding tour. Yep! I've been on my *wedding* tour. when Clyde promised to love, honor and obey me he also promised *me* he would go with me on a trip to the lakes which are about thirty miles away and are at an altitude of 1400 ft.[?] So, Sept 4th 1920 We started on the tour that followed the wedding which occured May 5th 1909. We went for the fishing of course, but the beauties refused to bite so I tired of angling and set out exploring. Evry one of the party were perfectly well-behaved except myself. As usual, I had to get in-to trouble, only it was no trouble to me, only fun. I heard a lecture on glaziers last winter. I had not explored very long before I saw signs and symptoms of a glazier. While eating lunch one day at one of the higher lakes we heard a land-slide. Evry few minutes there after we could hear a roaring, cracking sound and although we were looking right at the mountain which was above timber line and less than half a mile away, we saw nothing move. It was a cold, raw day and I feared I might become tired and need a fire so I took a few matches and set out to see what the mystery of the mountain was.

The lake country has at one time been a favorite camping ground for Indians, years ago—so has an enteresting aspect for that reason. So when I set out Clyde supposed that I was merely going along the margin of the lake. So he and Ernest, our returned soldier boy went on casting

[64]

for trout while I went on my way thankful that the children were safe in the tent two miles away with Miss Prindle. From the lake to the base of the mountain was a morain and walking was neither easy nor safe, on the other side of the lake where the fishermen were was solid and dry for it was piled high with slabs of stone.

When I had crossed the morain I encountered my first snow bank of the eternal snow. I walked on this snow bed a part of the way around the base until I found a favorable place to start up. Then I had to wind about to find footing. I climbed shoulder after shoulder this way. At last I did what I then supposed was going over the top. But no! Picture to yourself a place about the size of six city blocks and all the surface covered with huge boulders—say from the size of an automobile to the size of a bushel measure—and also picture this wild surface sloping to the center from all sides and beyond rising steeply the crowning peak of the mountain. And also picture a large person starting across this boulder bed for the last final climb that should show what was on the other side. That's me.

When I had gotten well out onto this place I suddenly became conscious of the fact that I had heard a subdued roaring all the while and had supposed it to be the wind. But there was no wind. A few more steps and the sound came from right under my feet. It was water. I stooped down and moved a few boulders to see what it was like. I must have moved the key stone for no sooner had I done that than the mountain fell in. For one confused, scared minute there was a roaring clattering thunder and *tons* of stone fell *into* the earth. I thought I would be killed and buried and remember crying out "Lord, I did not pray for the rocks and the mountains to fall on me." But when the falling did cease I found my self clinging like a leach to my big boulder that I had been on in the beginning. It had never moved but at my feet yawned a cavern no telling how deep. I was too weak and scared to move, but I could not help noticing details. I saw that the underground stream or tunnel did not go straight down into the mountain but with the slope of the mountain, so while an object that had fallen in would not be many feet from the surface it might tobogan hundreds of feet and drop at the end into the very bowels of the earth. And I saw that the rock was cemented together with *ice*.

When my nerves had quit their frantic jumping I crawled away from the hole and stood up. I could only see a few feet into the hole either way but it was just the same either way, just boulders cemented with ice—with a rushing stream at the bottom. So I began to pick my way over the treacerous place listening all the while for the water. I had a great desire to see where the water came from for, you see, the snow all lay below. It blows off the tops of these mountains and lays in hollows along the sides and at the base. Not one thing grows here, of course, not the tiniest blade of grass, there is no soil except rock-dust. When at last I topped the mountain I saw just a rock strewn waste, perhaps miles in extent and I saw with alarm that it was nearing sundown. Although I could still hear the water I could find no source. Along the craggy top were ice caves with ice cicles many feet long, looking almost like pillars but I had no time to investigate so I began to retrace my steps. I had supposed that I could get down faster than I went up but I could not make much better time. When I was about half way down I heard them calling and yodling and I answered but it seemed to do no good.

When I got down it was almost dusk and a frantic Scotchman was tearing madly along the lake edge, calling and calling. I answered but made the discovery that no sound came. I hurried to him as fast as I could. He was too frightened to do anything but stare and pout for he though I must be sunk in the quagmire. Then we started back to camp but it was growing dark. Ernest had gone back to camp to break the news to the family and to try to bring a horse. There's no trail. You see he thought I must be dead. Jerrine came back with him and such a yowling as they set up. Where they had expected to find me dead they found me safe so the tears were dried and only the Scot looked dour and glum.

But it was more than two miles to camp and Ernest had failed to get the horse. I soon found that I could not keep up so asked them to go on ahead and come back to meet me with a lantern. I thought I knew exactly how we came that morning and the men had six head of horses to attend to or else they would go home and leave us. Also supper was to get and the little boys to see to so I sent Jerrine on with them. I found myself uneaqual to the climb of the hill   I would have to go over to follow them so started around the base, then night settled, thick and murky, but I kept on because I knew that the lake we were camped on lay just beyond this hill, so I plodded on, thinking that I could not be far from the trail or way they had gone. Presently I stepped into an oozy place—the water and mud came past my shoe tops. I knew we had passed no such place that morning so then knew I had lost my way. I

scrambled up the mountain side but could not go far. This hill is heavily
timbered, lots of down timber and huge boulders. I had not strength to
climb over them so I remembered my matches and made a fire—I had a
long night to reflect on my sins but when morning came I made my way
back to camp where an irate Scot all but licked

Your friend
Elinore Stewart

You see, it was only about two miles home *across* the mountains but
five miles around. It didn't seem it *could* be far to me but then I had
never been around it and only across it that once in the morning when I
went from our camp on the lower lake up to the higher one. And so I
thought I would be in calling distance of the way the men took through
the forest but each step took me farther so when they came back for me I
could not be seen or heard and the mountain is so densely wooded that
they could not see my fire even if they had gotten over on my side of the
mountain. So after searching all night they had gone to camp for a cup
of coffee and to plan the obsequies. No wonder they were a little upset to
see me bob up serenely in time to cook breakfast. The Stewart looked his
indignation when he solemnly said "Wooman, I'll *never* take you on another wedding tour, *never*."

But then he had eight days of fishing and not nearly the luck fishing
that I had exploring. I feel a regret though, for I suppose I will never get
to explore my ice mountain or to solve some of its' mysteries. Next day
after I came in that morning we started home. I had more fun than any
of the party except perhaps, Jerrine. She turned Spiritualist while we
were in the hills but that is a *long* story. Will you forgive me this long
story? Please accept my love and write me real soon. By the way, your
friends did not show up. I wish they had but hardly expected them for
we live in such a remote spot. With much love, dear Woodsy Person,

Your friend
Elinore P. Stewart

That same year, hoping to relieve the family's financial stress, Elinore
began work on a novel entitled "Sand and Sage," an adventure story of
sheepmen and cattlemen, rustlers and Indians, set in the ranchland of
Wyoming. She wrote the manuscript as she usually did, in longhand,
skipping lines and writing on only one side so that she could make

corrections. However, she often ran out of paper and would have to
continue her new chapters upside down on the backs of the preceding ones
until a new supply of paper arrived. Then she would begin again on clean
sheets. Although all of her other manuscripts had been submitted in
longhand, she decided that this one needed to be typed, so she found a
typewriter and hired someone to type it. The woman, a wigmaker from
New York, had read Elinore's work and had come to the ranch to visit the
author. Unfortunately, the family had problems with the middle-aged New
Yorker. She not only declined to help with chores around the house but
also refused to bathe. Elinore literally dragged her to the creek and attempted to give her a much-needed scrubbing. Needless to say, the woman
stomped off the ranch in indignation. After many problems, both personal
and secretarial, Elinore completed the manuscript in the summer of 1921.

Burntfork, Wyo.
Aug. 9, [1921]
My dear, dear Woodsy-Person.
    I am so very busy that I can-not write you a letter but I can take time
to send my love and very sincere thanks for my little crown of love, the
dear little Hat. You make me very happy, my Woodsy-Person. To think of
you thinking of me, you away there in that busy town, K.C. and me
away off in this lonely, remote Wyoming.
    It is good to have some-one to love and to dream about as I mow the
long, even swaths of hay. I think "what would happen if I walked in on
my Woodsy? Would she ever write me any more dear, encouraging letters?" We are so busy haying that I do not find time to write, Jerrine got
thrown from a horse and hurt but will soon be able to write you.
    The new book is written, only I must go over the type-written pages
to correct them. The typist did the best she could but mistakes will creep
in. Iwillw I [end of original typed letter—remainder in script] I will
write soon.

Love
Elinore P. Stewart

    By the fall of 1921 the family had decided that they could not maintain
both the ranch in Wyoming and the residence in Boulder, so they decided
to lease the Wyoming land to their neighbors and live year-round in Boulder. It was difficult for Clyde to leave the ranch, especially when it needed

rebuilding, for he dearly loved the ranch and the life it offered. Yet he loved his family more, and he acquiesced to Elinore's insistence that the children attend the best schools possible. Furthermore, Grandmother Stewart, unable to care for herself any longer, needed full-time care. Elinore, Clyde, Jerrine, age fifteen, and the three boys, age seven, nine, and ten, crowded into the open wagon, along with their necessary provisions and possessions, to make the five-hundred-mile trip through Rabbit Ears and Berthoud passes to Boulder.

While in Boulder that winter, Elinore attempted to sell her novel, mailing it first to Sedgwick in the hopes of publication by either the *Atlantic Monthly* or Houghton Mifflin. Both rejected the manuscript. Nevertheless, Elinore remained undaunted, planning still more adventures gleaned from her journey across the Rockies to Boulder. She wrote to Sedgwick asking for advice. He replied on May 20, 1922:

> I am ever so glad to have your letter, for even though the news is not particularly cheerful, at least it shows that nothing very disastrous has happened, and that you are all still in the land of the living.
>
> I have heard nothing of the manuscript of your novel since it was returned from Boston. If you have any luck with it in New York, be sure to let me know.
>
> Overland in a wagon across the Rockies sounds like a cheerful subject, and I should think there was a very good chance of such an article finding its way into The Atlantic.
>
> I had no idea that you were sending material to the House Beautiful, but I could have told you that there would be but little chance for it. You see, the House Beautiful is almost a technical magazine. It covers, or is supposed to cover, the interests of a person building, improving or renovating a house, and does not give space to stories or narratives which have nothing very definite to do with the serious business of building.

Some time after Houghton Mifflin rejected her novel, Elinore, remembering F. N. Doubleday's invitation years earlier, sent the manuscript to his company. Doubleday, Page, and Company responded by wiring a telegram to Boulder, purportedly offering five thousand dollars for "Sand and Sage." Elinore, however, had already returned to Wyoming to help Clyde with the spring work on the ranch that year. The messenger pushed the telegram through the slot in the front door and it fell onto the floor in the foyer. Several days passed before the children noticed it. Jerrine immediately forwarded the wire to Burntfork, again delaying it many days because the Stewarts picked up their mail only when it was necessary to go into town for supplies. As a result, Elinore could not accept Doubleday's offer by the deadline specified in the telegram, and the novel was not published.

Not getting the book published was one of the greatest blows in Elinore's life. One day, Jerrine happened to walk into the kitchen and saw Elinore attempting to shove the manuscript into the kitchen stove. Jerrine grabbed it from her mother's hands and begged her not to burn her years of work. Elinore handed the manuscript, its edges charred, to Jerrine and said she never wanted to see it again. Jerrine stored it in a trunk in the attic with other keepsakes. Later, when the homestead was vacant, vandals broke in and stole the trunk, including the manuscript and many of Elinore's cherished books. Fortunately, a rough draft of the novel and another typed copy have survived.

The financial straits of the ranch and Elinore's failing health magnified the stress and disappointment. Perhaps *The Outlook,* in its August 1, 1914, review of *Homesteader,* foresaw the results of Elinore's attempts at commercialization: "It still seems almost incredible that such brilliant talent should have its only literary outlet in occasional letters. Conceding the indorsement of the publishers, however, we hasten to say that it will be a sad anticlimax if the author attempts to write to order. Her extraordinary freedom, her delicious humor, her unrivaled naturalness of impression and expression, could hardly escape the deadening influence of formal writing for print" (26–27).

Elinore published no known letters between 1919 and 1923, although she continued writing stories to send to her friends, often as gifts. However, she continued to hope for another chance to read her work in print.

1525 Arapahoe St. Boulder
March 2, [1923]
Beloved human Being.
     Here is your tardy, delinquent friend. What are you going to do with me? I wanted to send these letters on to you a month ago, but just monkeyed around and didn't. Now you see how worthless I am. But at last I am getting to it. These letters are addressed to Mrs. Coney's sister. That was done to lend enterest if ever we should decide to send the letters to the publishers but that is a remote possibility so if my beloved friends can get any enjoyment out of them they shall as fast as I can find

time and energy to get them in readable shape. It is little enough to do for you and all the rest who are so good to me. If you think they are worth while will you, after you have read them, send them on to Miss Ida Howorth, 17 Grove St. West Point Miss. That is, send the last two letters. She has had the first one, keep *that* until some time when you write me and tuck it in if you will.

I *do* hope you are feeling well, I don't like to think of my own little Woodsy-Person not feeling well. I am jealous of those who do things for you when you can't do them for your self. I want to do them and can't. But I can *love* you, dear Little, and I *do*. I send you a World of love in this very letter.

Your friend
Elinore P. Stewart

One of the story-letters Elinore sent to Missouri pleased not only her southern friends but the *Atlantic Monthly* editors as well. "Snow: An Adventure of the Woman Homesteader" appeared in the December 1923 issue.[3] In this mystical adventure, the woman homesteader becomes stranded in an abandoned shack during a blizzard on her return home after delivering a neighbor's baby:

My Dear Friend,—
When Mr. Stewart asked me to behave myself while he was gone, I promised. I really thought I should. He cautioned me over and over not to go on any wild-goose chase and get lost or frozen, and I had no desire to do so.

But no objections have ever been made to my helping out when a neighbor is in need; so when young Melroy Luke came for me very early one bitter morning I felt no guilt in going. It was not until we were well on the way that he told me he had moved and now lived ten miles farther on. "I thought maybe you would not want to go so far to help and we need you so!" he pleaded. Any twinge of anger that might have stirred me left when I saw the concern and anxiety on his boyish face. We made our way with what grace we could; but grace is a scarce quality on such a ride. I had a very likely tale outlined to tell Dad to account for the toes I felt sure would be missing when all that seemed frozen were off.

3. "Snow: An Adventure of the Woman Homesteader" was published in the *Atlantic Monthly* of December 1923. Reprinted by permission of the *Atlantic*.

At last the frozen miles were over, and we took our cold stiffened
bodies into a cabin in a remote cañon that I had never seen before. Another neighbor was with young Mrs. Luke, and later the baby came. The
neighbor had already been gone from her home longer than she should
have stayed; so next morning she left, saying she would send someone to
stay on. So I stayed that day and the next. I knew that at my home bread
would be out, and the boys would be with the men who were feeding for
us, so I felt that I must go.

Luke could not leave his wife, but he said the way was perfectly plain.
"Just you follow the telephone poles after you get over the first hogback.
They are right along the mail road to Linwood, and you have only to go
west along the road to Burntfork. You can't possibly miss the road, and if
you did get off there are plenty of houses along to set you right."

We had taken a short cut in going, and I had not noticed the way at
all; it was so cold that I had kept my face as much covered as possible. I
set out with all confidence. I should not have minded at all if the
weather had been pleasant, but it was still very cold, with a veil of frost
hanging over the mountain. A sudden gust of wind swept over the bare
mountain, carrying with it a sheet of snow. My horse and I were enve-
loped in a whirling, driving mist of snow. It was strangling, smothering.
It penetrated my clothing; it drove down my back, I gasped for breath. It
struck us from all points at once. In a flash it was gone. I turned to look
as the flying mist of snow swept on down the valley. "If it were not broad
daylight, the sun shining brightly, I should think that a snow-wraith, a
ghost of a storm long dead. But no respectable ghost would be so uncon-
ventional as to stir out in the day!" Almost before I had so assured myself, another ghost of a storm assailed me. I was not alarmed, I had been
to Linwood, to Manilla; I knew the road once I reached it. The sun
shone with a gleaming lustre owing to the flying snow. I don't know how
I could have been so careless, but I rode along enjoying the scene, the
snow-wraiths traveling down the valley.

I had been conscious of a muffled roar for some time—wind in the
mountains; but the full meaning did not strike me until suddenly the
sun went out; I was caught in a whirling, blinding gust that did not pass
on down the valley. I could not force my horse against the storm; he
turned tail to whatever direction the capricious wind came from, and in
so doing must have turned round many times.

I saw to my dismay that the snow now flying was not old snow. A
storm was now on that might last for hours, days even. To remain there

meant to freeze, so I urged my horse down the hill, intending to go back to Luke's. When we reached the bottom, I could see in patches where the snow had blown off what seemed to be an old road; better yet, in a lull I saw a telephone pole. I started to follow that, but the storm increased and I could not see a yard ahead of me and it was growing darker every minute. I believe that I am as courageous as most women, but at last I almost gave up. Wherever my clothes touched me I was wet with snow. All outside clothes were frozen stiff. I had n't an idea where I was and I could not force my horse to move when the wind bore down upon us. I was so tired and sleepy that I began to wonder dully what would happen if I never came home. I felt a decided relief that Jerrine was safe in Boulder, but, foolish as it sounds, my chief worry was that the children might not let Whiskers, my cat, sleep in the house.

I don't know how long it was, but it seemed ages that we plodded on. I must have been half asleep when something brushed my head and at the same time scratched my leg. I was stiff with the cold and my frozen garments, so I tumbled off. For a moment I lay in delicious drowsiness, and then I remembered that freezing people always go to sleep. I bestirred myself with whatever energy is possible in a half-frozen state. To my surprise I saw the roof of a shed. We had come back to Luke's, I supposed, so I called and called for help, but only the roar of the storm replied.

My horse went to the shed, and I tried to follow, but I was a long time getting there. However, I made it; but my gloves were so frozen that I could n't unsaddle, could n't even take the bridle off. I went to the door and called, but no answer. I saw a cabin only a few feet away and, filled with anger, I staggered out to it. The storm hurled me down, but I crawled to the door and pounded. I could n't lift the latch, but I kicked and pounded till the door opened and I fell into the room. A rat scampered across the floor but there was no one else there.

I closed the door and leaned against the wall, panting and sobbing, with a sharp pain in my throat and in my chest. A trickle of water crept down my face. The snow in my hair had begun to melt. I walked over to a stove in the corner. It was rusted with disuse. I began a search for matches, but there were none to be found. All this was my salvation, had I but known it. If I had been able to get a fire at once, I might have lost some portion of my hands, face, or feet.

Failing to find matches, I decided to go to bed. I could n't get in with my frozen clothes and I could n't get the clothes off. I began another search for matches, and after I had looked the cabin over again I remembered that I wore Clyde's macakanaw. (That is wrong I know; but you will understand.) Clyde never is without matches; so, after getting my now sodden gloves off, I began to search the inside pockets of the coat. I was rewarded with two matches and a piece. I had little use of my hands, so I wasted the two matches, and was about to weep when I remembered a piece of candle that the rats had partly eaten. I waited as long as I dared, slapping and rubbing my numb hands trying to get them so they would be a little more steady.

At last I succeeded in getting the candle lighted. In a few minutes I had a roaring fire, and was foolish enough to get as close to it as I could. As my fingers limbered, I removed my frozen skirts and hung them to thaw and dry. When I began to thaw, I was in agony. Of all the itching, burning, and stinging! I suffered terribly every time I went near the fire. Some snow had blown in through the ill-fitted window-frame, and by accident I touched it. At once a soothing relief came over that part of my arm. I had begun to think a little more rationally now, so I took great handfuls of the snow and rubbed myself over and over. At last, after what seemed hours of work, I was able to move about in moderate comfort as long as I stayed away from the fire. I did n't dare let the fire go out; there were no more matches. It was long since dark, so I filled the stove with the largest pieces of wood, closed all the drafts, and made the bed so as to be sure that not a rat shared it, then crept into bed, thanking God and my unknown benefactor for plenty of dry wood.

My bed was dusty and smelled of rats, but was not otherwise uncomfortable. I had not expected to go to sleep; I thought I should get up at times and replenish my fire; but when I awoke it was morning, and the sullen, gray light told that the storm was still on. I was tender and sore, but not so badly off as I had expected to be. Enough of my fire remained for me to kindle. I soon had a roaring fire; then I thought I had better see how my horse had fared.

The snow was waist-deep and still falling steadily. I made my way to the shed, but was unable to get in, the snow had drifted around it so; but I peeped in through a crack, and saw that Brownie was very comfortable indeed. He had rubbed the bridle off and helped himself to someone's oats which were stacked in one end of the shed. I knew that if he were very thirsty he would lick the snow that had drifted in, so I went to the house with a clear conscience.

It is strange that when we are under great stress we are mindful of small comforts, but when we are not under stress we are more mindful of small discomforts. When I was really in danger of death, I was thankful even to fall from the horse; but now I began to fret because I could see no place to get water. When I was safe in the cabin once more, I remembered that I had had nothing to eat since breakfast the morning before; and as I have never cared for much breakfast the memory was not very filling. I was hungry. A ransacking of the shelves revealed no food, and the cupboard might have been Old Mother Hubbard's.

But I found plenty to divert me. By the fuller light of day I saw a card tacked over a shelf. "Welcome, friend. You are at home. Help yourself. All I have to eat is in the cellar. I may never need it. I am off to war. EMIL GENSALEN." But where was the cellar? The drifting snow covered the ground so that none could be seen out of doors, even if by any chance any of the mentioned refreshments remained. I knew that I could never find the cellar, so I sat down to read a battered magazine that the rats had spared. I guess they were not literary, or else they preferred the *Atlantic Monthly*. Certainly almost all of an old copy of *Everybody's* was there to help.

I read, I viewed the storm, I wondered what it was all for. I explored the cabin and wondered about the friendly Emil. I had not known any Emil. But I reflected that it was not necessary for me to know him for him to exist. After a while I noticed a ring in the floor. A ring meant a trapdoor. Of course! The cellar. How bright I felt! Ring in the floor. Cellar. Food. Who says a woman is not logical? Who says we cannot make deductions!

The door yielded unwillingly and I was half afraid to descend the mouldy steps; but I did and saw a neat set of shelves almost empty, but with enough cans to awaken hope in my stomach. The labels had long ago given up the light with rust and mould. I selected two cans and sought the upper world. I have known for a long time that breakfast need not begin with an iced melon or a grapefruit. I have even suspected that oatmeal and toast might be omitted, but I should hardly have supposed that coffee was superfluous. I found no coffee, but I found a hatchet with which I opened my cans, one of corn and one of Vienna sausage. The frying pan was ratty; I had to take time to scrub it out with snow, but I did not dally at my work, I can tell you.

I expect that you have had better breakfasts, but I never did. Even the thought of ptomaine did not scare me. But, true to my former assertion, no sooner was I comfortable than I thought of four more discomforts. How long would I have to stay? What if the wood gave out? Maybe I was snowed in. Would anyone ever think to look for me? Would they be in time? I knew perfectly well that the children would be cared for. The two men would be there and both men could cook. I was restless as a mule colt being weaned. I tried to see out of the window, to see if the snow was too deep for me to try. As I leaned against the rough casing, I saw some written words.

"When you make any charge against Providence, consider, and you will learn that the thing has happened according to reason."

"Well sang the Hebrew Psalmist. 'If I take the wings of the morning and dwell in the uttermost parts of the universe, God is there.'"

"Nothing happens to any man which he is not formed by nature to bear."

Every bit of available surface was covered with such writings, English on one facing and some other language on the other. The door the same way. I hunted for a pencil, a piece of paper, to copy it down, but none could be found. The three I send you seemed to fit my case so exactly that I memorized them. All that day I tried to picture to myself what Emil would be like. Not old, else he could not go to war. Not young, for no young man is wise. Kind and learned. That of course. An ideal host, for he attended to his guest's needs even when he was no one knew where. I was astonished to see dusk gathering. I knew that I should lack courage to go into the cellar after dark, so I brought up another can. I tried again to get to Brownie, but could not get in.

As night settled, the wind rose, and such a tumult as was outside! I ate a can of tomatoes and banked my fire and went to bed. Except for being dreadfully sore, I seemed to be none the worse for wear. I lay in the dark listening to the unearthly noises and thinking of the absent philosopher whose guest I was.

Some way, my troubles did not seem nearly so unbearable as I had thought. Perhaps Providence had sent me there to learn those very truths. I needed just such reflections every day of my life.

When I awoke next morning, all Nature was smiling. Deceitful jade, after all the turmoil, to flirt with her outraged victims! Just like young Mrs. Luke—raise all kinds of hurricanes until the baby came and then settle down to quiet. I kind of wondered that Dame Nature had given birth to. After a breakfast of apricots and Somebody's pork and beans I hunted for a shovel. None to be found. Not even a board that I could use for a shovel. I took the hearth off the stove and scooped the snow away from the shed door till I could get Brownie out. I removed the saddle and curried Brownie with some straw; then I resaddled and tied my horse outside the door. I carefully made the bed, put out the fire, and closed the cabin door securely.

I dared not ride until I reached the hilltop; the snow was too deep anyway; so I drove Brownie ahead and followed in his tracks. The going had nothing to recommend it. Certainly it was disagreeable in the extreme. The horse lunged his way, often falling, but as we neared the top the snow became less deep. It was nowhere so deep as at the cabin; it had blown off the hill and drifted around the pines that were about the cabin.

On the hill I took a survey and tried to locate myself. I was so completely turned round that the sun seemed to be in the north. I knew that the mountains lay east and west and so, keeping that in mind, I set my face northwest and mounted.

We plodded on down the hill and over another bare hill—that is, bare of trees. Slipping and sliding, panting and falling, we made our slow way. I stumbled on after Brownie most of the way. It was unsafe to ride. When we reached the top of the second hill I could see a mile away to the north the telephone line. Brownie too found himself and took courage. We made what haste we could, and soon found ourselves on the mail road. Snow had so drifted that even the road was all but impassable, but we knew where we were.

We reached home in the purple dusk. Not a thing was wrong, supper was on the table, and the men had a guest. After he had talked of everything on earth it seemed to me, I asked him if he had ever known anyone named Emil.

"Why, yes. Emil Gensalen. He was a queer duck. He came from Switzerland. I guess that is where the Swiss come from. He had a claim down the country a ways. He had a notion that goats were the thing to raise. Said he was going to try grapes too. He was a dandy good fellow, but queer. He went to war and has never come back. I never heard that he was mentioned in the casualty list, but no one has ever heard a word from him. I guess he went West."

I asked what became of his things.

"Oh, he just left everything. He was a little foolish about his cabin. At the dance that we gave for the boys who were leaving for war, he said publicly that he wanted everyone to feel welcome in his cabin, but that if anyone misused the privilege, some great misfortune would overtake them. Belham went over there to make some moonshine, and you know how quick the prohibition officers got him. Hanson went over after a load of logs that Emil had cut and piled up there, expecting to build a stable. He did n't get home with the logs before he broke his leg. That is where the sheriff got Dave Peters. He had made that his headquarters while he was in the rustlin' game. Did n't last long, though."

The men had so many other things to talk of that no one wanted to discuss Emil. I had much to think of, and Emil had a place in my thoughts. I am not superstitious but I could n't help wondering.

All those misfortunes were merely coincidences. What misfortune will overtake me? None has, and I feel just as if I had had an adventure that is deeper in significance than appears on the surface.

But I have no feeling of fear. Can two paths of life cross each other invisibly? Why?

I must stop this long jumble. You won't love me pretty soon. Perhaps I shall never get to mail this to you. The postmaster has had no envelopes for a month or more. That happens often. With much love to you and tenderest remembrance of the day.

Your friend,
Elinore P. Stewart

Pleased by the acceptance and the seventy-five-dollar payment, Elinore thanked her friends for their part in the publication:

March 22, [1924]
Burntfork, Wyo
  Now my Dear Miss Wood, See what you and my dear Mrs. Tidball have perpetrated upon the American Public! As it is Lent they *should* do penance should n't they? If I had my way they would be doing that kind of penance all the time. With Love.

Elinore P. Stewart

Although Elinore appreciated the educational opportunities and the easier life in Boulder, she deeply missed her Wyoming home. She filled her time with gardening, taking care of Mother Stewart, visiting with her Colorado friends, and, of course, writing to friends across the United States. Two of her Denver friends, Miss Josephine Harrison and Miss Emma

Adelaid Davis, had cabins in the mountains near Boulder. She shared her letters and stories with them, despite Miss Harrison's complaint that Elinore's letters contained too much fiction.

Full O' Joy, June 4, [1924]
You two Dearly Beloveds at Miramonte.

Happy Greetings. The birthday was a great success. I must tell you about it but first let me love you, kiss you and love you again. My joy has kicked up such a golden dust of happiness that I know that some of it will settle on you at Miramonte. Consider "yourselfs" breathless from being loved and powdered with happiness that gleams and glistens and settles on every one you think of—Friday the boys went down to get their certificates. Mystery prevailed when they came back. I thought perhaps they had not passed so refrained from questioning.

Saturday we planted corn and melons all day long. Still mystery, still no questions. I meant to call up on the phone and see how the boys came out but waited and was busy, too. I sent to the mail-box but recieved only a catalogue. No matter, I had *much* to plant and Dad worked away from home all day. We all worked until dark; Dad ate supper and then went to market, Mrs. Boatright called and spent the evening. Later Daddy called up and said he would not be home, that he would stay with Mother. After Mrs. Boatright left we washed up a little and the boys begged me not to make them go to Sunday school and all of us go to the hills instead. So, we went to bed with that arrangement to dream of. In the dim light of early dawn June 3, I was awakened by the sound of little bare feet pattering about. Soon the sound of a broom came to my ears. Excited, shrill whispering, enough to waken the deaf came to my ears. I sensed that some thing very secret and very unusual was going on so, to be obliging, I slept on very soundly.

After awhile the Trio bounded into my room to awaken this sleepy head. Multiply forty-six by three and find how many black and blue spots I have dealt by loving little fists unconscious of their strength and hardness. But happiness survives. Such a wonderful breakfast! Eggs in all stages and degrees of hardness, some not hot through, some that had been boiling an hour. But the coffee was good. You know Jerrine, how that made up for everything else. But better than any thing else, my plate was heaped with the mail that seemed to be lost the day before. The card and letter from you two blessed lovelings. Funny! A letter from the electric light company, a *bill* I should say and one from the Smith Shoe Co.

That furnished the laugh which the trio didn't know I had, and now comes the solving of all the mystery. In an envalope was the boys' certificates together with Robert's honor certificate! Yes Ma'm, he was the honor pupil at Lincoln. And Junior tied for first at Central. They every one passed with "heads up and tail over the dash board" as grandpa would say. And the dear little fellows had mowed a lawn and recieved twenty cents. With it they bought some peanut candy entending to give it to me for a birthday present.

From Friday afternoon til Sunday morning is a long time for candy to remain intact in the keeping of three small boys. One piece the size of a dollar, much sampled remained. It was the very sweetest bite of candy any body ever tasted and the flavor will remain with me always. And the precious words from you two! How I love you both. My coffee had many tears in it yesterday. Just big, crystal drops of joy. Oh, how I wish I could be worthy of all the happiness that comes to me.

But more was yet to come. Daddy came pretty soon with the groceries. he couldn't go on the hike, he had to irrigate while he could get the water but he brought some good thick steak so we revellers set out. When we came to the foot of the hill I was requested to keep my eyes shut while I climbed because in honor of the day I was to be admitted into the Tom Sawyer-Robin Hood-Indian Chief gang and we were on the way to the hide out. I *did* shut my eyes once in a while, I was admonished every few minutes by shrill, boy voices, away ahead to "keep your eyes shut, Mama." Steep hillside Rocks and stones and prickly pear, a fat lady and a beaming sun! We reached the council rock where Robin Hood became Tom Sawyer or an Indian, wily and brave with equal ease and astonishing rapidity. By common consent Sir Knight Mama became a member of the gang. Leaving that I was allowed to open my eyes which was well for the way became more steep and hard to climb. The stepping stones furnished a great ceremony. Next, I was envited to sit in "The Seat." Bending, crawling, using every care that my one and only dress didn't tear, I scrambled under some pine boughs, between great boulders to the den where by taking "The Seat" I swore eternal fidelity to Robin Hood and became on of his Merry Men. The same process made me a member of the Sawyer gang and a great Indian brave. Then we emerged and became ordinary American citizens again. That is, to the causual eye. We of The gang know how much more than that we are.

We climbed on up over the hill. On the top of a great rock we made a fire and fried steak and potatoes—a friendly, pine-scented little breeze cooled our heated bodies while we rested and looked at the beautiful view. Boulder and the surrounding country lay, a lovely picture to inspire us. We went on over into "the Valley of enchantment." Being allowed the use of my eyes, I recognized among the plants and flowers many of friends of childhood. Many of them I had not seen for twenty years— They opened a storehouse of memories that further sweetened the day. And "the Valley of Enchantment" truly named. It was a fairy land, a very bride of loveliness. Barberrys, haw, choke cherrys, wild plum made the whole canon a bower of white. Under foot, sand lillies, mountain phlox, blue bells, lark's spur, Johnny-Jump-ups, daisys, white and yellow, ferns and many flowers that I have loved all my life but have no name for. Overhead a sky of matchless blue, on the hillside a lark pouring a song of joy, the great, friendly hills "from whence cometh my help." The pines, giving their blessing with their incense. Three active, happy little High-landers whose feet are at home on the hills . . . [?] . . . thought of their Mother's full day.

You two precious beloveds away over the hills, a quiet, silent man, puttering away at home, that home in order for once, made so by my own boys as an offering on that happy day. It is all too beautiful, too *wonderful* for a blunderer like my self to *try* to tell. To most people I would seem insincere if I tried to tell what the day meant to me. But it was my beautiful, precious day to take on into eternity with me. And now I must watch for the post man to get the rug. It will come today I know. How I love you two lovelings for it. I would not trade it for the finest Persian rug on earth because the story woven into my rug is Love's old, old story, the sweetest on earth to me. I inclose a dollar for your re-turn to Boulder, Jerrine dear, when your visit is over. Kiss my Josephine Harrison very gently for me, and please, Miss Harrison Kiss my child for me—

> From happy
> *Elinore Stewart*

3136 9th Street
Boulder, Colo.
Oct. 20, [1924]
My Dear Woodsy-Person.

You can't escape me, you see! I have been wanting to write you for a long time but the less I have to do the less time I have to do the things I want to do. I *hope* you believe in mental telepathy for I am constantly sending you love thoughts. Still, I suppose you need an occasional letter as sort of an anchor to stay the thoughts so you can look 'em over.

This morning when I peeked out of my window the world was white with frost. The leaves have not fallen yet. As I stood looking at the rosy dawn I decided to go for a walk out to the hills. Funny thing to do, go tramping off before breakfast, but I had been up all night with my croupy Robert and mother who was restless and unable to sleep. Every one was asleep so I drew on a dirty, favorite old sweater and slipped out. There is no pavement out this way and the grass and weeds were crisp with frost. The air was so keen and had a tang of pine to hearten me. And there are many patches of spear mint which, when I tramped through them gave me a whif of perfume.

The hills are not far from my door but it is a long, hard climb to the top. I wanted to reach the top before the sun came up. Things that had been things of beauty not long ago had on a winding sheet of crystal frost—tall holly hocks, mullens, sear and brown but frosted. Some asters and snap dragons were defying the cold and valiantly lifted beauteous heads. The last house was soon left behind; tall, golden leaved poplars, (Carolina poplar) hid it from view. Exulting, I climbed on.

What at first seemed to be a cemetery, though I knew it wasn't, turned out to be beehives, dozens of them. Some enterprising bee man had set his hives out on the hill side and so got his little workers near the mountain flowers. It was too cold and too early for them to be astir. Not a bird, not even a rabbit was about. My fingers and toes stung with the frost but my heart sang. Out of breath but joyous I reached the top *before* the sun came up. It was so calm—and still, just as if all nature waited reverently for the miracle. I gazed away over what was once the plains, now all orchards and farms. 'Way off a train whistled and rumbled. The town lay at my feet, soon black smoke shot up from the tall, white smoke stack at the Sanatarium, trucks began to rattle out; Boulder awoke, it was as if the shreiking train had awakened a sleeping world. It was glorious. In just a breathless minute the sun popped up. It hung like a red ball for a moment and then shot shafts of rosy gold after the fleeing, purple shadows.

I stood up and spread exultant arms to greet the sparkling new day. The pines offered incense, a little breeze came and took the toll of them; the pines were asleep I think, for the wind shook them to arouse them, the same little wind shared the pine perfume with me as it tossed my graying hair with friendly fingers. And I, negligent mother, bad housekeeper and poor example of decorum that I am! Why was I not busy in my kitchen as hundreds of other mothers were in theirs at that moment? Because the Scot was away from home, Mother and Robert would sleep for hours, and the other kids can fix their own breakfast and I had gone wild, eloped with the morning.

I decided to wash my face in an ice fringed spring so went further into the hills to find one. Climbing up, down and around, I conquered another line of hills and saw a spring branch. Also I smelled smoke, a willow-fire. That, of course meant that someone was camped on the little stream. I soon saw the smoke rising and made my way toward it. A *very* melancholy man was broiling some bacon. some coffee simmered in a can. I don't know what gets into me, I sometimes lose all sense of good behavior. I had *none* this morning. "Hello, pardner" I hailed. "Have you enough for two?"

He didn't answer at once, he just looked at me, wonderingly. I felt embarrassed and began to wish I was less forward. I felt I should not stay and was ashamed to leave. The morning lost some of it's glory, things began to look common-place when the magic of the man's voice restored the wonder. "Are you hungry?" he asked kindly. "There is plenty for us both. I expect this to be my last meal on earth and I have more than I can eat; I was going to leave all I didn't use here for the chipmunks. It is better to have you to eat with me." His last breakfast! I suspect I looked wild eyed.

"I was overseas, twenty-two months my discharge says. I don't know, myself. I've been in Fitz Simmons hospital. I can remember that. I can remember, too, that they say I am hopeless. I was wounded, they tell me, four times. And I was gassed. Some times I can remember very well, I can this morning. I know my name is Willis Jerome. My family live in Massachusetts. I don't know their address and I had not remembered the state for I don't know when. I forget my name but the discharge shows that—if it *is* my discharge. Any way the Chief Mogul at Simmons told me that my only hope for life lies in the great out doors, out on the mountain tops. But I can't get work. I've *got* to eat but no one wants a lunger [a person who has tuberculosis] or a crazy man. I'm both."

The pity of it! He passed me a carton of Crackers to open, "Take half, and maybe you could eat better if you cooked your own bacon." he passed me the carton of bacon. I unwrapped two slices, strung them on a stick and we were soon munching. he carefully divided the coffee, pouring half into his cup and handing me the can. I sat on a stone, he on his neatly rolled blankets. I drank my coffee from the blackened can. We enjoyed our breakfast but I kept wondering about the last meal. The soiled, worn khaki clothes almost brought tears. He kept up a line of talk, snatches of over seas experiences, what he did once when he was a boy, where he was yesterday all so jumbled that it was hard to follow him. "And now" he said after he evidently thought he had finished his discourse, "I have come to this. No work, no prospect of work or of help of any kind. I *cant* beg. I can *work* if they'd let me—".

"But" I interrupted "you must surely have a pension."

"I guess I have, but I don't want to be paid for doing my duty. Unless I can help myself I don't want to live. Would you?"

"But why did you say this would be your last meal?"

"Did I say that? Maybe I was hoping that it would be. Still, I would be all right if I could only land a job. But I don't know what I can *do*. I must have made a living once but I can't remember how. And I tell you, he ended pettishly, "no one wants to be bothered. *No* one."

I couldn't dismiss the idea of his suicide. He *must* have meant to. He loved everything so, the clouds, the pines softly singing, even the chattering magpies. I had to think fast. Suddenly it popped into my head that I was invited to go to the Courthouse to hear the arguments in a mining case, one of the contestants is a friend of mine, it was he who envited me. I thought "If I can get this Willis Jerome down there some one can take him in charge. So I began talking hard, telling him of the case, trying to enterest him, trying to *hold* his enterest. "And I want to go so badly, but I feel queerly about going down alone. I need an escort."

"I will go down with you but—it's a long tramp back. I don't need to come back tho' I can chance luck in some other direction."

So, we set out to walk back to town. We climbed slowly, stopping often to rest, to admire the beauty every where flaunting. I hated myself most cordially and dreaded to be seen. My mind was so benumbed that I could not think of a way out of my predicament, hatless, unkempt, wearing the white sweater you sent, but now sadly dirty. And what could I say? To whom say it. I felt crazier than I had thought the man to be. But we went on, there were odd, disjointed snatches of conversation. There was much we both loved. The golden banners of the poplars. A great, silver leaved maple, other maples. It was a wonderful morning but my feet were leaden. At last we reached the pavement; belated breakfast smells were in the air; A man futilely raking the lawn, a woman sweeping the walk. A portly, dignified old gentleman came out and sought the morning paper. A cedar wax wing and a robin hopping along the lawn. And *your* friend hopping along on a fool's errand.

But no one paid any attention to us. We reached the courthouse grounds and I contemplated a sneak; My newfound man stopped to read the honor roll; The names of Boulder's over-seas dead. I went on to the courthouse feeling very foolish and wondering what next to do. Just as I reached the steps Mr. Baur, my mining litigant friend came out. He had come early to the Courthouse to get some copies before Court opened. Hurriedly I told him of my trouble. He said, "Get in my car, I'll drive you home and I'll see after your soldier. He sauntered over to where the man was reading the names. Soon a conversation was in full swing but I didn't get much of it. I could tell that Mr. Baur was telling of the lawsuit. Presently they came on over to the car; Mr. Baur was telling of the difficulties he experienced in keeping the opposing side from dismantling his mining property.

"I have good cabins, abundance of wood and water, every comfort for a man, but I cannot seem to find a man who will stay and hold possession through the Winter months. I've been obliged to close down mining, owing to the adverse mining condition, but these fellows seem to think my mining apparatus is public property. Most fellows find it too lonely up there in the mountains but it is a quiet, cosy home with every thing furnished and small wages, too. All a fellow would have to do is to take care of himself live in my house with my Belgian Police dog—Do you happen to know of a good man who would like such a job?"

Bless his dear heart! I *hoped* no one saw how near I was to kissing him! Friend Jerome got in the car and they talked it over while they took me home. I am so glad. Mr. Baur has a good watchman to guard his enterest, Mr. Jerome has a good warm home, plenty to eat and a chance to "come back". And all because I am irrational.

Now that I have thought it all over calmly, I don't think the man meant to Suicide, perhaps he meant nothing, but any way, he had no work and needed it, and any way I had a pleasant breakfast with him. I don't dare tell Mother Stewart my adventure, she would find it hard to over look such utter irresponsibility but I tell you and hope you get a gleam of the happiness that was born in my heart that glorious morning. It is wonderful to be a little bit crazy.

Oct. 23

It is a gray, sodden day here today, but it is a cozy day to read, to think of one's friends, to *love* them. It is a good day too, to make some ginger cookies for my three darling hoodlums and for my very dignified 'Prep' girl. She is very fond of biology and history. she likes Latin a little better than she did last year because she finds it useful in biology. Well, I find a cook book more enteresting.

Have I tired you plumb to death? Forgive me and love me.

> Your friend
> *Elinore Stewart*

Boulder, Colo.

Feb. 19, [1925]

My Dear Woodsy-Person.

Each time a letter comes from you it sets a little bird singing in my heart, visions of beauty immediately arise before my mind's eye. That's what makes me liken you to a flower, you just *are* to me.

There is something primrose-ish about the thought of Miss Locke Arnold. Every time I think of her a vision of pale yellow, sheer fabrics and a faint, sweet perfume comes to me. I always vision her as in a garden, at dusk, just after a summer shower.

I guess I'm crazy but my mental pictures of my friends are my keepsakes. With you there is always a little twittering song-bird. I think it's a wren.

Anyway, I'm fond of you, very. And I haven't even a snap shot of you to tell me what you are like. Still, it would be only to satisfy my curiosity if I had one, for I know the sweet spirit of you and I can clothe it with rose leaves and dew drops and set the thought of you a tingle with bird songs.

But I can't clothe my own fat body with anything more romantic than unwanted avodopoise. That's the reason I don't like me very well, I want to think pleasant things about myself, but no bird songs twitter and trill in my picture of myself. All I can see is a fat person, nagging boys about mud on their feet, or wet feet, or a ball through a window. Worrying about what to cook for dinner, how to keep the light bills within bounds, trying to get out of dusting, knowing if I don't dust some one will be sure to come, trying (vainly!) to keep the boy's sweaters darned, their stockings darned, buttons on their clothes, trying (vainly!) to keep my daughter's paints and brushes, charcoal, pencils, sketch pads and such things picked up and where she can find them when she wants them. I have just been looking at myself in the mirror. I'm homely! I am glad I don't have time for much looking; Better yet, there is much that is beautiful to see. For all the flying snow and spiteful quarrelsome winds threats, glad Spring is on it's way.

I see a few tulips coming through under the window, and the after-a-while hate dandelion is cheerfully announcing growing weather for dandelions. It won't be any time at all til there'll be greens to gather, that's one of the beautiful things to look at and for. And how I do love the wild flowers that will soon be peeping, the children's donkey ate my big rose bush but I think it needed pruning anyway.

And my plum trees are full of heavy, brown knobs that will be blossoms after awhile. I am just praying that gentle spring won't be in too great a hurry, for I do like plums and I'd hate to have my plums freeze.

My desires are contrary-wise, I want spring yet fear to have it. And Robins are such little liars! One has been promising spring to me for a month. He is no coward, if he is a prevaricator, he braves the storms and fights my cat and I believe he'd fight me only he won't strike a lady! You make me ashamed when you write as you did about my letters, please poke them in the fire and forget 'em. But please don't forget to write me soon and often. Do you remember that precious cake you sent me once? It's flavor is stored in my heart and many times I can taste it. It has a distinct flavor of friendship, the best flavor on earth.

I am wondering if there is not somewhere about your home, a bed of those little English violets that cuddle down under their leaves and have sweet, blue blossoms long before any one would look for flowers?

Is there? Well, if there is, will you please take as many pinches of their sweetness as you can and lay them on the grave of Mrs. McCausland. Do it for me. And when the lily-of-the-valley- comes please take as many as you can to the sweet spot that means Miss Henry, and say to her; 'These represent the thought of you that lives in the heart of your friend.' They both loved you and will both know we are sending them our love.

My only quarrel with life is that it will not be long enough for me to get my loving done up. I just love people, I just love to love them. When

they have gone on, I still love them. I've been lovin' you for ten or twelve
years, I loved you before I knew you but I didn't know it was you I
loved. I didn't entend to write this long a letter, but I have and so—Bye.

Elinore P. Stewart

During this period in Boulder, Elinore began a correspondence with a
blind man, a Mr. Zaiss, who apparently lived on Cape Cod. He had read her
books in Braille and had written to her. She responded, and their long-
distance friendship endured until her death. Nothing has been discovered
about this Mr. Zaiss except what can be learned from the letters. Elinore
mentions a friend of his, Miss Viola Allen, of Harwich Port, Massachusetts,
who may have been related to Mrs. Florence Allen, Mrs. Coney's daughter.
She also refers to a Miss Coney, perhaps another relative of Mrs. Coney's.
These letters, noteworthy because of their vivid sensual description, document in specific detail Elinore's daily life and blossoming social concerns.

March 4, 1925
3136 9th St., Boulder, Colo.
My Dear Mr. Zaiss.

I know you haven't forgotten me for that lovely Christmas greeting
told me that I still have a place in your recollection in spite of the fact
that I feel that I do not deserve it.

But I had lost your address; your card at Christmas time gave no address. When I went back home last May I put your address down in a little book, meaning to write you. The book became lost in the general
upheaval and I have just now found it.

I wonder if I can make you see the mountains? I so ardently wish you
could. Try it this way. Think of the soil you stand on, at the beach,
maybe, where you could hear the waters, like wind in the pines, think of
the ground as slanting upward. At first the walking would not be tire-
some, but it would get increasingly hard for you until at last you could
not walk upright but would have to bend over and finally crawl.

Think of stones within your grasp, against your feet, of putting out
your hand to grasp rough surfaces of logs, branches.

That would be one physical feeling, that would be what your sense of
touch would tell you of the mountains; but there is still another feel as
Opal of the understanding Heart would put it.

If you were in our Rockies the wind on your face would have a different feel; after you were a part of the way up you would feel exhausted but elated at the same time. You could feel that. You would find yourself too weak to stand upright, the muscles in your limbs would ache and feel so weakened that you would sink to the ground but you would be ecstatic, joyful.

Whatever worry had been with you at the bottom of the hill would seem of little consequence, would seem as small as the trees and houses would seem to you at a distance. You have noticed that the farther away a sound is the fainter or smaller it is; that is the way it is with sight. A thing that looks large at the foot of the mountain seems very small when it can be seen at all from the top.

I have gone up among the pines and tried to sense the feeling for you. Perhaps green color is just a name to you, there are greens and greens, too. All of them different.

But the green of the pines away up on the mountain would convey a feeling of serenity, of peace. Even if a great wind were blowing, so that the great trees were tossing their arms in agony, you would get a feeling of courage and brave strength.

As you climbed your hand would touch tender things, anemones, columbines, little, short stemmed daisies, pentstemons, Their beauty could not speak so clearly to you but their feeling is tender courage.

You would also touch unfriendly, rough, prickly things. But you'd keep climbing and presently you would reach the top.

You could tell by the feel when you got there. Such a joyous rush of clean, sweet wind! Such exaltation. I have always been glad that the Devil (or should I say Satan?) took Jesus to the mountain top to tempt Him. It is so much easier to want to do right when we are on the heights.

Poor Adam and Eve lived in the low lands; if their garden had been on Mount Ararat or Mount Sinai the serpent would never had bothered them.

One thing you might not have thought of if you have never seen a mountain is that on the tops there is no sound but that of the wind. If we speak, of course, there is that sound, but the peaks are wrapped in silence.

You get the feeling of exalted peace, of high courage, of tender compassion, when you reach the tops.

But for all the glorious feeling on the mountain, no one would want to stay there.

The Woman Homesteader: Elinore, who self-consciously avoided having her photograph taken, posing beneath the "whispering pines," ca. 1925.

This photograph of Clyde Stewart and his first wife, Cynthia, shows the Burnt-fork homestead with the new living room addition, ca. 1905. The original cabin is to the right, and beyond it is the stone cellar where the winter food supply was stored. The dog, Bob, greeted Elinore on her arrival in 1909.

The Green River, viewed from the south. For supplies the Stewarts traveled three days north over sixty miles of sage-covered desert like that in the foreground. The trail suddenly dropped into the Green River valley and the small Wyoming town.

Henry's Fork, a tributary of the Green River and the setting for Elinore's Culberson family stories. Burnt Fork, a smaller branch of Henry's Fork, flows past the original post office and the Stoll homestead and helps irrigate the lush hay lands of the Burntfork Valley.

"Our Three": Robert Clinton, Henry Clyde, Jr., and Calvin Emery, ca. 1914.

Mary Antin (left), Jewish Russian immigrant and author of *The Promised Land*, on one of her summer sojourns with Elinore, ca. 1915.

"Sweet girls, Sweet flowers." Elinore's daughter, Jerrine (left), and her friend Josephine Antin, daughter of the author Mary Antin, among the flowers in Elinore's garden, ca. 1915. As teenagers, Jerrine and Josephine, with their mothers' support, considered taking up a homestead claim themselves.

Robert, Calvin, and Clyde, Jr., ca. 1918. Elinore entitled this portrait "Ranchers."

" 'The mon' bet me five dollars that he could find a weed in my one acre garden. After his inspection he reached around to his pocket to get one he had stored for the emergency but I had 'beat him to it,'" commented Elinore about this photograph, ca. 1921.

"I keep the weeds out of the garden, Frank the porcupines," wrote Elinore on the back of this photograph, ca. 1920.

Topping out the fireplace on the Stewart home as the garden awaits a new crop, ca. 1928.

Jerrine and her father loading cream for the Lucerne Valley creamery. *(Photo courtesy of Herb Aldridge)*

Elinore on the mowing machine, ca. 1926. "Oh, I'm glad I can mow and rake and even stack hay," she had once observed to Miss Wood. "I have been having a perfectly lovely time helping. And we have had a perfectly glorious fall." *(Photo courtesy of Herb Aldridge)*

It is more painful to get down a mountain than to get up; one seldom falls in climbing up but falls often in coming down. The peaks call out something more than human in us, all that is finest in us responds to the call of the heights, but it is very comforting to get back to the human level. It is very satisfying to come back to the hurry and scurry of every day life, even to the little meanesses. (I wonder if I spelled that right!)

Anyway, back to detesting one's neighbor for emptying her ashpit on the windy day when one washed all the blankets, back to wondering where to plant the sweet peas this year, what to get for the girl's graduation dress, threatening to change grocers.

My typewriter has gone crazy and I'm glad you can't see that awful line. [This sentence is crossed out in the original manuscript.]

One thing I took up to the peaks, enjoyed there, brought back down and enjoyed here, is the love of my friends. Maybe I meant love *for* my friends.

What ever the way it should be said, the feeling for friends remains the same on the top or at the foot of the mountain. I am so glad of that, some of these days, dear Mr. Zaiss, you are going to be my very good friend.

I am not going to lose your address any more.

Will you please write to me? I like to think of you being a friend of Dear Miss Coney, it seems a point of contact for us.

I shall be looking forward to a letter from you some of these days when you feel like writing to this 'wild, woolly, Westerner'.

Most sincerely your friend

Elinore P. Stewart

Raised a Catholic and far from any organized congregation, Elinore subscribed to an eclectic religion. Her constant reading, her conversations with visitors of many denominations, and her own experiences fostered a personalized faith founded on the Golden Rule, guided by a benevolent God, and encouraged by an insistent belief in a happy reunion of friends and family after death.

Theosophy also intrigued Elinore. In her letters she mentioned reading two books on the subject: *At the Feet of the Master* and *The Key to Theosophy*. Not a religion but a sort of brotherhood among all humanity, Theosophy had as its chief aim "to reconcile all religions, sects and nations under a common system of ethics, based on eternal verities." The Theosophical

Society adopted the motto "There is no religion higher than Truth," and espoused reincarnation.[4]

Many of the fundamental beliefs of the society, Elinore discovered, were incorporated in her own attitudes toward life. J. Krishnamurti, in *At the Feet of the Master*, urged his disciples to set their feet on the path of the Master: "Never allow yourself to feel sad or depressed. Depression is wrong, because it infects others and makes their lives harder, which you have no right to do. Therefore if it ever comes to you, throw it off at once. . . . Use your thought-power every day for good purposes; be a force in the direction of evolution. Think each day of some one whom you know to be in sorrow, or suffering, or in need of help, and pour out loving thoughts upon him."[5]

The Key to Theosophy, with many horticultural and garden images in its explanation of doctrine, must have instinctively appealed to Elinore. "For every flower of love and charity he plants in his neighbor's garden," the book explained, "a loathsome weed will disappear from his own, and so this garden of the gods—Humanity—shall blossom as a rose." Theosophy also emphasized the importance of each person, not organized religion. "Act individually and not collectively."[6] With such a doctrine, Elinore, in her remote corner of the world far from any church or minister, could feel at peace.

Elinore probably borrowed what she agreed with from the Theosophists, just as she did from the Catholic church of her youth and from the Baptist, Episcopalian, and Presbyterian friends she encountered in her "adventures." From all of these sources grew a strong belief in God made concrete through good works. She worshipped Him in her garden, on the mountaintops, and in the retreat she called her "cathedral," a small group of spruce in the willows and wild roses near "Aggie Creek" a quarter mile south of the ranch house. Nearly all of her letters reflect her spiritual beliefs.

Boulder, April 27, [1925]
My Dear Woodsy-Person.
We seem to do our remembering each other by spurts and jumps the way we write. That is not just what I mean either, but there is something

4. Blavatsky, *Key to Theosophy*, 2–3.
5. Krishnamurti, *At the Feet of the Master*, 42–43.
6. Blavatsky, *Key To Theosophy*, 53, 244.

kind of odd about the way we correspond. Still, we have been friends for a long enough time to be a little priveleged have n't we?

I just *love* to count up the years I have loved you. It is very sweet to me to have folks to love. I *am* fond of you.

This is Enchanted April and I have had a drive about town; it is lovely, so bowery and flowery. All the fruit trees in bloom lilacs just bending under their heavy load of beauty. It is very dry and spring is very early, the lilacs are past their prime, petals are falling from the apple and plum trees.

There are so many things to fill our hearts with joy, the larks, blue birds and finches and across the house tops come the music of the bells calling people to church. I think the Theosophists must be right. We surely must come again to this earth. There is so much to enjoy that no one lifetime could embrace all the delights, there is so much to do. I can think of a dozen things I would like to do any one of which would take a life time. My dear, My dear the longer I live the greedier I am for life. I dread inactivity. I am glad I was born into the "hewer of wood" class. But what do I mean by boring my dear you! Just 'cause I can I guess. Now then! Do you seat yourself and take your pen in hand and drop me a few lines. I am going to pull out of here about the end of May. My three sons and I are going to "Westward Ho!" as soon as they can get out of school. Did I tell you that I am going to drive back over the road we came?

The Scot is in Wyoming now. Jerrine and Mother will stay here until August 1st then come on the train. Bye—dear Woodsy. Love to you.

Elinore P. Stewart

❧ THREE

More Adventures (1925–1930)

As soon as school was out in May 1925, Elinore moved back to Wyoming. The Stewarts had stopped leasing the ranch in the spring of 1924, and Clyde had returned to the ranch earlier to help with the spring calving. Elinore and the three boys, now ages eleven, twelve, and thirteen, set out for Burntfork with their team and wagon. Snow still lay along the roads, none of them paved, and twelve to fourteen feet of snow clogged the passes. The family acquired food for the trip along the way, storing it in a chuck box that made into a table in the back of the wagon.

Three boys in a wagon traveling at three miles an hour demanded firm discipline, and any violators of the "No Fighting" rule walked. Sometimes the boys walked voluntarily, running up and down the mountainsides, exploring streams and valleys. They hoped to find another old coin like the one Robert had discovered on an earlier journey, a halfpence dating back to the 1600s, perhaps lost by the Spaniards or early fur trappers.

In many places, the road was only one lane wide, and Elinore had to keep a close lookout for approaching cars and wagons. Fortunately, not much traffic complicated their progress, perhaps a wagon every few hours and occasionally a car. Rain, however, caused problems, making the roads slippery and dangerous and the ride uncomfortable. The boys could crawl under the tarp covering the contents of the wagon, but Elinore had to continue driving with only a coat as protection. Her varicose veins and the bleeding ulcer on her leg pained her greatly, adding to the discomfort.

Their route took them from Boulder south to Central City in the Rocky Mountains, then northwest through Berthoud and Rabbit Ears passes. They angled west until Vernal, Utah, where they headed northward through the Uinta Mountains and west of the Flaming Gorge area, signaling the last leg of their journey. Later that summer, Grandmother Stewart and Jerrine also returned to the ranch by train.

Elinore gleaned many "adventures" from her trek. Several letters and stories, probably composed in her head as the wagon slowly inched northwest, attest to her keen observation, innate curiosity, and creative mind. She wrote most of these story-letters, usually addressed "My Dear Friend," to Mrs. Coney's daughter, Florence Allen, in remembrance of Mrs. Coney's March birthday. Elinore referred to the letters as "keeping our day."

[1925]
[to Mrs. Allen]

We started on our five hundred mile journey on a bright, sunny, Monday morning, May 25th. I had asked our school superintendant about the boys getting out that early and he had said they might quit school, that they would pass. I had been calling the Chamber of Commerce almost every day asking about the passes, when they would open and at last came the welcome news that Berthoud Pass would be officially open June 1st.

It was with happy hearts that clothed a small ache of sadness that we climbed onto our well loaded wagon and started—for it was sad to leave dear, gentle Mother knowing that we might never see her again. She stood out on the steps waving . . . [?] . . . as long as she could hear the rumble of our wagon. We saw her dear, silvery head glistening in the morning sun as long as we could see through our tears. But, we were going *Home!*

We were taking our dearly loved horses home, home where they were borned, home from the bondage of town life. We started as early as we could in order to escape the thunder storms that are so terrifying a little later in the summer in high altitudes. We escaped the lightening but we did *not* escape the snow which was just going out in the high places.

At Idaho Springs we were joined by a young fellow who was moving from his home in Denver to Hot Sulphur Springs where he had a homestead. There by hangs a tale but not this one.[1]

All the road up this side of Berthoud was like a paved street but as we neared the top drifts of snow appeared though the road was clear. On top the snow was deep, it had been shovelled out of the road and

1. See March 15, 1926, story-letter.

ofcourse that made it deeper on each side but it was almost like a tunnel, higher than the horses' heads for, perhaps, two hundred yards.

After that we saw only drifts and pockets of snow until we climbed Rabbit Ear Pass—just this side of Steamboat Springs. But I didn't start in to tell you about snow and blizzards. I can't get away from weather for it was rain that introduced me to Mollie-Jane Patton and it is she I am going to tell you about. It was June 8th. It had been raining all day long and we were soaked.

We all like a playful, dashing shower but this rain was the Spirit of Hegate. Isn't that the name of the woman in the legend who sat in her cave weeping and enviting her friends to come and enjoy sorrow? Well, that was how this rain was; it *forced* us to stay out and *endure* it's sorrow and our own. Say what you will, there is something saddening about slow falling rain. It shut off the landscape and made us feel that we were alone in the world.

The stretch of country through which we were passing is just beyond Elk Springs Colo—and there are few houses near the road. The country has been deserted owing to what people there call Mormon Crickets devouring their crops.

Another reason for our discomfort was there is a scarcity of water along that road, in fact none, tho' one might think the rain would supply that need. But it didn't. We were wet outside but dry inside. Our patient horses were thirsty, we had no water with which to make camp; that didn't bother us much but there was no shelter to be found so we dragged on over the road.

We came to a bridge across a deep sandy gully. We stopped and unhitched the horses, fed them and stood under the bridge and ate a lunch of bread, cheese and ginger snaps.

Water kept dripping from our hat brims and draining from our coats. We had a dog along and it was so miserable that we tried to make a fire so that Gyp could warm and dry but the sage was so wet it refused to burn, the air was so damp and heavy that the smoke refused to rise so hung in a stinging pall around us. Discomfort bade us "move on".

That seemed a very long day, since then I have had a deep sympathy for the Noah family. But after a while the clouds parted a little in the West and showed us that the sun was about to set. There was not a house in sight, not even a strand of wire to encourage a belief in a settlement.

Our prospects were decidedly damp but we took comfort in the thought that we could become no wetter and might as well stop one place as another. Just then Mollie-Jane and a Collie dog came into our lives.

A thin little woman, as wet as ourselves, riding a *resigned* looking animal she called a nag and followed by a beautiful dog came riding slowly out of the cedar brakes. She drew rein and looked us over appraisingly— "Well, you look like Baptists!" was her greeting.

"That is on the outside." I answered—

"That's good. If all that water were inside you would either drown or burst. Where are you going?"

I told her.

"You'll hardly get there tonight. You had better come on up with me, get dried and have some hot supper and you will feel more friendly toward our country. I feel like I kind of owe it to you to take care of you for I ordered this rain. It has been so very dry that the whole country was about to burn up. There is no road from this side up to my home but you can get there. Come on, follow my horse."

We were glad to do that and after zig-zaging around through the cedars for a mile or two we came to her rude looking home. It was built of shaggy cedar logs. Shaggy, because the bark had not all been removed and still clung, rude, because cedars do not make long, or shapely logs as do the pine and to get the cabin long enough three lengths had to be used and these were spliced together.

The house was low, squatty, the stone chimney was wide and low. The small yard was fenced by deer horns and elk horns with a thick growth of cactus making a hedge four feet high—That don't sound as if it could be beautiful but it was. The cactus were full of great yellow and crimson flowers, drooping then like bits of bright, wet silk. All about were fine cedar trees. Evry thing was so clean looking about the grounds. There was no barn or stable, just a shed under which I drove the wagon.

My Heaven sent hostess came up leading her unsaddled horse. "Now that you are here and are going to stop with me, we will have to have something to call each other by. I am Mollie-Jane Patton."

"I am Elinore Stewart—these are my sons, Junior, Calvin and Robert."

"Boys, take your horses out and turn them into this pasture with my nag. Be sure you fasten the gate. Then; take your dog into that sheep-shed and *tie it up*. Be sure you do that for I have sheep and I cannot have

a strange dog loose. When you get that done come right on in at that
back door and we will see if we can't find some dry clothes."

So that started a friendship which I hope never ends.

I suspect I should, to make this a good story, tell you that the inside
of the cabin was a marvel of beauty in finish and furnishing; it was not.
It was very ordinary. The walls were covered with some bright flowered
calico, two pictures, The Lark and the Stuart baby. Neither went well
with the calco walls. On the mantle over the fire place was a queer old
clock, that is the case was very odd. The Great grandfather of Mollie-J—
made the original clock, the works "quit work" but Mollie-Jane had new
put in so the case does duty. Every thing else seemed just about what
would be found in any such ranch house. There is no use in writing
about the house, it is Mollie-Jane that is enteresting.

There were no clothes in the house large enough for me except some
that had belonged to a perfect giant of a man—these I thankfully donned
and provided merriment for the entire group. In just a little while we
were all too busy with . . . [page missing]

" . . . But never for a moment was I a willing captive and I now know that
all my life I *planned* for escape some day. Subconsciously. While my two
sons were growing up it took all my time to instil in them a respect for and
belief in all the traditions of their father's family and to try to bind them as
securely as I had been bound with as many of our own rules of conduct. I
don't know why I did it. Poor children! They never had a sign of a chance to
develope individuality and I should be the last to complain now that they
have both grown into men who are incapable of even an impulse. I didn't
expect just that. As children they were both *delightfully* mischievous.

Fowler, the oldest just reveled in fighting. One day, after a particularly
streneous fray I said 'Fowler, you should not mix in such brawls. The
Fowlers don't do that. Gentlemen don't fight.'

He answered; 'I *am* a gentleman. I am a Patton. *They* fight.'

Secretly I gloated and thrilled but all that passed with the school-days.
And then the long illness of their father made me duty bound. Both sons
married lovely girls, girls rich in traditions and as convention bound as I.
Then, suddenly, I found one of the bonds broken. My poor husband
died. I regretted his death more than I can say because I know he could
have had more out of life if he *had* not shut his eyes to every thing that
the long line of Pattons back of him wouldn't have done. He never really
lived and I so wanted him to *feel* life.

Some way, after his passing, I felt so let down. I seemed half dead. I had no desires. I felt so uncertain and so lost. Besides that, almost at once my sons and their wives began to urge me to give up housekeeping, each wanted me. At last I yielded and spent six months with Fowler and the next six months with Talton. And they were good to me. Both Elizabeth and Louise watched my every move.

I was n't allowed to do one single thing. The girls tucked me into bed just as if I were about two years old. One night, just for fun I said 'Now I lay me down to sleep.' The next day when Fowler came home I overheard Elizabeth telling him and he said: 'Mother is childish, she is so old.'

When the war came on and all the world seemed so topsy-turvy I was a little awed by the sudden freedom of the young folks—then angry with them because so many of them misused their freedom and cheapened themselves. Seeing how the young folks tore down the old traditions and conventions, trampled them and yet gained nothing amazed me. I had n't wanted to tear down or to trample but I *had* wanted to break away.

That and the children's constant coddling me made me doubt myself. And my grand children were *so* perfect! They were constantly waiting upon me. It took a long time for me to see what was happening but at last I did see and I resented it all just as much as if I and not they were right—I had become a kind of punching bag for the development of my grand childrens manners and morals. I was a splendid foil for my sons' wives—I was a wonderful back ground for all the traditions that I, myself, had brought my sons up in. I hated it all. I felt cheated—and yet, I could hardly say what I felt cheated of—Just freedom, liberty. Nothing bound me but oppinions and they not my own. One day I spoke to Talton about how I felt about our family restrictions. He became so allarmed that he called Fowler and at the council which followed they decided I was losing my mind.

Their watchful care increased. So careful were they of me that I knew I should have to put myself beyond this pale of their forgiveness or I should *never* get away from it all. I thought of many ways but I had lost self confidence if I ever had any. One day, while reading the paper I glanced at the 'Personals.' Instantly a plan leaped into my head. I sent in my name and description as I had been at twenty to a matrimonial bureau. Many letters came and were carefully kept hidden for the future of my plan. I should never been able to remain undetected but for the janitor of the house in which we had appartments.

Of the number who answered my appeal for a husband I selected Jan Palik because his very name would be an offense. I answered every one of his scrawly, misspelled letters and I kept each letter carefully hidden. When the time was almost ready for me to make my break for liberty I suggested to my sons that I make over my property to them. Wonderingly they consented. I kept a few hundred dollars they knew nothing about. All the rest, burned bridges.

One day Jan Palik came from his Dakota home to see me. I didn't see him but Fowler and the janitor did. Poor Jan. I have always been ashamed to have made a cats paw of him. Fowler didn't believe him, of course. He said nothing to me about it but the janitor managed to tell me.

The time I had worked for had come so that night while the children were at a concert I ran away. I asked a taxi man to buy my ticket. I left all Jan's letters, tied with a pink ribbon in a little drawer of my desk, all the other letters scattered about my room. I was riding away into the black night. I felt a little lost and uncertain but that soon passed. I threw away my age with my past. I refused to be sixty years old. Thirty was a better mental age so I adopted that—just to myself, ofcourse. I joined a party of tourists and had one glorious year touring New Mexico, Arizona, California and Oregon. Then I joined another party, the men of the party were going to visit the new oil fields in Wyoming and then prospect down Green River for oil shale; we went by auto and the women visited the oil fields with the men.

I invested a few hundred dollars, almost all I had but that investment brings me an income sufficient to keep me—I don't need much. Money, any property binds so. But I must have a home, I love the West so I bought this little wooly place and I am *happy*. No, I am not lonely at all. I have two little Mexican boys with my sheep. They have no parents, no home so I am filling in a gap for them. I wrote the children but I didn't tell them I was not married to Jan Palik. The only thing I regret about the whole thing is I was unable to see the faces of the children when they found the evidence I had so carefully left for them.

I shall stay here. If I went back I should be a bound old lady. Seventy one. I should lie 'on the shelf.' I believe no one is on the shelf until they find the shelf comfortable. I never found it comfortable so I refuse to be on the shelf. If I remain here I can be as old as I feel. Thirty exactly. I can live and die and lie down for my last sleep in the great out doors, unbound, *free!*"

The shelf argument won my heart. There is so much I want to do, so much I *have* to do that I have been afraid that by the time I get the *have* to dos attended to I should be too old to attempt the want to dos. But I shall fix my age at thirty like my friend Mollie-Jane did—I think that pretty sound philosophy—

I am sending you much love in this letter—Please forgive my tardiness, you cannot regret it so much as I. It rests my heart to keep the day with you. Always I do whether you get a letter or not. I really do keep our day.

Your friend—
Elinore P. Stewart

Burntfork
July 26, [1925]
My Dearly beloved Josephine Harrison

It will be more than a card you will get! Bless your dear heart. I expected to write you many times before this—I don't know why I have not written before, I have been home since June 13.

We came in perfect safety although at times I wondered what would happen. I had been afraid of some of the passes, the Virginia Pass at Idaho Springs is particularly dangerous but we came down safely although our brake blocks caught fire, the friction was so great.

We camped on Fall River at Idaho Springs and were then joined by a fellow whom the children called "Goofus." He hung on til we reached West Portal. Thereby, or to, hangs a tale but it is too long for this communication as is the adventure I mentioned at Hot Sulphur. *That* was an adventure with a moonshiner. By then we had come in safety across Virginia Pass and Berthoud Pass—those are the Passes I told you we had passed when I sent the card.

I am sorry you did not recieve the Wild flowers; There was some anemonies in memory of Elda. Some sage and Indian Paint brush from Wyoming and eight other varieties the names I don't know.

Evry one we talked to tried to persuade me not to attempt Rabbit Ear Pass but I *had* to keep on for I had only just enough money and each day had it's allowance.

So after a series of small adventures, most of them pleasant we came to the dreaded Rabbit Ear—

There had been much snow on the Berthoud tho' the road was clear,

it had been shovelled out and was deep enough so that I could reach it
from the seat on the wagon and we had on double sideboards.

Well, we reached the foot of the Rabbit Ear in a driving rain. A sign
board by the road side informed us that food and shelter might be had
one and a half miles further on the road so we labored on, the roads
were a bog of mud and the wagon skidded frightfully. There were long
drifts of snow, it was just going out, that was the reason the road was so
bad. Night over-took us but we had to go on for there was no where to
stop, mud, snow and water every where and steep slopes on which to
stop.

Finally we came to the Columbine Lodge, the sign board had told us
about but the proprietor would not let us stop because we had horses.
He told us that a short distance further there had been a road camp and
that it was a good place in which to camp. We dragged on. By this time it
was snowing hard and was almost dark—We could hardly see to un-
hitch. Luckily, the road crew had left some wood cut and in our mess
box was a dry cracker box with which to kindle the fire. We soon had a
roaring fire and the rain changed to snow.

We unrolled our tent and our bedding, both were soaked through.
The tent, being wet, was so heavy we were unable to raise it; We dragged
it up over a pole the road crew had left up. We dried up as best we could
and cooked a very satisfying meal. A big fire and a hot meal *do* help
wonderfully when you are weary and your spirits are dampened. The
boys were soon quite happy and drying out blankets. We made our beds
under the tent as soon as we could and went to bed. The children were
soon sound asleep but a little, blue devil sat astride of my conciousness
and dug spurs in.

The wet tent sagged tightly about us and the snow had a sinister hiss
as it came down through the pines. If I could only have wept I should
have felt so much better but tears have never come easily to me. Of
course the lodge keeper's unwestern behavior hurt me. We *were* a tough
looking bunch and he was probably afraid we had no money with which
to pay him. I don't think *that* was what grieved me and in trying to locate the cause of my sorrowing I questioned my self.

Though some what worried over the road ahead I was not afraid; I
was not hungry, I was warm and comparitively comfortable. Finally I
came to the conclusion it was the horses I was sorry for, they had had
such a terribly hard day, up hill and through mud and muck and with

such a load. You see, we had two wagons, one loaded on the other. We had come twice the distance that day as we had made in going over in any one day—I could hear them contentedly munching their hay, I knew they were warmly blanketed and their blankets were waterproof if ours were not. So, in a little while I had run down all the possible reasons for me being blue and found none valid.

Still the snow kept hissing and the pines kept whispering of sad things that had happened or were going to happen. And I thought of you, my dear you. I was happy in thinking of you, safe, warm and dry even tho' lamed. And I went to sleep with you in my heart. You comforted me.

Next morning I awoke in a beautiful world. The sun was shining and the trees were covered with drops of water, just like heavy tear drops. But the snow that had dwelt on the mountain in the night had gone with the storm and as far as I could see where on the ground was bare were thousands of fairy bells, golden things of beauty glistening joyously in the sun. If you could have seen them!

Presently the lodge keeper came to get me to sign in his record book, it seems he has to keep one to justify his being there to the Forestry Service. I asked him if he thought he had rendered us a service—he said his lodge was for Autoist and that he could not have horses around. Of course, that was a flimsy excuse and I told him so. I would n't write our names but I asked him the names of the flowers. He said they were dog tooth violets. They were not violets nor of the violet family. They were six petaled and bell shaped, often as many as six on a stem and their leaves were much like tulip leaves.

Many, many things happened to us. When I can I will write or tell you but just now I am a very busy person. I cook for six of us, milk two cows twice each day, separate the milk, churn and run a mower every day. We are doing all the hay work ourselves. Our whole crew consists of Clyde, myself, Junior, Calvin, Robert and Ernest—the boy we raised.

I can mow easier than I can do any thing else so I do that. I have to keep ahead of the rakers and stackers. Ofcourse, evry one helps me do the house work, the boys make the beds, sweep, help wash dishes, scrub the floor. I need not milk but none of the rest are as careful and I like to have plenty of cream and butter. There is such a hay crop here that men are scarce; even if we could afford to hire them. I feel that we cannot spend the money that way.

Mother and Jerrine will be here next week and we will return to Boulder August 29th. School opens the 31st. Please, *please* get well, my Josephine Harrison. I know how you love the hills and their most lovely time will soon be here. I feel guilty every time I enjoy something out of doors—I know how you would thrill to the beauty of that particular view or thing and my heart aches because you can't have it. How gladly would I bring it to you. All I can do is to send my love. I do that—

Your friend
Elinore P. Stewart

Diamond Mountain near Brown's Park, Colorado, had always intrigued Elinore because of the many stories she had heard of the great herds of cattle and the "notorious outlaws" who often wintered there. In her search for background information on such desperadoes, she wrote to her friend Grace Raymond Hebard, librarian and professor of political economy at the University of Wyoming.[2] In a January 17 (1926?) letter, Elinore asked: "How can I obtain dates and data of the express robbery that occured at Point of Rocks, some time in 1899 I think. Where and how can I get a line on Butch Cassidy's activities? I am unable to go to Rawlins to see Carlisle, how can I get his story? All this sounds as if I were becoming blood thirsty. But no. I am just kind of subconciously planning, *hoping* to enter some of the many contests being conducted by the publishers." Her fascination with such tales prompted the following imaginary journey.

Aug. 20th, 1925
Some Where on the Road
My Dear friend. [Mrs. Florence Allen]
    Yesterday I was tired of the road. I found myself regretting that we didn't take the train and reach our destination in less than twenty four hours instead of this long, lonely crawl over sand ridges and waterless alkali flats. We had stopped at noon, the sun pouring it's rays down without stint. I got a shadscale thorn in my foot and the water in the bags was almost slimy and tepid besides having a most distinct mineral flavor. Mrs. McPike and I were putting the victuals where those who wished might eat but I was doing my part wholly from a sense of duty.
    I was tired of the trip and I said so to Mrs. McPike. "I am glad you say

2. Larson, "Wyoming's Contribution," 10.

that for it is a sign I have been looking for all day. Just as the darkest hour is just before dawn, so is the dullest hour just before adventure. I can expect something to happen any time now since you find the road dull."

"Our wagon will break down. We may have to stop and set a tire, or the horses will get away," I answered.

"My! You've got it bad," she laughed. "I *know* we are close to an adventure. I can't trust my own feelings when looking for a sign because I really enjoy every minute. I like the glowing sun, the great purple reaches of the distance—"

I was rude. I felt that way so I interrupted, "And the shadscale in my foot, the brackish water, the never ending jolting, the sunburn—"

She wouldn't listen, she put her hands up to her mouth and shouted "Chow! Come get it. Luncheon are served."

I think that I was merely trying to find reinforcement for a secret hope when I found so much to growl about for, in my heart I admire the purple distance, I like the shimmering lights on the desert, the lonely buttes, the castle-like palisades we sometimes passed, although there is no river there now there must have at one time been water there to leave the rock and earth so washed as to show the strata.

After "luncheon are served" we took up our journey. The long, brown road looked *tired.* It didn't beckon a bit, it played no merry game of hide and seek as mountain roads do, where only a short distance of the road is to be seen at a time. Mountain roads are always hiding behind the shoulder of a hill or running away from you up a canon or leading you into dim, green forests. This road lay tired and neglected far, far ahead. As the afternoon passed the country became more broken so that hope could build on the hills that began to appear. I began to speculate on what would lie beyond the next hill or what would we see when we passed around this long ridge of crags. That was a little more enteresting than being sorry for a tired road. We came to a place where the craggy ridge broke and a narrow valley showed between the stony walls. A line of fence appeared in the distance. Our road didn't go that way and the sun was not yet down but water had to be thought of for we had drained the bags at noon so we pulled off the road and followed the dim outline of a road into the canon of high stone walls.

We rumbled along for half a mile before we caught sight of any dwelling. The valley widened as we progressed and we saw what appeared to be quite a pretentious place. Along the road we had just come it was at least sixty miles to the nearest neighbor and more than one hundred miles to town. As we drew up we saw that the out buildings were more pretentious than the dwelling which was one of those long, low log houses of the earliest days, sod roof, or what *had* been sod. It had become just loose soil and the thought came "it leaks" followed by the thought "Perhaps it rains only on travelers."

I was in a detestable mood; almost by the time the wheels stopped a man came out of the house and let down the bars of his corral which was also his door yard. "Come in, come in. Damned if I can ever have any privacy any more. This old road has become a thorough fare—" was his rather unfriendly greeting.

"We only came to find a camping place where we could get water," the Stewart explained.

"You don't need to tell me. I know exactly what you came for. You aint the first offender but it's damn hard on a fellow that cares for a little privacy. It was only last Thursday that a fellow came here just as I was about to take a bath. And now you come just as I was about to take the bath I didn't get then. If this keeps up I won't get to bathe this year."

"Well," McPike spoke up, "if we can water our teams and fill the water bags we will drive back to the road and you can clean up, but Gosh! this is Thursday. You've had a whole week to bath yourself."

"My weeks aint made up of Thursdays and Thursday is my bath day."

The Stewart took up the argument. "Isn't there water enough for our needs and your bath too? If not, how far is it to the nearest water?"

"It aint a question of water, it's a question of privacy and system. I aint never bathed in public yet and Thursday's my day."

Mrs. McPike giggled, I giggled, Jerrine did so and in another moment the whole bunch were laughing.

"Man, it's almost night, your day is almost up. We will fill our bags, water our teams and pull on so that you may become as Godly as you like," said the Stewart.

"Unless you want me to stay and wash your back." Mr. McPike offered.

"No. Nobody was ever turned from this ranch and your horses are tired. You drive in and either unload your outfit at the camp bunk house or at the door here. If you'd *rather* camp you can have the bunk house but if you want to visit me just troop in."

I wondered which he had given up, the bath or privacy. With so many buildings around it seemed a useless sacrifice either way. Mr. McPike accepted at once and I found my self scrambling down off the wagon torn between a desire to stop and the wish to go on and not accept the hospitality of so unwilling a host.

He left the children, Mrs. McPike and I standing before his door while he piloted the men to the proper corral for the horses. He seemed filled with amazement when he returned to find that we had not entered and made our selves at home. The room he ushered us into was a large one, four large windows and two doors. In it were a range on one side, a heater on the other of the room. A long table in the center, two or three smaller ones against the wall, several chairs in different stages of decrepitude, cooking untensils of every kind.

Each chair I tried protested loudly so I walked about looking at the objects on the wall. An antelope's head, a deer's, a splendid one of a mountain sheep and a dog's head, all beautifully mounted. Over each door were cow's horns forming a rack for guns. I offered to help prepare supper but mine host curtly refused. It wasn't long before he had the meal on the table; seeing no other place to wash our hands, we had gone out to a ditch.

"He's a queer one, now don't you think so?" whispered Mrs. McPike.

Even the children felt the restraint, they were quiet enough to please any one and even Jerrine asked no questions. Every one felt it and as we were seated at the table Mr. McPike tried to loosen things up a bit. We hadn't been introduced and as we found our chairs the Stewart said "My name is Stewart. I don't think I've heard yours—"

"No, I don't think you have, tho' that aint no fault of mine. I've lived here nearly sixty years and my father lived here before me."

We waited a moment but he said nothing so Mr. McPike said "My name is McPike, this is Mrs. McPike. We are on a wedding tour."

Our host gazed at the pair for a moment then said, "Well, you aint no baby. If you've lived this long and get into trouble like that, deliberate trouble getting married is, why you can't expect no sympathy from me."

He seated himself and began carving a lovely roast of what I thought was a leg of mutton. What ever else our host lacked he has good fare and plenty of it as Josiah Allen's wife would say.

Jerrine is wearing overalls. Our host kept calling her Buddy. She was afraid of offending him so didn't tell him of his mistake. The Stewart said, "This is our daughter. Her name is Jerrine."

He looked at her curously for a moment. Jerrine was embarassed but she tried to smile it off. Suddenly the man smiled back at her and said "You are about the age but not very like my little sister. I will show you her picture after supper."

He was just as pleasant as he could be all the rest of the meal. It was marvelous to see the change. We could see he wished the meal over but it was hard to hurry. When we were through he lighted a lamp and asked us into another room. It was not dark out of doors yet but quite dark in the room except for the light of the lamp he carried. "This is my picture gallery. If you ever read I expect you know that all old English families have them. Well, about seven generations ago we were English but I am American now. But some of the old English ideas stay with me so this is my picture gallery. In Mother's day it was the parlor but I don't think it was used half a dozen times in her life. This is my father."

A gloomy countenance glowered down upon us from a heavy, over ornate frame. Three or four more solemn visages represented other male relatives; some faces of women, what ever of beauty they may ever have possessed carefully done away with. I racked my brain for satisfying lies to be polite and was glad to have such help as Mrs. McPike gave. As might be expected neither Stewart nor Mr. McPike said a word.

The last picture needed no lying. It was beautiful. It was of a girl about sixteen and I think it the loveliest thing of the kind I ever saw. It was in a white frame. The face seemed alive. Actually the expression seemed to change. The blue eyes were so merry, the mouth so wistful. But you will get an ugly impression if I try to describe the face. We stood silently gazing, I could not find a word to say, I dared not lie. At last Jerrine said "What is her name?"

"Jessie."

"Where is she?"

"She died for *me*."

There was a sharp intaking of breath. No one spoke and the man, holding the lamp nearer the pictured face allowed the sorrow that filled his heart to creep into his face. Silently he lowered the white curtain that covered the picture and as silently led us back to the kitchen. I was glad that the men went to see about their horses. I knew they felt as if they had looked upon another's naked sorrow. The children went out to unroll their beds. Jerrine and I began to pile up the dishes. Mrs. McPike settled herself in the one rocker, the man lighted his pipe.

We three washed the dishes, no one spoke until the dishes were done. Our men came in but conversation lagged. I wanted to go out and make beds but it seemed uncivil to leave just then so I sat on the step and watched the big stars come out. It was all so lonely, so remote and yet tradgedy seemed to fill the air.

Jerrine began to admire the heads on the wall. Our host went up to her as she stood looking at the dog.

"He was Jessie's dog. The antelope was hers, he was a pet. I killed the mountain sheep one day while she was with me on the fall round up. Jessie could ride any thing that could be saddled; I could never beat her at daring. No broncho caught from the wild herds could scare her. There was *never* a girl like her."

He was conscious of no one but Jerrine, surly and taciturn to the rest of us, he was human to Jerrine. No one spoke. Away in the crags an owl hooted and down the valley a coyote barked. Jerrine seated herself by one of the small tables. Our host sat down near, relighted his pipe and began.

"My father settled this ranch in the days when the fur trappers were leaving. I never knew why he settled so far from any possible touch with civilization but I think it was because he foresaw that settlers who crowd along the streams to get irrigation while these isolated spots like this would be free from crowding for many, many years. There are springs and seeps where cattle can get water where it would be impossible to get water to farm with. He must have foreseen that he would have free range for one hundred miles in each direction but he did *not* forsee that some other cattle man would also see the natural advantage of the land and heartlessly squeeze him out."

"Further on you will find the country very rough, cedar hills rise upon cedar hills. They furnish excellent shelter for cattle in winter, shade in summer and they afford some thing else not quite so innocent. It is very broken, *very* rough country where Colorado, Utah and Wyoming join. No one not used to the country could ride through, they could not drive cattle. But for one who knows there are trails unseen and places and places where droves of cattle can be held for days with only one or two herders."

"The lay of the country and the state lines made it a paradise for cattle thieves but no *small* cattle thief ever made a go of it. A man getting a beef now and then should not be called a thief. My father never called one that, the man is only providing for a need when he kills a beef not his own, but the *thieves* are the big cattle men who take on every hand just to feed their pride and arrogance."

"One of the biggest cattle outfits in Northern Colorado (Haley) was such a man.[3] His men had orders to brand any thing that had hair on. They did it, too, (Haley) himself was in Europe for two years; He had a rustling foreman and the time came when all his men were rustling—for themselves. When the big cattleman returned of course there was much to explain which the men did by naming every other settler as the rustlers. The cattleman in question was only one among many. Their headquarters were at Cheyenne Wyoming and all the others had suffered or professed to have, in the same way, so they formed a protective association."

"Perhaps you have heard of Tom Horn? He was hired to get evidence on rustlers and to shoot them when he had it. Tom Horn is the only one the public knows about but there were scores of such Judas'."

"My father's losses were heavier each year so he went up to Cheyenne to try to join the association. But (Haley) the cattleman named him as a rustler. My father dared him to produce evidence. It couldn't be had of course so my father was allowed to come home. I never saw any one so angry and so hurt. He said the country was getting to be too thickly settled and that he would close out and go to Alaska or South America."

"So we began the fall round up. We had corrals built in many places in order to brand, hold special cattle and such things. Most of the cattle were held on the flats, that is herded, but often we wanted a special shipment at one time and another later, so when the round up was on every thing was gathered and the cattle we wanted first were held in the corrals the night before we started for the railroad. We had a shipment of three year olds in a corral over on Diamond Mountain. It was a dry year and the spring there had failed so our mess wagon was at another water hole half a mile distant."

"It had been a hard day and after we corralled the shipment we shod horses as long as we could see, getting ready for the long drive to the railroad to begin next day. It was ten o'clock before we turned in and every man was dead tired. We had to be up before daylight next morning."

3. The name Haley appears in parentheses in the original manuscript, perhaps because Elinore intended to change it later.

"As the cattle were safely corralled we concluded there would be no need for a night herder and as the days and nights ahead were to be strenous ones we were all glad to get a chance to sleep."

"We had our breakfast before it was light next morning. I heard the mess wagon rumbling off just as I got off my horse to let down the bars to start the cattle. In order that the cattle could not rub against the bars and knock them down I had wired the bars, but I found one of the bars unwired. I thought I must have over looked that wire so soon had the bars down and the steers out."

"My father and I with three other fellows were to drive. We were a mile from camp, the sun was just rising when two men rode up. One was (Haley's) foreman. He greeted us pleasantly enough, asked us if we had seen any of their brand while riding. We told them all we knew. The foreman hesitated a moment then said "We would like to look through this bunch if you don't mind." My father told them to go ahead but he was white with anger. I wasn't so old then as I am now by a good many years. I resolved to pound both men when they came from among the cattle."

"We were amazed to see them cut out a steer. More amazed to find it had their brand; they cut fifteen, every one with their brand. Now, it is customary among cattlemen to gather for the neighbors. All do it when they are riding and exchange afterward but my father was too angry with (Haley) to do that so we had not been picking his up as we gathered. Also, our corral system made it impossible for other brands to stray in, besides each animal had been culled and reculled to get the best for this shipment, those that would best stand the long, hard drive. So we *knew* we had none but our own. Then I thought of the missing wire and I knew what had happened."

"For reasons of their own they had put their cattle with ours in the night. My father would not allow me to fight. (Haley's) men merely turned their cattle loose and rode away. We went on but both father and I rode again and again through the herd to be sure that no more of (Haley's) were among ours. Some one was with the cattle every minute from then on."

"We couldn't think what the game was but we found out soon enough when we got to town. We were loading the cattle on the cars when the sheriff arrested Dad. I went on with the cattle, Dad went to jail. They cuiched [?] him. My old Dad went to the penitentiary and died there.

Mother died the night the news came. She asked me to take Jessie and leave. I was n't much more than a boy and I swore to break (Haley). I swore he should die on the scaffold, a pauper. Jessie agreed with me and together we started to gather evidence against him. We rode by day and we rode by night. We had evidence enough to send an army to the pen but always some poor devil of a tool was the one who would get the sentence if we had acted. Our own herd was decreasing rapidly."

"At last Jessie begged me to stop, to leave as mother had asked us to. Each defeat left me more angry and determined. Jessie quit riding but I kept on. At last I found a corral so hidden among the cedars that it was by accident that I happened upon it. I stationed my self near and watched day in and day out. At last I had my reward. (Haley) himself came with his foreman and a bunch of yearlings. They branded them, altered brands already on and altered the marks. They drove them into a box canon where there was a little feed and water to hold them until the brands healed."

"I was too elated for words. I put out at once for those to whom the cattle belonged. But I reckoned with the wrong man. The chief man was a (Haley) man and would not beleive. Next a price was on my head. I was a marked man. I had to sneak about my own range. Added to that I could not understand Jessie. She begged and pleaded to go. She wouldn't go out with me. She wouldn't ride with me any more. Life was tough enough. I never gave up my idea of squaring things but I thought I might start anew some where else and finish my work here some other time so I set out to find a new place to start. Jessie refused to go until I had found a place so I got a woman to stay with her."

"I was gone several months and when I came back Jessie asked me to go to Denver to purchase a tombstone for our mother. I told her I would later, she coaxed and when that failed tried every way she knew to get me away. Finally she begged me not to ride any where east of our range boundary. She was terribly unhappy I could see but God knows we had enough to make us unhappy."

"One day I determined to look over some range to the east. Jessie begged and plead with me not to. I told her I had ridden there many times since coming back and meant to go again. She turned all the horses out of the corral but I succeeded in getting a rope on one of the worst of the bunch. He was a big black stallion that had been ridden only a few times. I saddled him, intending only to run the others in to get the horses I wanted. He was a murderous beast and I came to the bunk house to get my spurs while I was buckling them on Jessie ran past me. Before I could say a word she was in my saddle and gone. She wore her riding togs and an old hat of mine. Helpless I looked at her disappearing and wondered what she meant by her behavior."

"It was night when I heard the horse at the gate. I waited a little and as she didn't come in I went out. She was hanging across the saddle, still alive but shot through, plucky little sister! Shot, dying, on a wild horse she came back to warn me and to tell me what she knew would break my heart. Repeated warnings had been sent to the house telling me to leave the country and warning me that hot lead was a sure cure for cattle rustling. She recieved the warnings but had not told me. I held her in my arms while she told me. Unknown to me she had met, loved and married (Walter Haley) son of the man who had ruined our family."

"At first she had hoped to end all the trouble that way but old (Haley) was more angry than ever and had posted men to get me. Young (Haley) had left his father then but he had no place to take Jessie and she would not leave me. Young (Haley) found out his fathers orders to his men about shooting me and told Jessie."

"She was desperate when she made that last ride, she was on her way to plead with (old Haley). All her pride was laid aside. It would have been a terrible ride for her had nothing happened but just as she came out of Irish Canon the bullet found her. The horse wheeled and came for home but she saw and recognized the man who fired the gun. She screamed back to him to tell Walter what he had done, told him she was his wife. The man thought it was I. She never told me who the man was. I have never known. She died in my arms, forgiven and at peace."

"Next morning brought Walter. I—didn't kill him as I once thought I would. I couldn't. He was too heart broken. He didn't know who did the shooting. The news had been shouted to him in the night while he lay in bed in the shack he had built to start a home."

"We buried Jessie. I saddled my horse and took that gun over the door and started out to clean up the (Haley) bunch. Walter rode with me. "He is my old dad but he deserves it." was all he said. We rode right up to the house. I took my gun and went in entending to get (old Haley) first but I waited for Walter to have his say."

After that death would not have meant any thing to (Haley). There was no need to shoot. I sometimes wonder if I *am* a coward. I just said to

(Haley) "You have ruined my family, *killed* my innocent sister. I came here to kill you but I wont. I want you to live to see *all* your hopes die. You shall never have a foot of range my father ran on. All the fortune you pile up will do you no good for in killing my sister you ruined your only son. Your only hope to save your self is to shoot me now."

"He didn't of course, and I have kept my word. His range is gone. Where he once had thousands of cattle a few, pitiful creatures live a starved life. I had to bury my pride to do it. I had to quit cattle but I run thousands of sheep on the old range and I have killed the cattle business here. Still, I am in the same fix as (Haley) for I have no one, no one. I am almost a sheep my self. Family gone, pride gone, almost gone myself."

Silence was the only tribute we could pay so great a folly, so terrible a grief. We left, one by one, sought our beds.

Next morning a very brusque host sped us on our way. "I see no need of encouraging loafing. I never do. If you run across any of my sheep camps you can stay for one meal but pull on after that. There's no feed for your horses at a sheep camp. Goodby."

Without waiting for a word he went about his business and with a rumbling and jolting we again took up the road. Not a tired road, a road over which tradgedy had passed.

My Dear Mrs. Allen, this is your March letter. Please think of me on our day of remembrance. Loving, grateful thoughts will be flying from my heart to Boston on that day.

This letter is tiresomely long, I know but it seems I could make it no shorter and I thought of you as I wrote it so I called it your letter. If you like it will you please send it to Mrs. Burlingame? Mr. and Mrs. McPike have been married many years but they are, they say, professional wedding trippers. They go on wedding tours for any of their family or friends who haven't time or means to do so themselves. Accept my love, give Miss Coney some of it and if you see Mr. Sedgwick tell him not to forget me.

Your Friend,
Elinore Stewart

Burnt Fork, Wyo.
March 15, 1926
[to Mrs. Florence Allen]

We had just stopped to camp on Fall River, just out of Idaho Springs. All day long we had been dodging autos, turning out for them, nosing up into hillsides or perching on perilous edges. We had not seen a team, not a horse; we felt like intruders in a world of autos.

My nerves were in a tangle; I was glad to stop and get down off the high seat of the wagon. It should have been a beautiful camping place, nature had done much for it. Roaring, beautiful, cascading Fall river on one side and wild hills all around. But the river was blue from the 'tailings' from the mines, all along it's banks were heaps of rubbish, disgusting in the extreme. They use the river edge for a city dump. There was no where else to camp so I looked out the cleanest place I could find and began to unpack.

About this time another wagon rumbled into view. It was a ramshackle affair, piled high with odds and ends of household furnishings.

Atop the load was a man who knew very little about handling a team. He was a young man, probably twenty five years old, he was awkward and fat. But he drove a team instead of a car and my boys hailed him as a welcome addition to our small defense.

The camping space was so small that it seemed a pity to have two fires and I had mine going, my boys attended to their team and helped the newcomer with his. By that time I had our supper of bacon and eggs ready so we asked him to have a bite with us. He told us his name but I don't remember it and as he also told us that his friends called him Goof that name remains in my recollection.

I awoke in the night; Goof was sprawled upon his wagon. I could see him clearly in the dim light, he had not even removed his shoes or his hat. But he was asleep, I could hear him doing that.

Next morning we had breakfast together and it came out that he had no food and no feed for his horses. I looked at him with suspicion in my eye. He came from Denver he said, had never been over the road we were travelling in the day time, had gone by auto and had supposed that grass would be plentiful for the horses. That early in the year! May 27th. And we had Berthoud Pass to go over. I asked why he slept as he did but he wouldn't answer me.

The morning's clearer light revealed much that was not noticeable in the dusk he came in; his horses were in bad shape to travel, his wagon was crazily loaded and the wagon tongue was *wired* in. A wired in wagon tongue to go over Berthoud with! No wonder he was called Goof.

I helped him to reload his wagon and while we were doing it came to kind of like the silly thing, he was so ignorant about his work that I felt sorry for him and he was so cheerful and good natured. Maybe it was a feeling of kinship after he told me he was homesteading near Hot Sulphur. But I wondered how he would manage, he knew so little about things.

Before I left Boulder I had found if the Pass was opened. I asked the Chamber of Commerce almost every day until they told me it would be officially open June the first. We had made better time than I had expected to and reached the foot of Berthoud three days before we expected to. Goof stayed with us for two excellent reasons, he couldn't get away and his wagon tongue made him afraid to try the Pass alone.

After we left Empire we met many stragglers quiting work on the tunnel at West Portal. I asked about the road on top and they said there was much snow and mud. So, when we reached the foot of the Pass I stopped to camp; I knew it would take half a day to get over and I didn't want night to overtake me on the mountain.

There's no place to camp, the road is graded and hugs the mountain so closely on one side that it is hard to get off the road and ofcourse, one can't camp in the road.

Even at the foot of the Pass there were huge snow drifts, real little streams running merrily from the melted snow. But we found a splendid place to camp, the children put our team out to nibble the dandelions just showing. My boys went fishing in Clear creek and I gathered dandelions for supper.

Poor Goof almost wept he was so anxious to go on. What a supper we had! My dandelions were delicious and the trout the boys caught were more so; the potatoes roasted with out a flaw. We had a clean, lovely spot in which to camp, we had pure, icy water and plenty of good wood, a clean, level spot on which to make our beds and plenty of room so that Goof's snores would only wake the echoes, not me. We were all happy, for, after he got over his disappointment about stopping, Goof enjoyed it all as much as we. After supper we put on our coats and sweaters, made a roaring fire and sat around in deep content.

We grew confidential. Goof told me he grew up in an orphan's home and had been whipped two thousand and eleven time for playing in the dirt. When he found they would make him work in the garden to punish him he became the worst boy in the Home.

He began to save his pennies to buy a farm with and when he was sixteen and had to get out of the Home he had saved seventy nine cents.

Different persons had got him jobs on ranches and truck patches around Denver but he was such a 'Goof' he couldn't stay with a job. One man fired him for sleeping with the pigs, another became peeved because he said 'Commence' to the horses instead of 'Get up!'

And so on and so on. He has reached man's estate and gained a few smatterings of knowledge that he may in time find how to correlate. He knows which end of a horse to put a collar on but he starts out on a week's journey with no feed; he knows how to harness and hitch in but he starts over a perilous pass with his wagon wired together.

There is much that is grand and inspiring about Berthoud Pass; I would like to tell you about it but I've tried so often to present a scene as it appeared to me and I have never been able to do it justice. We began to climb as soon as we could get started after breakfast. The road was perfectly clear of snow or mud, it had just been cleared of the stones and tree branches that fall in the Winter time. Even the rake marks showed, so recent was the work.

Upward and upward we wound, often we dragged a mile to gain fifteen or twenty feet. The road doubled so to make the grade. We kept climbing and climbing. At about half past eleven that morning we made the top. Snow and snow, on every hand stretched slopes and fields of glistening snow. An army of men were frantically shovelling and dragging to clear the peak of the road. Seventeen autos were stalled or waiting in the snow.

Among them was a great old made over affair, a kind of house on a truck. In it were a man, his wife and four children and his step-daughter. The man had been working at the tunnel and had been dismissed; no wonder he was dismissed for he was a sullen, grouchy thing. The step-daughter, Nina, was about seventeen and rather a pretty girl but very ordinary. She was kind and helpful I noticed. We decided to cook and have our dinner while we were waiting for the jam to loosen up. But it was snow every where underfoot.

Goof found an empty gasoline can and made a fire in that so I could boil coffee and fry some steak. We were closest to Nina's outfit so I observed her closely. So did Goof. Goof and my boys fed the horses while I fixed dinner. Nina came over to admire the horses (*And* Goof!) With a magnificent 'the world is mine' kind of gesture Goof invited her to share our dinner.

The snow was so wet and heavy, shoetop deep where we were. We sat

up on my wagon while we ate the steak that was so tough we had to use
our fingers, the coffee got cold before we could enjoy it. Neither Goof
nor Nina noticed it, he was telling her his hopes and plans, making every
thing out very rosy and fine.

She was giving us little sketches of her history and that of her family,
all of it drab enough, common-place enough but enteresting to Goof and
herself. One or two cars moved up and sped on the way down the road
we had come, thankful to be out of the mud and snow of the North side
of Berthoud. The government man in charge of the road motioned Nina's
party forward.

The great old ark of a thing lurched forward and sunk axel deep in a
'chuck'. All the heaving, pushing and snorting did no good. It began to
look serious for us all. For all there were more men than he could use to
push out the stalled box car, Nina's dad made her come and help push.
She pushed and sloshed around in the snow but it was useless. The more
useless it all semed the more frantic Nina became, the more she tried to
help the more foolish things she did. Some one had placed a rock under
the wheel to keep the old ark from rolling back down the hill; Nina took
the rock away and the thing began to back down. Dad slapped her ears
and Goof called out; "Hey! You stop that! Jump on some one your own
size, why don't you?"

There was really something dignified about his uncouthness then, I
really admired him.

Well, the government man took some chains and our horses and
snaked the whole bunch out. Nina refused to go on with her people, she
said she would go back to Portal and wait table in the boarding house. I
think a girl's place is with her mother so I refused to let her ride with me,
I thought she would go on if she got no sympathy from me. Not so. She
said she would walk the few miles down to the place. I wanted nothing to
do with the affair so I pulled into the road the minute I could and went
rattling and rumbling down. I wanted to get away before the parents did.

Getting down Berthoud was much worse than gettin' up. So much
mud and many stones in the road. We passed West Portal, we passed
through Frazier, through Tabernash and still no Goof. We found a good
place to camp, had supper over and our beds made when we heard a
wagon rumbling. We knew then that Goof had come down Berthoud
safely. He didn't come to our camp; we could hear him whistling very
happily. From my vantage point I could see him moving about. Some

how, there was a new springiness in his step, the slumpiness was gone, he was another creature.

This looks like a love story, the natural thing to say would be that they married and lived happily as long as the groceries lasted, I confess that is what I thought as I saw Goof moving about. At the same time I wondered what about his meals and his horse feed.

I hadn't long to wonder; very soon we could hear the horses munching their hay and smell the ham frying. But Goof stayed away from our camp, Next morning my boys wanted to fish in the little creek we camped on and Goof pulled out ahead of us. He was whistling very merrily as he passed us, he never spoke, waved a hand or even glanced toward our camp. We had been jogging along a couple of hours before we caught sight of Goof again.

The expected had happened. His wagon tongue had pulled out. He was very plainly distressed. We stopped to help if we could and his distress increased. At last he said; "Say, I got sore with you when you turned that girl down, I don't think I ought to let you help with out tellin' you that I think you acted kind of raw."

I told him I didn't care what he thought, I wanted to help so that the wagon could move on and let others use the road. As we worked he got over his grouch and we talked quite comfortably. He told me that Nina had gone on with her people but had reproved him for trying to get on without 'food or feed' and had made him promise to take care of himself. Hence the ham and the hay, bought at Tabernash. He confided that he had two reasons for his homesteading venture, one he wanted a home and that kind of home, that kind of work. The other, he expected to take kids from the Home as fast as he was able and as many as he could to start them to happiness and independence. I didn't tell him I had thought he had found his woman there on top of the world, I still think he did but it may be that I will never know.

Just as the sun was burnishing the bosom of the great Bear river with sunset glory we left Goof. We couldn't have accepted his invitation to stay all night with him for he completely filled his small domicile. And his personality more than filled it, he had changed. There on the snow wrapped mountain top he found some one who respected him and he suddenly grew up.

I had started in to tell you about our adventure with the moonshiner but when your letter came I thought I had better tell you about Goof. I had not forgotten you or our dear day. I never shall. You say I have an unusual knack of meeting extraordinary people; Miss Harrison once wrote me that she didn't like a letter because she didn't like the fiction. So I had a session with myself to determine whether I do fictionalize or how it happens that others seem not to see what I do in those we meet in passing.

I have come to the conclusion that it is because most of my friends are cultured people and I am not. I have absolutely no manners and therefore can and do ask questions, can mingle with anybody and every-body since I have no standard to support.

In proof of this; there is here in this town a woman who wears a mask all the time, she never takes it off, she dresses in mens clothes, she is a finished musician, was trained for the opera, she speaks French and Ger-man fluently. She has a magnificent home, furnished most expensively. She raises goats, does all the work with them herself. She has Nubian, Algerian, Swiss and many other kinds that I know nothing about. She has peacocks, all kinds of geese and turkeys. She has Malay ducks, Chi-nese ducks, Pekinese, Australian. I don't know half the names.

She has a girl about Jerrine's age that is as wild as an antelope, actu-ally runs from another girl. No one knows what the girl is to the woman, there are all sorts of stories. Money seems no object, there's always plenty of it for every whim. The house has a most perfect radio. Radio fans here have sometimes caught things coming from Chicago where the husband lives and is said to be a millionaire. But the messages are always in code. They may not be to Mrs. Gesper at all, she gets the credit though. Those passing her house after midnight hear the most exquisite singing; four o'clock in the morning is her bedtime, she arises at ten.

These are just a few of the oddities of this household; if I were to write this to Miss Harrison she would think I am fictionalizing, yet it is true and is right here for the proof. I can see her house from my back yard. Some day I may get the story and then I'll write you. In the mean-time I will be thinking of you, of a dear, gentle presence that once smiled from your Mother's eyes. She was, is, more to me than a friend. More even than the help, success, that she gave me. She is an inspiration.

She is just as much alive in my heart today as ever she was, I have a little, loving expansion of my heart every time that memory presents her serene, smiling face. I love the memory of her thin, silvery hair. I loved her humor, her kindness and her patience.

I must stop now and see if the children have left me pen and ink so I can sign this. You have my fondest love.

> Sincerely
> *Elinore P. Stewart*

Often the real men and women who populate Elinore's letters evolved into the characters of her fiction. The delightful "Ma" Mary Alice Gillis and her son, Dave, lived near the Stewart family. Although Elinore often deliberately borrowed from several acquaintances to create a composite character, Ma Gillis alone was the basis for Mrs. O'Shaughnessy, Ma Dallas, and Mrs. Pond. As the years went by, these characters became more irascible and earthy, perhaps because Stewart grew less concerned with her public image, or perhaps because she was reading more realistic fiction.

Burntfork
Aug. 29, [1926]
Dear Mrs. Allen.

The children have gone back to Boulder, they left early in the morning of the 26th. The place seemed so desolate after they left that it seemed I just could not stand to stay. I had a wild impulse to run after the truck on which they were going.

Ernest, a young man who lived with us for years but now has a homestead on which he has to stay most of the time, came up to see the children off. But he came too late, they had gone, so he came just in time to see how it hurt me. We are great friends, Ernest and I. When he saw what I couldn't hide, tears on my face, he said, "You need to go some where. You've hung out too long around this joint. You take Topsy and get out for a few days; I'll stay and help Clyde. I'll attend to the cows and milk."

The breakfast dishes were unwashed, the "makings" of the children's lunch yet on the table. The beds were unmade, the separator waiting to be washed—much to do but there always will be, heavenly chances to roam and explore fewer and fewer.

It didn't take much persuasion, the opportunity was too good to let pass. Although I had no idea of going any where a few minutes before I was very shortly clothed in a pair of corduroy trousers and a wool shirt, more, both Clyde and Ernest helped me off. As Ernest was opening the big gate to let me out Clyde came hurrying with the field glasses, a kit containing my microscope, chisel and mallet. And a gunny sack in which were a few tools.

"If you should go by Ed Aldrich's leave this brace and bits. I promised him to send them over so he could fix his stacker for his late hay. I let the kids get away with out sending it over so you take it."

It was a very definite shove away from the Green River road and I smiled as I rode away, adjusting my cumbersome, jangling load. The tools, bits well wrapped meant a short visit with Ed who says he had a fever when he was a child that settled on his mind, that is why he is queer. The field glasses always taken on excursions, the "hope kit" with chisel, mallet and glass could only be useful in the "Bad lands." I *might* find an enteresting hill. Two parcels of lunch showed up among the various bags and bundles bedecking the saddle, each man had seen the "makings" on the table and each had put up food enough for two or three. Topsy jogged along cheerfully and I felt a little more cheerful myself as I remembered the injunction not to come back until I had had an adventure.

But still, I was so sorry for myself that I felt a little resentful because I had had no time to plan my outing but I quickly remembered several places that I had long wished to visit and decided to visit the chimneys. These chimneys are plainly visible at our place but I had never been close to them, our place being several miles south of them. They range along the rim rock of a mountain lying east and west on the north side of Henry's Fork.

I could see them as I rode through our meadow and that determined me to go there. Then on the way back I could putter among the Badlands and later deliver the tools to Ed. So I spured up and was soon cantering along the big road outside all the fields. I had forded the creek and headed into the hills when I saw Mrs. Pond ahead. I have known her for almost twenty years but have not cared for her, hardly respected her. She had seen me or I should have turned back rather than ridden with her. I took a grip on what ever little politeness and patience I have and rode on up to where she sat waiting for me.

"Good morning," she greeted. "I couldn't make out who the devil you were, chugging and clanking along like a tinker going to war. What you up to? Where are you going?" I told her and she promptly envited herself to go along.

"I *was* going after wild currants, gooseberries and choke cherries but

I've been wanting to see the chimneys, too, so we will just picnic and have one hell of a good time today." It must have been ten o'clock by this time and the sun poured down hotly upon us. Sweat dripped from our horses as we toiled upward. The soft, crumbly bad land soil made the going worse, there is no road and we wound our way around the ashy hills up this little wash, along gravely shelves, through clumps of odorous cedars, finally out upon a cool plateau where the breeze could reach us and we could rest our panting horses.

Mrs. Pond removed her saddle and carefully wiped the sweat from her horse's back. She let him loose to roll on the dry dirt and while he was enjoying his freedom she turned to Topsy. She cast a scornful glance at me and demanded, "Why don't you attend to your horse? You ride like a big, fat bag of sand, you just sit in the saddle and don't try to save your horse at all, it's got to drag you and carry you both, the way you ride. And now that the poor thing has got you up here you flop down and let the sweat dry on the hair. It will make his back sore." Before I could reply or do any thing else she was removing my saddle.

"Judas Priest! What the hell have you got in all these sacks and bundles?" I explained and she seemed satisfied, seemed even to enjoy her self imposed task of grooming Topsy. Afterwards we sat for awhile under a cedar, resting and chatting. I wanted to get on to the chimneys and I sat looking toward them. Mrs. Pond got the field glasses from my pack; she looked out over the valley far below us, sought out the different ranch houses, saw that John Briggs had painted his house, had a red roof, made caustic, stinging remarks about what she saw and handed the glass to me. I adjusted them and turned to the chimneys. Whiter than the hill against which they stand, they looked like giant mud dauber nests. I remarked that and she seized the glasses and after a moment became almost petrified, she scarcely breathed and when at last she lowered the glass she was very excited and she made no move toward returning the glass to me. She seemed so jubilant that I looked at her in wonder.

"Say," she said, "Would you do some thing to please me? Would you help a little, do as I say and ask no questions if I promise to explain every thing later? You needn't be a bit afraid and you will be helping a good cause, too. Will you?"

I told her that I would like to help her but that I had started to see the chimneys and that I hadn't much time. She said, "I know that most ranch women have more than they can do, especially at this time of the year, but if you will help me for just an hour I will leave it to you whether you want to go on and besides I will come over to your ranch and help you for a day to pay for it."

That seemed generous and fair so I said I would do as she said. "Well," she said, "some one is knocking about up under the rim rock and I am almost sure I know what they are about. They have not seen us, I don't think they can for the lay of the land.

"I want you to turn back to the big road, go West through Burntfork, don't stop to gab with any one, tell them you're going to see the chimneys. Go on up past Hank's then turn North and cross the creek at Harding's, keep going north 'til you come to a dim road, it looks like an old wood road. When you get to that ride as slowly as you can but keep going. If nothing stops you you will get to the chimneys in time to see all you want to. If you get there just wait for me. If you get turned back, just act natural and turn back, just like you were going home. Don't arguy at all and above every thing else *don't tell a human soul you saw me*. Don't mention my name or even own that you know me."

All this time she had been hastily saddling the horses and removing most of my bundles. She left me only my hope kit and a coat tied to the back of my saddle. I mounted and she gave Topsy a slap as she said "Scat now, do just as I said and you'll never be sorry but if you don't others will be sorry and we'll both be. Now hurry, don't fool around."

Topsy thought she was going home so she clattered along at a good pace. As I passed the few houses called Burntfork a dinner bell rang and I saw some men coming in from the hay field so I knew it was noon.

I did exactly as she said and after about an hour's ride found the dim old road and followed it. It was pleasanter and more easily travelled than the way I had started up. My mind was in a turmoil, thoughts of the children would bob up but I resolutely chased them away. I tried to remember *all* I was to do. If I were to turn back I was to turn in at the Old Anson place cross the meadow, ford the creek and follow an old wood road. If any one were spying on me they would think I had gone home after I passed the school house where as I would only have gone on so far as the old Anson place. It was all so mysterious that I felt shivery in spite of my wool shirt and the ardent sun.

I have never yet given up the hope of some day finding a prehistoric man in these fossil fields, perhaps a mate for the Neanderthal man, so I

enjoyed riding along slowly and when I saw an enteresting, dark out
crop in a recent wash out I was off Topsy and at work with mallet and
chisel in spite of the fact I had been told not to fool around. But I hadn't
been at work long before I was frightened stiff and that by a pleasant
voice right at my elbo, "Well! If it aint Mrs. Stewart! Are you lost?"

Reed Hawks, a young neighbor whom I have seen grow from child
hood to man hood, a pleasant fellow, I had always considered him harm-
less enough. With him was another fellow whom he called Wick. Each
had an axe, they said they had been up in the cedars cutting posts to
fence their stock yards. I told them I was fossiling and was going up to
see the chimneys. They were both helping me dig, Wick said nothing but
Reed said. "You can't get there. The last big rain we had caused a land
slide and I'll bet it is twenty feet from the bottom up to where you could
get onto the level where the chimneys are. You would have to have a
ladder."

I said I could go around the slide and find a place further on. Besides,
the slide it's self would be enteresting, might even have uncovered fossils.

Reed laughed and said, "You have never been up that far, have you?
You see, there has been lots of such slides, this last one was the only
road to that level. All that bare rim rock was once covered with soil. This
mountain is a flat plain on top and the wind blows the soil over this rim,
right on the hard, slanting rock, but there always comes a time as now,
when a slide moves it all. I suspect you'll have to wait several years to
see those chimneys."

"Well, I can go see the slide. I *might* find a fossil." I said.

"It is all wind blown dirt. There's no fossils in that." Reed said.

"And it's—dangerous. You might get shot." said Wick as he arose and
brushed the dirt from his knees.

"You see, those Wops from Rock Springs are out after sage chickens,
they are careless with their guns." Reed hastily explained. I suddenly remembered that I was not to "arguy" and having found that the out crop
was stone, *not* bone petrified I cheerfully allowed my self to be turned
back. I couldn't hurry, for both men were afoot, they walked along with
me after they had helped me to mount, chatting pleasantly. I would like
to know what Topsy thought as we came once more to the "big road".

The Hawks house is right on the road, both went in but they didn't
invite me in for some thing to eat as is custom in the country. I
wondered.

It seemed to me that I had been riding up and down the big road all day and when I came to where I should have turned off to go to my home I was tempted to do so, particularly as I began to feel the need of food. But I had been foolish enough to let Mrs. Pond get away with the tools sent to Ed and with my prized field glass, so I followed directions and turned the disgusted Topsy into the Anson place, crossed the meadow, forded the creek and found my way up to the old road where Mrs. Pond was waiting for me.

"I knew you'd get turned back. I stayed to watch those two fellows. As soon as they sighted you they started down to head you off. Who were they?"

I told her, told her also what they had said.

"They are both damn liars. How the hell could the Wops get there if you couldn't? You certainly are a dumb bell if you don't know that you have just met a couple of moonshiners who have herded you away from their still. Just you come on, lady. We're going to have some fun." I don't know why I followed, I certainly didn't want to, I was even afraid but trotted right after her like an obedient little dog. Much of our way lay through the cedars, they slapped, scratched, gouged me unbearably. We had left the road and had to ride single file, we both had to lean low on our horses to avoid the vicious cedars all we could, we were going up hill all the time and hurrying our poor horses all the time for Mrs. Pond said we would have to get out of the cedars before the sun went down. At last, after it seemed that we neither of us could have a stitch of clothes or an inch of skin left on us, we suddenly came out of the brush and found our selves right up under the rim though a long way east of the chimneys. Dusk was already purpling the slope up which we had come but sunlight flooded to valley beyond.

Mrs. Pond surveyed the country through the glass while we let our horses blow a bit. Just for a few minutes–she was in the saddle and going before I could mount. Again we were on comparitive level ground and with no brush to contend with. We trotted along briskly toward the chimney. But presently we turned into a narrow gap in the rim and after a little floundering over shale were out on top. Lovely, lovely. The level plain, the lowering sun, the distant mountains, not a thing to mar the beauty—but Mrs. Pond didn't see it, all she saw was the need for haste.

"We are going to camp, you know. We must hurry on so as to find a good place."

I should have liked to have ridden nearer the rim so as to get all the picture but she wouldn't have it that way.

"We might be seen and you know they told you it was dangerous; that was a threat as well as a warning."

The sun hung like a great, coppery ball when we reached the spot where we were to camp. Rabbit brush grew thickly along the slope, a spring oozed sluggishly a little below that, while above it a dry, sandy kind of a shelf projected along the slope.

"You take this knife and cut a lot of those rabbit brush, pile it up on that dry sand for us to sleep on. I'll attend to the horses." Mrs. Pond ordered. I meekly obeyed. She cut the gunny sack in which I carried the tools and made two pairs of hobbles which she deftly and quickly put on our horses and turned them loose to graze and to get water in the small water holes made by the spring. My face and hands were smarting and burning, I was *very* tired and faint with hunger. I wanted to eat supper, but she said, "We can't waste a minute of this precious day light, we can eat in the dark. You fix us a place to sleep while I explore around a little." It was only a few yards to the rim, she soon disappeared over the edge. I hacked away at the rabbit brush and wished I had stayed at home. In a little she was back, a perfect whirl wind of excitement.

"Come here, come on! Let me show you some thing, *do* hurry, bring the brace and the bits."

She darted past me and got them for herself and I followed her over the edge. I could see that we were still quite away from the chimneys but she hurried along to where a fringe of Service berry bush, wild currants, rabbit brush and gooseberry bush hung over the edge of the rim. She waited until I lumbered up then pointed silently at the brush. The ends of a tier of barrels were plainly visible. "You see what we would have missed if we had stopped to eat? Woman! This *is* a find! Twenty of 'em. There were twenty four but they rolled four of 'em down, that's how I ran on to these, I saw their tracks and where the barrels rolled, you can see where the barrels laid. You see there are two tiers. Woman, *woman!* This *is* great."

All this time she was fitting a bit in the brace. She attacked the thick oak kegs with such vigor that she broke the bit. She swore a little at the delay and the wanning light as she fitted another. At the bottom edge of each barrel head she bored a hole. The whiskey gurgled and spouted, ran off in streams down the slope. It soon grew dark but she counted and

felt the barrel and bored tirelessly. I stood shivering, cold, weary and
frightened but I couldn't leave her of course. At last she said, "And God
looked on his work and called it good. He looks on ours and calls it excellent. Come on, let's go eat a bite, get a little rest and then get away
from here."

Painfully we made our way back to the alleged camp. I crept into my
pile of brush, pulled my saddle blanket over my feet, my coat over my
shoulders, pulled my hat on closer and stretched out. She felt around til
she found the lunch bags, brought them over to me, moved her own
brush up beside me, made herself comfortable then lay down to eat and
talk in low tones. The sandwitchs were good and as soon as I got warm I
felt better. She was so elated that a blizzard wouldn't have daunted her.

"Turn over on your belly. You won't ache then. You can sleep in comfort any where as soon as you learn that. You know, I never expected to
find a casche, I've been looking for a still ever since the officers destroyed that one over here last year. When I saw them fellows today I
thought it was funny they would have a still this high up, no water and
the smoke could be seen for miles. I never dreamed of finding their hide
out. They've got to hide their stuff well or it would all be stolen, besides,
they might be raided. Some time, when I can, I will tell you why I hate
whiskey so. It is not a moral or legal reason. It's personal—."

But it had been too streneous a day for me, I went to sleep with her
vioce in my ears. Early in the gray dawn she awakened me. Stiff and
sore, we set about breaking camp. We had to sky light to see where our
horses were. We finally got them saddled, every thing tied on, the brace
and bits, even the broken ones, securely wrapped in the hobbles and
firmly tied on. Then we scattered the brush we had lain on, mounted
and rode eastward. We were miles away when the sun came up. Neither
of us wished to try the cedars again so we kept in the open 'til we struck
the Green River road then turned southward and homeward. We saw no
one about when we reached Ed's so we put the tools in his mail box. She
rode a little way further with me.

"You'd better go home and get some sleep. I've got some important
work to do and you're not going to another round just yet. I'm going to
ask you not to tell *any* of your neighbors any thing about this affair. I
suppose you will have to tell that bald headed Scotchman of yours but
he is as close as a clam so you *can* tell him. But not another soul in Wyoming." I promised and we parted.

Home *is* a lonely spot now but oh, what a haven of peace, comfort and safety it is. I came back as *soon* as I had my adventure and I find that I am not so adventureous as I once was. Still, I *would* like to see the faces of those moon shiners when they find their kegs empty. Two hundred gallons soaked into the sand last night. You, safe in your beautiful Portland could hardly get into a similar scrape and I don't believe you'd like to; but already I am beginning to feel quite important, I saw done a work that "God calls excellent."

Will you think of me on our day? I shall think of you and be thankful always that your beloved mother was my friend.

Your friend.

Elinore P. Stewart

Elinore continued her vigorous activities, gardening, milking, and helping with the ranch work, until she had a serious accident in the fall of 1927. For nearly six months, she could hardly raise herself out of bed; she never fully recovered from her injuries. She unburdened herself to Mrs. Coney's daughter, perhaps the only person to whom she wrote as herself, not as The Woman Homesteader, and the one friend to whom she revealed the truth of her life.

Oct. 17, 1927
Burntfork, Wyo.
Dear Florence E. Allen.

Your letter is kind of late getting started to you this year and is going to be a regular bore now that it *is* started. This one must be so personal, tedious and trivial.

But it will be the last of that kind and I am sorry to have to unload all my troubles on your frail shoulders. I *have* worried you. I know that and I am sorry. Thanks to you, we now think we will not go under, but before we go into all that I want to set your mind at rest about my self and the accident.

I had gone out with a team and a mower to cut some alfalfa for the hogs. I had driven the horses all summer, done all the mowing all through haying. Having no fear, I was perhaps careless. Anyway, I was driving leisurely along looking out for the tallest second cutting so as not to have to waste time with short hay.

Suddenly an owl flew up from almost under the horses and struck

against the head of one of them. They leaped forward and struck a small
ditch with such violence that I was thrown from the seat, I held the
lines, ofcourse, and my fall jerked them so that the horses backed the
mower over me.

They were thoroughly frightened but they turned in the way they
should have had they been mowing but that brought the eight hundred
pound mower back over me and one of the horses stepped on me. I had
to let go the lines and was having great concern to stay off the knife. As
soon as the horses found the lines free they ran to the house where
Clyde was just starting out with the binder to cut grain. Clyde and Jerrine came out to the field and some way got me home and in bed.

Then followed ten days of entense mysery—(that word don't look
right!) I was unable to help my self at all. I knew that wouldn't do, Jerrine *must* go on to school and to her brothers who had gone on before
that. I was so uncomfortable in bed too, I could only lie on my back, so
one morning I caught the bars of the head of the bed and so managed to
get up. I was in less pain by getting up and by sitting frequently and by
sleeping in a rocker I was able to get Jerrine to go.

After she was safely away we had the real examination. I was terribly
sore and bruised but had no idea of all they say is the matter. Three ribs
broken, a cracked shoulder blade and, worse than anything a spread
thorax. Pneumonia was feared but none of the ribs punctured the lungs
and I'm safe from *that.*

But the unfeeling doctors pronounced doom when he said I could not
work for a *year.* He claims that any lifting will keep the breast bones
from uniting properly.

All this is foolishness, of course. I cannot possibly lay off for a year.

It is a critical time with us and Mother Stewart is just like a little
child, she could not go along without me.

So that's that! But when we knew I would be unable to help with the
fall work we hired a man and I am doing all I can to get back to where I
was. After all being all broken up *could* be worse, I am doing some reading that I have wanted to do and I find it very pleasant to have excuse for
long naps. And I'm steadily growing stronger and better. Still have to lie
on my back but can get up and down without help. I can attend to
Mother's wants and putter about the house quite well. But I can't dig up
my flowers, put cabbage in the cellar, store the celery, beets and
rutabagas. Now that I have bally hooed about myself, I must write you

some of the doings of the last two years. But first, Clyde is very, very much better. There is very little trace of the old trouble, the worst that remains is lack of confidence in himself and loss of faith in others. But all that is slowly passing and I have no words in which to tell you how happy and thankful I am.

With so much neglect and mismanagement our affairs became as bad as they could be. I could not help. I just had to wait for the worst be-cause no one could anticipate the next move. To most persons Clyde seemed normal tho' he did the craziest things. If I could have taken hold I could at least have stopped such things as his going on other people's notes, buying worthless things, making mortgages and getting absolutely nothing to show for it. And at the last he was here at the ranch and I ag-onizingly stranded in Boulder. But two friends, Mr. W. A. Carter of Fort Bridger, and our minister, Mr. J.A. Roeschlaub took things into their hands. They talked him into getting the state loan and engineered the business. so that saved the ranch for awhile at least.

But nearly all the stock was gone, only two old cows were left of all the cattle. so this same Mr. Roeschlaub and another friend, Mr. Keith Smith, Linwood, Utah, further took matters in hand and made arrange-ments whereby we became possessed of one share of creamery stock of a creamery then being started near. And four thoroughbred Holstein cows. But that didn't restore health and was just that much more debt. Then Mr. Roeschlaub came for me. Mother had always declared that she would not live in Wyoming and I had paid too much attention to what I know was a mere whim. Now that she is here she is satisfied. Then when I came the real battle began. The whole time was a seige of horror that seems like a nightmare now. The long, long nights of watching, hoping, praying. Not knowing if Clyde would awake my own self-reliant, clear-minded man or be an embecile. Perhaps a raving maniac.[4]

It had been largely pride that had suffered all through the years be-fore, I didn't want him to seem to others less than the man I knew him to be. And there were so many ends to be kept up. I could n't appologize for my husband, for our shabiness and lack. Then came a period when I would rather have died than for my children to guess the truth. I didn't want *any* one to know but the time came when I *had* to tell my fears. But

4. Although the family did not know it until later in his life, Clyde suffered from hypoglycemia, an abnormally low blood-sugar level.

when I came home and saw what a year had done to make matters worse I saw myself as I was, foolish and sinfully proud, dodging issues instead of meeting them. Lying and pussy footing instead of acting. Having taken invoice of my own short comings, I went into action. Circumstances had never before been so I *could* get at the business end of things or get at the cause of it all. The help I sneakingly *tried* to get for Clyde were either skeptical or unenterested, they thought it was I that was unbalanced, I had so little money to work with that I was sadly hampered.

I came to the pass where I didn't care *what* happened, what loss we might suffer if only I might have Clyde back. Things came to look so badly that I prayed he might die rather than live insane.

So that dreary, blizzardy night when he awoke and asked me what it was on his head, I held on to my self until he was safely asleep again then I went down to the barn yard, into the shed among the cows and gave way. I don't know what foolish things I did. I was thankful that I had sense enough to get far enough away so that Mother would not be disturbed. I can't tell you the joy and relief. But fires had to be kept up, covers had to be kept straightened and it was very cold. As I came through the snow to the house the morning stars were twinkling, rejoicing with me and I suddenly thought "I am free. It is *I* that am well. I don't have to lie or worry any more!"

And that joy stays with me, I exult each day in that knowlege—Ways and means are still a problem but the old load is gone. Then, Clyde's recovery was rapid. that is his general health. Just once in a while his mind was a little foggy or he had a fit of depression, He began in a very business like manner to mind our fortunes—He went out on the country road and worked until he had enough to purchase nine more cows. All Holsteins. They've all had calves and some of the original four have twice had calves. Little by little we are getting things together for a real try—I did the milking while he was on the road and until I was hurt we both milked. We milk eight cows, ship the cream to the creamery. Once Clyde would never ask a man for what he owed. When he took the young neighbor in with him the great drouth year, he took him in with him in an effort to save the neighbor's herd.

That is how such a great debt started—Clyde used his credit to buy hay for both, and both lost everything. But the neighbor never did pay for his part of the hay. Since his recovery Clyde went to the man and we are a few head of cattle the richer because of it.

To me that proves his sanity. I *am* happy. And the children are all little bricks—they are real stays in time of trouble, all are helpful, reliant children and I really think our dark experience has helped instead of hindered them.

Her teachers say that Jerrine has real talent in art. They believe in her so much that she has a scholarship in the newly opened art school of U.C. [University of Colorado]. She may do something. she entered a soap carving contest put on by the *Ivory* soap people and all four of her carvings were sent on the tour of cities to be exhibited. she had hoped to win a prize offered but to me it is wonderful that she can do such acceptable work with out the least training. All the children are back in school after a summer in the hayfield. They earned enough to take them back and start things there. Every time I count my blessings, and it's many times these sleepless, painfilled nights, your wistful face comes before— You've helped me so! You *have* helped me so much. I am embarrassed for words, I don't wish to seem silly and I don't know how to thank you. Please, *please* forgive me for so nearly spoiling your summer, I know I must have and that when you needed every loving care and thought that could be given you.

You know you have my sincere love. And please don't worry about me now. I am getting well and I am happy.

Gratefully, gratefully,
Elinore P. Stewart

The boys had left for school in Boulder. Clyde, Jr., sixteen, had worked all summer on the Stoll Ranch and had purchased their train tickets with his wages, leaving six dollars to spare. The boys arrived safely, expecting Jerrine two days later, but Elinore's accident delayed her departure. With the help of the six dollars and the ingenuity inherited from their parents, the boys supported themselves for a month.

Jerrine and her brothers had a hard time making ends meet that winter. Jerrine had a scholarship in art at the university in Boulder, and she and the boys worked to support themselves and help pay off the mortgage on their home in Boulder. But their earnings were not enough; the bank repossessed both that house and Grandmother Stewart's. They then rented a little house on University Hill, paying the rent and living expenses themselves.

The next summer, the children returned to Burntfork and the duties of the ranch. Clyde, Jr., added a large window near Elinore's cot in the original kitchen, and Clyde, Sr., had a stone fireplace built in the sunny center room to keep Elinore and Grandmother Stewart comfortable. Although both women enjoyed the new view in the kitchen, the fireplace never proved satisfactory. Elinore kept telling the mason that he was building it all wrong, that it had to have a smoke shelf and it had to have a throat, but the mason continued to stack the stone higher. As a result, the fireplace never did draw properly, much to Elinore's dismay. That same year, Grandmother Stewart died, and Clyde accompanied his mother's body back to Boulder for burial beside her husband in the Columbia cemetery.

Elinore's injuries from the mowing accident, in addition to problems with an ulcerated sore on her leg, varicose veins, and sciatica, substantially affected her health. She still did not stop her activity, although she now had to take a chair to lean on while she gardened. Through it all she rarely complained. When she could no longer ride out in search of material for her stories, she had to live her adventures in her imagination. However, Elinore continued to write her long story-letters to Mrs. Allen in memory of Mrs. Coney's birthday, and her letters to her other friends increased in frequency and in length.

March 25, [1928]
Burntfork
My Darling Woodsy Person.

It was good to get your letter, I *could* have stood a longer one. And we each thought of the other about the same time, didn't we?

If you could see how snowed in, ice bound I am! I think Alaska or Siberia has no more snow than Wyoming. Did you see in the papers where a whole caravan of trucks loaded with families were marooned in the red desert and were fed by airmen dropping bags of food to them? They were finally rescued but it was after days of suffering, they will *never* forget that experience. But this big, fat friend of yours has really had a good time most of the winter. We couldn't get out very well and no one else could get here, snow, *snow;* But, tho' I miss my neighbors I am/was not lonely. I've read stacks. Some good, some bad and much indifferent. I've sewed a little, mended a lot, a whole apple basket full of socks with yawning heels and gaping toes. All mended, rolled and laid away for the boys next summer. (if any!) And when Winter redoubled it's efforts and the snowy outlook *too* discouraging I turned to the seed catalogues. Tomatoes, *tomatoes.* Beautiful red. Each winter I resolve to plant none but red flowers, such a relief from snow, White snow. But in my memory garden I plant white sweet peas to represent my precious little Mother Stewart, white sweet allyssum for my little boy that's gone. And I have a very beautiful white dahlia, (Delighted) that I would not miss for anything.

But I think the Theosophists are right about us coming again and again until we conquer all our failings. It was not the "Key to Theosophy" or "At the Feet of the Master" that convinced me, it was the seed books. I think the seedmen will have to reincarnate until they grow things that come up to their own description. Seven pound tomatoes! One such tomato should fill even the Stewart.

It has taken me twenty years to learn to grow tomatoes in this high altitude but I *have* learned. I used to reason that a small tomato would mature sooner than a large one, so I tried every human way of growing them. No good. Lots of green ones for pickle but never a ripe one. Then a seedman put in a packet of mixed seed—they called it the kid's garden. I took all the tomato plants and most of them were large kinds. I expected no ripe ones so gathered them when the freeze came. They ripened in the boxes and we had fine sliced tomatoes in Nov. So I learned how to do it. This year I shall have six varieties of *large* tomatoes.

But there hasn't been much time to waste in longing to grow melons at an altitude of 8000 feet; it has kept all hands and the cook busy trying to save the lives of the poor brutes dependant upon us—Ernest, the boy who used to live with us came back to Winter with us, and Ed, another derelict has been here all Winter. Most of the time it took all three men all the time to keep the stock shovelled out, fed and watered. We had to check up on every thing we let out of the stables and when any were missing turn out with shovels and dig them out—Hog houses, chicken houses, cellar, All under ten feet of snow—tons and tons of snow. But my cellar has been a joy this Winter—Each day we have enjoyed fresh salads made of Witloof, endive, celery, Bermuda onions and cabbage and we have an abundance of potatoes, beets, carrots, parsnips and salsify. Of course we have plenty of cream, butter, milk, eggs and meat.

I suspect all this sounds pretty silly to you but you'd count *your* blessings if you lived sixty impassable miles from a market. No freighting can be done and there's a food shortage on. We have to divide with each other and I am powerfully glad of my big cellar.

My four Highlander Hoodlums are *all* well and doing well in school. All counting the days when they can come home. And my big cat, Nibs, sends you his love. Some way I have the feeling that you do not care for cats—You would love Nibs, he is part Angora and has a ruff like a Collie dog. Now, my Woodsy-Person, wont you please write me all about *you*. What you are doing, what you read, whom you love, *every* thing. *I* love *you*. Happy Easter to you.

> Your friend,
> *Elinore P. Stewart*

May 15, [1928]
My Dear Friend [Mrs. Florence Allen],

Although I vowed that never, *never* again would I deliberately run into discomfort and danger when I came home the other day, I find I cannot trust myself or believe my most earnest avowals. And I was in such a resentful frame of mind, angry and disappointed over the failure of my outing.

My outings are so rare and I feel that I *earn* every one I get. So to have been defeated and turned back, to be so sunburned, scratched and bruised and to be called a damn fool filled me with ire but there was no one on whom I could vent my spleen so I attacked the job I hate worst, cleaning the stove. I had just emptied the soot box. An agravating little breeze had thrown it back over me so that I looked like a chimney sweep when Mrs. Pond rode up and hailed me.

"Hello! You look like the devil sued for murder. Is that your idea of beauty?" Uninvited, she slipped easily from her horse and came on into the yard. She seemed not to notice my lack of friendliness, went about among the flowers, picking one here and there. "I like poppies, especially these Shirley poppies. They are so bright, silky and cheerful—"

"Come in." I envited. Some how she looked so wistful and little and old that my heart melted and my anger vanished. Soon the soot and ashes were cleaned away and the stove was as clean as I could get it. We were chatting gaily and she had called me a damn fool tenderfoot two or three times. I told her frankly that I felt cheated.

"Of course you were but hell, woman, I didn't do it. You would never been allowed to go up to the chimneys alone if you went at all. One of them moonshiners would have gone along just to steer you away from their cache. I had an idea they had a still there, you know the Agents

burned Ave Hank's big still and outfit over there two years ago. I thought
maybe they had rebuilt it but I didn't think of a cache 'way up under the
rim like that."

"It cost me the only outing I am likely to have this year and when one
stays at home month in and month out even a day in the woods count
tremendiously."

"Don't worry over what it cost. The moonshiners can do that, it cost
them. But let's take a little time away. Let's go up to Hoop's lake and see if
there is not some wild rasp berries. There used to be lots of huckle berries up there too. Then on over to Beaver Creek there were worlds of
choke cherries. Let's go up and stay all night. Are you afraid to camp
out?" I wanted to go terribly. We couldn't start that day, too many neglected tasks to do but she went to work and right good help she is. It
ended in our getting an early start next morning.

If there is any thing to open the heart to the whole wide world it is a
long ride in the hills these golden September days. Golden aspens in little hidden places in the hills fluttering in delight in the friendly sun, blue
haze, distance; views of little brown homes. I loved it all. We were both
silent but the numerous pails we had tied on our saddles jangled and
clanged like a tin pedler's cart. Mrs. Pond led the way but when we came
to where we should have turned off into the bald range she kept right on
past the fork of the road.

I called to her, thinking she had not noticed. "There's another trail on
up past Hank's. I want to pass the Hanks place so they and every one else
will know we are not out on any secret mission. That is why I wanted so
many pails. They make enough noise and glint so in the sun that we can
be seen for miles and every one will know that we don't care if we are
seen." A few minutes brought us around a shoulder of a cedar hill and almost up to the Hank's door. The plain, travelled road runs between their
house and the meadow. The two men we had seen the other day were
out hammering a tire on a wagon wheel. They were sullen and furtive-
looking but Mrs. Pond was very pleasant. She told them where we were
going and why, told funny fibs about me, called me a damn fool tenderfoot repeatedly, her fibs illustrating my greenness.

"But I've lived here a good part of nineteen years, can I be called a
tenderfoot?" I asked.

"Look at the face of her, peeling with sunburn, she doesn't know
enough to powder when she goes out in the sun and wind. She caught

that trying to get up to the chimneys the other day. Is the road open up that way? Could we get up there if we should want to as we come back?"

"The road is open pretty well a few wash outs but we've been hauling posts out. But you can't get to the chimneys. There's been a slide," Wicks answered.

After a little we rode on, this time we turned off into the high hills leaving all the ranches and homes far below us in the valley. It was glorious, I was happy, happy. That day will be a beautiful golden page to put into the drab book of Winter. We scouted around hills, up little draws, some times up narrow canyons, through pines, out again on to rocky flats. A few choke cherrys, a *very* few raspberrys, a handful of service berrys rolled about in our pails. Always up, up. Away from all the cares and worries. Suddenly I was aware of Mrs. Pond's voice, talking, but not to me. "Yes, I'm coming, God, right up to where I can almost touch the hem of your garmet. I know you are near and I love you, Father. No matter what I am in the valley, I am your child and you are my dear Father when I come to the high spots—."

I drew rein and dropped back for I felt it was a holy communion. She rode on, not missing me. I saw her gesture. Slowly I followed and when I came up with her she had alighted in a little shimmering grove and was briskly unsaddling her horse. "Get off your horse and attend to it so it can rest while we eat a bite. This is a good place to noon."

A little spring gurgled up from the earth, the water cold and sparkling. Grass and weeds grew among the aspen and our horses cropped eagerly. Mrs. Pond had put up the food for the trip while I did the many chores that must be done before I can leave home. She handed me a generous sandwitch and this is what it contained; one thin slice of whole wheat bread covered with cheese, on the cheese a pinch of raisins, on that a thin slice of buttered white bread. The reason I am telling you is because on all my outings it has been a real problem to take enough food. One eats ravenously on these trips. But this one sandwich made a delicious and satisfying meal. The few berries we had gathered furnished dessert.

Our grove was on a high, sunny slope. We could look across the gorge at the real mountains rising in solemn grandeur one after another, the snow peaks gleaming over the wooded hills. Faintly across the gorge came the sound of the wind in the pines but only the dappling shadows of the quaking leaves showed there was any wind on our sunny slope.

After our lunch we lay resting on the warm earth. I was wondering whether the hard ride would affect the breaks I had last year.

Suddenly Mrs. Pond said, "If every one lived on a hill there would be no sin. No one could live this high up, this near God and not love him and all the world too much to even think of doing Wrong. I firmly believe that all wrong doing is just ignorance, any way. Of course any one doing wrong knows he is but he thinks it is going to lead to better things and then he will do right. But wrong doing is like a chain, one link leads to another. If tempted persons could only get away to the mountains, 'way up to where it is quiet he could *feel* God."

I lay watching a hawk away up in the blue, the sun glinting his wings to silver. There seemed nothing to say to her observation so I made no answer. After a reflective moment she went on.

"I *know* that sin and wrong doing is only ignorance. Many people doing their very best to do right do irreparable wrongs. My father did. You might never guess it but I was most carefully brought up. My father was a minister and he was so narrow that if he had been any thing else but a man he would have been a shoe string. He worked with out a salary on a circuit that he mapped out himself. Every Friday he left home on his old brown mare with his saddle bags filled with his bible and what ever else he had to take. He would preach that night at Sarotelle. Next day he would reach Grafton in time for service, Saturday night he preached at Bonville, Sunday at Rockford, Sunday night at Burnside. All these were just communities, not towns. Monday he got home and Wednesday night was always prayer meeting night in our meeting house. We were renters. We lived in a little house of Squire Haddam's and tried to farm. We had a cow and our other horse beside old Julie that father rode. You can see how much time father had to help make a crop. We were poorer than any church mouse, we had only the plainest, coarsest food and not always enough of that. There were three of us children, Bart, the only boy, then Lottie. I am the youngest.

My mother was a saint. She couldn't be any thing else. Both my parents belonged to the old school that believes a man is the head of the house. Mother was so meek and humble and father was so determined to live a godly life, he firmly believed in a burning hell and he tried to save his own family and every body else. Well, we grew up that way. Grace was a good deal longer than the meals. Clothes were a hit and miss-come-by-chance. Every summer there would be a big revival meeting

where my father fondly believed he garnered souls for God, where
Mother, under instruction would always start the shouting and shout until she was exhausted and lots of others in a frenzy. Father would call for
mourners—Well, he *was* a good man but I can remember when I began
to think that he was working more for his own glory than for God's. Lottie and myself were expected to be models for all other girls and father
was determined to make a preacher of Bart. There had always been a
preacher in the Taylor family, so Bart would *have* to be a preacher.

Up the creek from us there was a small settlement that my father had
long given over to hell. I guess they *were* a rowdy lot; they were woods-
men and tho' they came to the revivals they never got religion. We used
to hear of dances they had. One night while father was gone I happened
to be awake and heard Bart creeping to his bed in the side room. Next
morning while we were in the cotton patch he told me that he had run
away and gone to a dance. Right then I became possessed of some thing
of my own. A secret. It was a very real some thing to me and I kept it
jealously.

One of our neighbors was Mary Maude Dixon. She was a widow and
older than Bart but she took a notion to him. She was what we used to
call "well fixed"; she could shout the loudest and longest of any one in
our neighborhood. Well, the next thing we knew, I found Bart in the cotton seed house very sick. I ran to Mother and—well Bart was drunk. Father came before we could get things straight. I don't know what was
said or done but I *do* know that that eighteen year old boy was *made* to
marry Mary Maude Dixon to save his soul. I never will forget the look in
his eyes the day father married them. He said "Father, you yourself, have
sent me to hell."

Lottie was sixteen then, pretty as a flower, quiet and shy. Both Lottie
and I helped out at Mrs. Haddams. The Haddams were the richest folks
in the county. Mrs. Haddam was always sick and always had a baby. So
Lottie and I helped her and were paid one dollar and a half a week.

Three of the children were wrong, couldn't speak, just idiotic. Mrs.
Haddam died, consumption they said. Mrs. Haddam and father had been
friends for years and after Mrs. Haddam died the Squire was at our house
a lot. Lottie got to acting queer. One day she disappeared. One day
Mother got a letter from her, she had run away with Willis Stokes and
they were married at the court house and had gone to Denver. It nearly
killed father, I know it hurt him but mother didn't seem to be upset at

all. When I was nineteen father told me that Mr. Haddam has asked for me and that he had told him he could have me, that I must set the wedding day soon and then get some new things to be married in. Lord! I couldn't stand old Haddam, he had more beard than Moses, and all the young ones, some of them older than I.

Well, I couldn't quarrel with father, he wasn't the kind you could argue with or reason with, his word was law and he had passed it. That night I eloped with Mr. Pond. We made it over the mountain to Aunt Lola Pierce's and were married in her house. She lent us the money and we came West to hunt up Lottie but we never found her. Mr. Pond came of a drinking family. We both thought he would be freer from temptation out West, but—Well, after awhile my boy was born—My darling boy. He was just every thing any mother could wish for. For sixteen happy years he made the world heaven for me. At first I thought his father would cut out the booze for Tate's sake. My boy's name is Taylor, but when he was tiny he tried to say Taylor and called himself Tate so we always called him that.

Mr. Pond would keep perfectly sober for months then go on such a drunk he was months getting over it. He was fine with sheep and I always went with him to cook for him until Tate was born. When Tate was big enough to go to school I insisted on a home. I washed, I cooked, I did every thing in the wide world I could to make an honest living for my boy. I did every thing I could to keep him from knowing his father's weakness. Often I have thought I might have got a divorce but that was *my* weakness. I couldn't cast off my husband. Tate was so quick and bright to learn, so eager to go on. He soon finished the grades and we planned, he and I, for him to go away to school. Mr. Pond was away with sheep. We hadn't seen him for months. I knew what that meant but Tate had not learned. But we figured out a way to get the money. We put in a big crop of potatoes then he went away to herd sheep while I stayed home and tended the potatoes. He didn't come back when he should have."

She turned over on her face and was silent for a while. Across the gorge the wind crooned and mourned in the pines.

"When next I saw my boy he was drunk. Sodden drunk. For two years it was a whiskey hell. Often father and son drunk together, too drunk to get out of each other's way. Every dollar they could get went for booze. Tate got a shadscale thorn in his foot while they were out with

sheep along near the end of the two years. he limped around on the sore
foot herding until blood poison set in. They got word to Hackitt, the
man they were herding for and he came out. He brought whiskey.

My boy was dead drunk when I got to him. I got him to the hospital
but it was too late. He awoke just before he died and asked me to get him
a bottle of whiskey. The doctor had told me he couldn't live but I couldn't
bear for him to die drunk. I—refused—him. He dozed off but woke
again, he stared right at me. He said "Mother, death is not what we think
it is. We do *not die,* we just quit this body. And hell is just wanting some
thing so terribly we can't stand it and not being able to satisfy the want.
But I will not have that to bear. I've conquered whiskey." He closed his
eyes, slept. I couldn't believe he was going but he never spoke again. You
have heard that Mr. Pond died of delirum tremens, he did, six months after Tate left me. Tate died of blood poisoning but *I* know whiskey killed
him. And—I'll fight whiskey til I die tho' I have to do it on the sly."

We reached the lake just at sundown—it is a lovely spot but there
were no berries. We made camp, broiled some bacon, had supper, and
larioted our horses out to crop the little meadow. Extra blankets under
our saddles supplied us with bedding. We cut pine boughs for our bed
and did all the camp work in silence. There was much to think of and
nothing to say.

It was too chilly to sit up, Mrs. Pond would not have a real fire, just a
smudge, so we crept under the blankets. I was tired, stiff and sore but I
couldn't sleep. Around and around my mind kept milling with the story I
had listened to. So much wasted endeavor, such futility, mysery. Our
camp was right in the pines and they kept crooning. It was easy to imagine that they were discussing the eternal Why—

We were up very early, coffee, bacon and toast, each of us held long
sticks with a slice of bread on the end over the fire. But we didn't dawdle
for we had decided to go further.

"In my sheep herding days I knew this country like we do our homes.
Over on Sage creek there is a long ridge, a kind of a bluff, where the
cherrys were never known to fall. We will not need to go back to the
road. We can just cut through the timber until we come to the open and
we will pass some real fossil beds as well as the Indian wall. The wall is a
rock face to a hill. The Indians once had a battle there, the Utes and the
Sioux, I think. Any way, they chiseled pictures on the rock wall that tell
the story of the battle."

I couldn't resist all that so we set out. We had turned North-West and were jogging along in the forest. Nothing much to see except as we came to occasional openings which allowed us views of distant peaks and dreamy beauty spread every where. Then a turn would plunge us again into the forest. We saw the ranger's telephone box fastened to a pine. Mrs. Pond got off to examine it. "Locked and no key in sight. What if I knew of a fire. I'd have to ride for miles to get to the station to report. It is a wonder they wouldn't leave a key here."

We came out of the timber, across a rocky mesa, down into the flats where the mesa's side made the rock wall. The pictures are there but the wall is soft sandstone so that blowing sand has almost worn them off. I could have spent a great deal more time studying them but Mrs. Pond is a fidgety creature and hurried me on, on across the flats to a low range of blue, badland hills, the fossil beds. So much of enterest to be seen, old diggings and quarries to be looked into but no time to do it in.

"Come on!"

"No, not yet. Let me examine this."

"Come on. We have to ride up if we are going to get any choke cherries."

"I would rather have one fossil than all the cherries—."

"Well, I wouldn't. You can't eat a fossil and our grubstake won't hold out for a week."

Exasperated, I followed her up the narrow blue trail, made by sheep in the ash like soil. The sun was scorchingly hot and I was thankful when we emerged out upon the bench where the breeze was so pleasant. A flock of sheep was being lazily tended by a herder, he was some distance from us but as soon as he saw us he came riding toward us. We rode slowly, Mrs. Pond eyeing the approaching herder, his sheep, the range. Not at all like the woman who told me the story the day before. The herder came on up, greeted us very pleasantly and began talking about how dry the summer had been. We agreed and Mrs. Pond told him that we were out for cherries, raspberries or huckleberries.

"Good Lord, did you think you would find any over here in the bad-lands?"

"We didn't know we were coming to the bad lands. We thought we had better get out of the timber and out into the open where we could see before we got lost."

"You came to the wrong place for any thing like that. I've not seen a one all summer, it's been so dry nothing could grow and the sheep kill out every thing, you know."

By now we were headed almost east and some way, the herder kept edging us along. There was no road, no trail, just bare, hot ground, heat glimmers in the air and the smell of sheep insulting our noses. Mrs. Pond rode along talking gaily, asking questions about sheep, did they pay well? Was it hard work? What did they do with the sheep at night? Just any thing that came to her mind and she had been out with sheep for years! Presently we found ourselves around a badland knob and right on the highway!

"Well, I guess I'll be leaving you folks, I got to get back to my sheep." Mrs. Pond waved to him as he turned the knob again.

"Bye-bye Mr. Sheepherder what aint," she said to herself; he couldn't have heard her. We rode slowly along the road, once more among the badland hills. "You see that white streak of road that goes over that rise away ahead of us? Well, that is the last place he can see us with out following us. He will be on some of these hills watching to see if we cross that. When he sees us go over that white rise he will think we are hitting for home. But I have been around in these hills myself and I know my way about. But I want to be *sure* I'm right before we make any change. You take my bridle and lead my horse right on. I want to sit back ward in the saddle so I can watch the hill tops." With out dismounting she turned face to tail and we rode slowly along the hot road. Pretty soon she chuckled.

"Right! He *is* watching but all his doubts and suspicions will be settled when we pass the white place."

Slowly we rode on, she still sitting backward. The very minute we passed over the high spot she jerked our horses around toward the west, out of the road, up a dry wash. We kept in the washes but kept as close to the hills as we could. It was past noon when we got back to the fossil diggings. We crept into the scant shade of a ledge and ate some sandwichs. Mrs. Pond took off all our pails and cached them with our food under the ledge. Then we mounted and rode west, still keeping close under the hills. After a while we came to where the badland range of hills narrowed to a point and a broad, dry wash ran north. We rode around the end of the point, came to where a ledge of rock, kind of a rim rock began. Buck brush and a few cherry bushes grew along, we found a shady spot for our horses and tied them closely where they couldn't get them selves into view.

We carefully worked our way through the brush to the north side of the ledge and began going east. The bushes grew taller as we went along but the going was hard and slow. We had to be so careful, not a bush must shake unduly, not a stone roll down. We didn't know what we were looking for or how soon we would find it. Cherries had to be our alibi and our pails were miles away.

Cautiously, slowly, silently, at last we gained a vantage point and looked down on a strange scene. We were high up under the ledge but there was sufficient brush to conceal us. Down below us the dry course of Sage Creek twisted its self into the letter S. In the curve of the S next to us we counted twelve log houses and a huge, low barn-like structure. We could see what looked like silos, not so tall as others I had seen but I can think of nothing else to compare them to.

As we looked a truck backed out of the barn, it was loaded with casks; presently another came and was driven into the barn. We could hear the thumps of the loads being placed, some filled wool sacks were thrown on and a tarpaulin was tied over each truck then both trucks drove away, right up the Creek bed. No road, not a sign of a trail or any thing to show there was a place. We had the only place from which the place could be seen with out walking right into it. I don't know how we made our way back, I was so excited that I couldn't talk. There was no mistaking what the place was, the smell betrayed it. It was not the smell of a sheep ranch. We mounted and just as carefully as before we made our way back to our cache. Still keeping in the draws instead of across the mesa we rode for the forest. Mrs. Pond forgot that I was with her, her face shone, she kept talking.

"Just let the daylight last, God, just let me get back into the woods, God, and you and me will raise hell with the moonshiners."

It is not easy to ride in timber, usually we have to pick our way. This time we didn't. We rode madly, recklessly. I never once thought of the ribs that have not ceased to be tender or of the chest that a jolt causes pain. More scratches were added to the collection already made. "We *must* get to that telephone box while we can see to find it. Oh we must! Hold the sun, God, just as you did for Joshua."

"Why not hunt up the road, go on home tonight and telephone—"

"Fool! All the phones are party lines and you know it. Every word would be relayed to them. The ranger's line connects straight to Evanston and is no party line——." We reached the telephone box. Madly she hammered and pried til' she got it open. She tried hard to control herself but her voice trembled as she called central and gave a number.

"Oh, Dr. Wilson, will you *please* come. The Tetlow baby is very sick. We've done all we can for it. We have given it sage tea. We used badland clay for a poultice but is does no good. I think it is the creek water they are using, it is not clean, it may be typhoid the child has. I think we should take it South but perhaps we had better go further West. But please come and if you can get it bring help, we're all worn out."

At first I was astonished. The Tetlow baby *had* been sick but was out of danger. We scooped out a little pool in a tiny little rivulet and caught water enough to give our horses a drink and to wash the sweat from their backs. We hung our saddle blankets up to dry and by that time it was too dark to cut boughs so we just rolled up in our blankets and lay down, no fire, no supper. We mustn't even talk where there was a chance for some one to creep near enough to hear, not about our find must we *ever* talk. I was so tired, so uncomfortable that I didn't expect to sleep but I was awakened before it was light by Mrs. Pond. "Get up. We've got to get home as fast as we can. We must get to a telephone where we can talk to as many as we can so as to let every one know where we are today all day. More than that the horses had a devil of a hard day yesterday and not a damn bite to eat."

Going toward home the horses traveled better. We kept away from the road so as not to be seen. By going through fields we managed to reach home without meeting any one. Mrs. Pond left amediately and I heard today that she is a silly old thing, that day before yesterday she telephoned about every body in the neighborhood. Today she came back.

"Lord, they've been raising hell with the moonshiners. Biggest raid ever over on Sage Creek. Seems the prohibition men were out after sage chickens and ran on to a whole town of moonshiners. They ran their still night and day. Had a big spring piped right into their plant. It was three or four miles off the road yet they had a thoroughfare right up to their very door. They used the creek bed for a road. Sage Creek never has much water and this time of the year it is dry. It makes a fine road and mighty little sign to show that it *is* a highway, not a sign of a road to show that any one *ever* went that way, just a few mangy sheep grazing about with a watchman-herder to steer non-wanteds away, a few families

here and there with party phones picking up every item of gossip that
may chance over the line. It seems that the government man had no idea
of finding such a *big* thing. They were not prepared to fight such odds,
they almost made a fizzle of their raid but a plant like that is too big to
get away entirely. They caught the four ring leaders. They apprehended
thousands of gallons of booze and destroyed thousands of dollars worth
of equipment.

And to think of *families* living in a moonshine dump; every thing as
modern as town, big delco plant furnished light, a great engine pumped
water so that every house had water, a sewer system, every thing!"

"I would like to have seen the raid," I said.

"Like hell you would. Why it was like a battle, machine guns even.
But it was a complete clean up, everything wrecked. They even had an
airplane. It was a great day."

Both the Stewart and I think the airplane must have been a mail plane
off its course. There would have had to be a landing field and there was
no clear space any where near the place. This P.S. is being written
May 15. Just home off a wild horse hunt. Sore, *sore*, stiff, blistered and
reblistered. Love, lots of love to you.

E.P.S.

Feb. 18, 1929
Burntfork, Wyo.
My Dear Mr. Zaiss.

You certainly have a right to cut me off your list of friends, I shouldn't
blame you if you did but I would be very sorry. That lovely calendar
came a long time ago and brightens our cabin wall very much. We find it
very interesting, neither Mr. Stewart nor I ever saw the sea or a ship of
any kind. And to think that our lariats and binder twine may be Colum-
bian!

Some way, the calendar seems to make a connecting link between our
West and your East. *We* like that.

I've been waiting, thinking I might have an adventure to write you but
the snow has piled so deeply that we are virtually snowed in, our entire
community. I can't wait forever to thank you. I *do* thank you. Also it occurred to me that you might consider it an adventure to visit me, that if I
could contrive a pen visit for you you might like it.

Well, you would leave the train sixty miles away, the long stretch of

snow would be very discouraging perhaps but if you got off the train at
Carter there are way stations and you would make the trip in relays.

You would ask for the Burntfork Stage, the Mail Carrier would say,
"All right, Mister, climb in". You would get into or onto a bob sled and
away you would go, the runners screeching over the snow, snow hitting
your face some times, the wind trying to elope with you. Westerners
have two outstanding traits, they take one for granted, do not ask questions, the other is that they are very anxious to point out every thing of
interest about their country. Your driver would say, "There's the hill that
Marsden, the man sent out by the Smithsonian Institute, got the dino-
saur out of, him and a lot more fellows, they dug in all these hills, just
gettin' a lot of petrified bones and things. Here we are at Fort Bridger—"

At Mountain-View you would stay all night in a big log hotel, next
morning another mail man would take you on his sled, he would tell
you the wonders of his section of the trail; you would have to sit in what
patience you could while your driver made frequent stops to shovel out
drifts so as to get through.

At noon, if you had good luck, you would reach the "Half Way
house", a little shack by the side of the road built for the stage men.
There would be a roaring fire in a great old box heater and a can of coffee would be boiling furiously. Another sled driver would be there and
the men would thaw out their lunches and you would all have a bite to
eat, great cups of poisonous coffee to help wash it down. You would hear
the drivers telling each other how bad the roads are, how much worse
they are going to be, how scarce hay is, how all the sheep men are going
broke. After lunch there would be a hurried scramble to get started.

You would feel refreshed, rested but a little doubtful as to whether
you would ever get anywhere. The two mail carriers would exchange
mail sacks and the one who brought you from Mountainview would go
back, leaving you to the mercy and loquacity of the new driver.

He is an ex-minister and he would tell you what a hell of a time people were having getting even the mail not to mention groceries or any
other heavy commodity.

Soon you would reach a little settlement called Lone Tree. Perhaps
you would warm a few minutes and you would be off again, this time for
Burntfork. You might ask your driver if he knew Clyde Stewart.

"Know *him!* Sure, everybody knows him. Bald-headed guy, big, fat
wife—"

Very likely our own sled would be at the post office. You would be bundled in, tucked in and away we'd come, higher, higher, swiftly.

You would be welcomed into a big log cabin; Walls bare except for cooking utensils, guns, coats. The kitchen serves as dining room, sitting room and library in the West.

You'd be seated in a big old rocker which it may be I would spare you the history of, seeing you'd have already been told the history of every badger hole and clay hill on the route.

You would wonder what kind of incense we burned and I would tell you that it was a tiny cedar twig caught on the top of the stove when we put wood in.

Presently a cool nose would be thrust in your hand. Jack, our old dog, would be welcoming you, making friends with you. A soft 'thump' into your lap would be His Nibs, my big cat, accepting you as a member of the family.

All the while I would be scurrying around, getting supper, hoping all the while that you would notice how tender the crisp endive salad, how savory the sausage, how light the bread.

Presently the Stewart, having finished the night chores, would come stamping, sweeping the snow from his feet. He might speak a half a dozen words to you but he would just mostly sit and smile across the table at you. You wouldn't be able to see that and might be wondering what manner of man he is. But you could *hear* me and I could tell you, would tell you, am now telling you that you *are,* would be very, very welcome. That your cordial coming broke the deadly monotony of too much isolation, too much reading. Then we would talk books probably. I would tell you what I think of Lord Haldane's "Relativity in its Wider Meaning," of "Jalna", the Atlantic prize novel, of "The Father." But you would be tired and I would know it; you would be shown to your room. The fire would crackle cheerfully and as you stretched out between the blankets you would be glad of your bed, a sense of well being would displace the feeling of disgust you had almost had. You would count over the things you had eaten that day that you had never liked or that had never agreed with you, you would be surprised to remember that the food tasted good, had not made you ill. Then you would remember that this air is tonic, that persons living in cold climates require more meat. You would recall, perhaps with pleasure, that a Western welcome is sincere and hearty. The incense again—crackle, crackle—comfort, warmth.—Boo! It's morning. A cold, white world, the smell of coffee, breakfast, The history of all Wyoming, each individual, chair, horse, cattle sale, everything, to be listened to! Oh dear!

Sincerely your friend,
Elinore P. Stewart

March 1st, [1929]
Burntfork
My Dear Mrs. Allen.

It is almost certain that I shall not be able to leave the place to hunt for an adventure for our memorial letter. It is like having to get up a company dinner with only the crusts and brown rinds at hand. All I can think to do is to give you just what I have. It is too little but I shall have to do just that.

This letter then, will be kind of a diary in which I shall record the happenings of each slow, snowy day. Our kitchen is the first old cabin built on the home stead. It is the largest room and the most comfortable because the constant fire makes it warmer. It has two windows and is furnished with an old range that belches smoke and spills ashes when ever the wind doesn't blow to suit. A huge wood box filled with fragrant cedar wood. All back of the stove I have the log walls covered with an oil cloth that served time as a table cloth. Against this blue and white back ground hang my skillets, pots and pans.

Next there are two five foot shelves of rough boards. These hold salt, coffee, soda, spices and odds and ends. Just under it is a large old milk can that will hold 100 lbs. of flour—it is my flour bin. Another old blue and white oil cloth covers the next wall space, against this hang my long spoons, forks, chopping knife, egg beater, cake beater, all the little things like that. Close against the wall under these is my cook table, native white pine which responds beautifully to soap and water.

The table now, is covered with sixteen quart Mason jars filled with kraut in the making. Some of my cabbage was beginning to burst so I made kraut which I can put in the cellar under the kitchen pretty soon. Being in the mason jars it will keep perfectly. Next the cook table is my cupboard—which the Stewart made before I came—just an open set of shelves on which I keep my dishes, this has two short curtains like sash curtains, made of the skirt of an old more white than blue barred gingham dress of mine. I have to wash these every week or they get pretty grimey.

Under the dishes is another set of shelves which hold cans of dried beans, oat meal, a few prunes, raisins and just now I have a cheddar cheese ripening there. On a long bench under my cook table is my home made soap curing. on a box next to the dishes is an old copper wash boiler which I use for a bread box and which I cannot keep polished and bright.

Next the east window with a perky little ruffle of a valance and two side streamer like curtains made of the same material as that of the cup board curtain, only the window curtains were Jerrine's dress. The separator sits before the window. Next the window is the table for the water bucket, then the door. Back of the door hang the coats.

We are now half around the room. We are to the south wall. This thing that looks like a cupboard is. it is where I keep the food. Next is the door to the rest of the house. Now we have reached the cornner that enterests me most. You see the clock shelf, on one end Clyde's shaving things, next the clock. On the other end all our household remedies and a jar of everlasting flowers. beneath the shelf is a cot on which I rest and some times direct the affairs of the kitchen. Established in broken leg days. Next is my library and a "news stand."

My "library" is a long narrow box nailed to the wall, just in reach of my hand when I am lazying around on the cot. It makes an admirable "five foot" book shelf. In the shelf are twenty little classics given me by the children one Christmas. On top of this box library are stacked my collection of government bulletins, I have kept all I could get for years and have never missed a chance to acquire them, so at a glance I can tell how to make an ice house, grow celery, make cheese, soap, jelly, jam, bread, butter, grow iris, dahlias, onions, strawberrys, make hog houses, can meat, cure hams, just *any* thing.

On my "news stand" is the "Atlantic Monthly, The Woman's journal, Boulder Weekly News paper, an occasional copy of "Time" which Jerrine sends and an occasional copy of Literary Digest which some one else whom I love sends, The lamp and our 'specs' are on the news stand. Just above the news stand is the west window, a broad sill which is a catch all, holds among the "messalaney" a can of earth in which reposes my big bug which I captured when we were digging potatoes last fall. Isn't larvae the right word? It is as long and as large as my forefinger. It is still alive.

Now, we have been around the room. A table from which we eat, two rockers and three kitchen chairs make up the rest of our implements of living. Ourselves, Ernest, the boy who used to live with us, the dog Jack and my cat His Nibs make up the family.

March 2—Snowing hard, so dark I can hardly see to write. I slept on the cot last night, it was so cold and cheerless in my bedroom. In the night I was awakened by queer thumping sounds. Morning revealed a poor old horse on the porch, a poor skeleton of a horse, he came in over the drifts and sought shelter on the porch. Poor, starving abandoned beast. We don't want him on the porch, though. He might break the floor and fall into the well.

March 3rd—If this storm doesn't stop and winter let up a little I shall be driven to desperation. Being snow bound is what my slangy young sons call "the bunk," I once thought it would be romantic, enteresting to be snowed in. I would study and read, write and sew, do just what I wanted to do since the deep snow made such a fine excuse for letting other things go. But "sich aint so," as my friend Ed says. It is fix something for the cow's frozen teats, heat milk for the calves, thaw swill for the pigs, thaw out and dry overalls, keep socks dried and ready, three pairs daily, dry and mend gloves. Shovel out the cellar door so as to get in to get some thing to cook for the men, they will come in exhausted soon, heat some feed for the chickens, wash milk things, heat some boulders for the icy beds. Round and round, the same thing *every* day.

March 4th—Everything good happened today, the storm passed in the night, the sun shining bright this morning. Mrs. Pond and Mrs. Brady here—Mrs. Pond is out of wood, none of us can get to the cedars to get any for her so she is going to stay with us until it gets so wood can be had. Fine, fine. Mrs. Brady came to bring her and has gone home. If we can get over the snow we are going to Logan's to hear the inaugaral address over the radio.

March 5th—We didn't get to go. We didn't mind it so much. We are having a great time visiting. It is so good to have another woman in the house.

March 6th—Gone again; Mrs. Pond left this morning to help out with the work at the McGinnis' where they have flu and a new baby expected any day. I inherited a lavender rayon dress from Aunt Mary. She was tall and slender, I am too large to wear the dress but I wish to keep it so I am making it into curtains for my bedroom windows, two windows and just one dress! I have a curtain that was given me, cream colored something, marquisette perhaps. Thin it is. I have cut it into three inch strips and am putting a border on the lavender strips—a narrow valance for the top. They look quite well and I shall be able to have my keepsake dress near me for a long time.

I have a pale green rayon that I have out grown and a kind of primrose cotton voile of Jerrine's that I am going to make up the same way for the one window in the sitting room. That's one good thing about this housed in weather. I *have* to do something so I am doing up the left over odds and ends.

March 7th—Happier today. A warm wind is blowing and has cleared the snow from some of the level ground so that I can see earth. I mended eight pairs of socks and a pair of blankets. Also I am making a quilt of two keepsake dresses and an apron. A blue gingham of Mother's, a red and white check gingham given me by Susie, my sister that is gone and a yellow gingham apron. It is making up beautifully. I shall keep on working until I get all these keepsake things worked up. I *must.*

March 8th—Still happy. Sun still shining and tho' the men's work does n't lighten because the wind keeps the snow drifting and they have to work steadily to keep things fed and watered and dug out of the snow, yet I feel more cheerful than for a long time. We had the mail today. A letter from the children says they are all over the flu safely and all feeling well, all at work in school and doing all they can get to do out of school to help them selves. Darling children.

March 9th—This is a lovely day. Not a breath of wind blowing, Serene—just as *she* was. Warm and mild—The sun shine falling like a blessing that it is. Of course my beloved Mrs. Coney is on my mind to-day, in my heart. I can see her gentle smile. How pleased she was over every little thing done for her. I loved her, I *love* her. It is worth the hardships of life just to have known her, to have her friendship. But I know that friendship was the least any one ever had from her. By that I mean that friendship is what she gave every one. Friendship and inspiration. I don't think it was possible for any one to know her and not long for her friendship and wishing to be worthy of it. I feel her influence after all these years. Many times I do something a little better because I know she would have had it done better, a little better work at darning or mending, a little more careful in cleaning, a little more kind—a little less hasty with criticism. Often when a thoughtless remark almost escapes me I think "I wouldn't say that in *her* presence," many, many times that happens.

March 10th—Mrs. Pond back. She is worn out, tired and sleepy. There is *such* a houseful of children at McGinnis' and they need a lot of soap and water. Disgust showed on Mrs. Pond's weary face. It was hard for me to keep from laughing for she preached a sermon on the sinfulness of birth control the night before she left to go to McGinnis'. "What do you think *now?*" I asked her. "Just what I thought before. God knows his business better than we do. I think it is time some of these damned reformers said a little about *self* control. That would help out a lot in regulating the size of these over-plus families. Can't you see the point? Folks set out to manage birth control which is God's business and never try self control which is *their* business. It is a pretty big jump from our own business to God's." How right is she?

March 11—Snowing again. The snow slapping up against the house, plastering like stucco. The porch posts are twice their normal size and as white as I wish they were. The old stray horse is going to stay; we found that he had been turned out to die by a sheep man who has lost everything he has. The deep snow is taking terrible toll. We call the old horse Boney Part because the bony part is all that is left of him, he has been a camp horse, has learned to piece out scant grazing with camp scraps. This morning he ate a pan of potato peelings and two chopped rutabagas, a basket of salsify tops four quarts of skim milk and two pancakes. The Stewart says he will positively *not* feed any more strays but I see Boney eating hay.

I *was* going to tell you about the house but this rambling letter rather got away from me. You can see how being snow bound robs life of romance, snow bound in that we are bound to shovel snow *every* day. But my thoughts travel southward to you and more than ever I am with you in thought and love this whole dark, snowy March—You let me share *her.*

Your friend
Elinore P. Stewart

March 29, [1930]
[To Mrs. Florence Allen]

I was snuggly rolled in my blanket on a clean bed of soft, white sand, listening to the voice of the river far below and watching the stars in their silent march across the sky.

My bed was under an overjut of rock that towered far above in a cliff that had once been at the river's edge before it changed it's course. I had had to climb a little to reach my very satisfactory camp but it was worth it. I was safe from storm or molestation of any kind, under cover yet outdoors.

I could see my faithful, tired old horse, twenty feet below me, resting in deep content, hear him munching his oats.

For me it was a perfect hour, I knew it then and enjoy it yet. To get away from every one is a blessing to be eagerly seized some times and I was deeply enjoying cave man freedom. But freedom too seriously taken ceases to be freedom so my occasional small doses of it are always sweet. I was happy. No one knew where I was but supposed they knew—The Stewart supposed I was with Mrs. Lyle who had gone with her son Richard on a wild horse hunt. Richard being one of a party, While the Stewart had been most reluctant to consent, he couldn't refuse since Mrs. Lyle was to be along. So I set out to join her and, later the hunters themselves.

But there had been so much last work to do up that morning that she had gone when I came to her house. She had driven the camp wagon so had to go by road most of the way. I set out cross country thinking to over take her more quickly by going through the hills.

When I came out of the cedar brakes and onto the desert no wagon was in sight, no tracks were to be seen. I settled myself to enjoy the view and to wait for her. A bunch of antelopes went past like the silent shadow of a cloud. The buttes were beautiful with the shifting colors coming and going. There has been much wind but very little snow this winter, that is why the horse chase could be two full months earlier this year. Usually they have to wait for snow to go. And they have to have their hunt before the feed comes, while the horses are in a starved condition. Being weak then, they are the more easily captured. I waited for more than an hour and as no wagon showed up, decided to remount and ride on. Numerous bags and parcels were tied on my saddle, remounting was not so easy and I had barely got seated when I heard a kind of subdued roar. Buck pointed his ears and pranced in great excitement so that I could hardly tie the parcel containing bread. And then—an avalanch, a huricane was upon us. A great band of wild horses going like the wind. I was amazed and too busy trying to keep on my horse to realize what had happened, then dismayed to see horses on every side and my horse going just like the rest. Too late I remembered that he had been a wild horse but even if I had remembered there was nothing I could do, for to check up meant to be run over. I found myself bending low over the pommel and, if you will believe, *enjoying* the wild ride!

I had n't supposed the old horse had it in him or that I could stay on in such a flight. Presently I noticed horses shooting past me so I knew that my weight was telling on Buck. Soon they were all past, I had time to breath and look about me. Far ahead the horses were breaking up into small bands, each band going it's own way. Back of us there appeared for a moment on the horizon the figure of a rider. Then I knew that some one had been after the horses, had driven them where the lay of the country helped to hold them together. That was why I had been caught in their midst. The ride had been great after terror had left me. When I began to think I reasoned that the camp must be east of the buttes instead of west as is customary. There would be some kind of canal and water. There are no trees on the desert except for a few in the deep rifts or splits in the earth, some times in which a few quaking aspen grow. Those that grow in the splits are tall and straight since no wind can shake them. Trees for fencing being few and far between, the natural lay of the ground has to be considered. If the horses can be headed into some of the narrow splits they can usually be trapped. Knowing all this I rode on undisturbed, thinking I'd see other riders or a camp some time soon. But no camp and no rider appeared. I was right at the river before I knew it, the sun was going down, I *must* make camp. But I didn't regret that nor that I should have to camp alone. I wanted to.

Much of what I brought along to eat was lost, the bread, butter, coffee—But a roll of spare ribs that I brought to roast over a camp fire stayed on. That would suffice. Sore, stiff and very tired, it was about all I could do to make Buck comfortable and gather a little wood for a fire. But I was happy and content. I had only a tiny fire and that back in an angle of the rock so that varying breezes could not blow ashes and dirt over my roasting ribs. They looked delicious and smelled more so but I made my bed and lay down. The moon came through a gap in the crags and began to strut her stuf across the sky, (the ribs not done yet). An owl began to tell who is who in the cliff across the river. Buck still chomping oats. Away off a coyote yelped—all the while the many voices of the river did a tale unfold. I was concious of so many things at once, the friendly contented conversation of the waters, the unity of things, the impersonal way every thing was, the crags, tall cliffs, wide sweep of desert, the lonely aloofness of the buttes in the moonlight, helpful, friendly, protective if we feel that way, austere, threatening even, if that's our mental attitude. Isn't life its'-self that very way?

Merry, happy, gay and helpful to others if we feel that way, every man's hand against us if we do not. I could see that my own moods had shaped my destiny tho' perhaps my surroundings shaped my moods.

Up from the river came this philosophy—Nothing matters—save only one thing—that we love the Lord our God with all our heart and our neighbor as ourselves. The world is as well off because of its bad people as it is for the good—they each do their allotted time, pass on and the universe continues—the stars in their orbits doing their part, the sun, moon, earth, water, wind—*every* thing doing their allotted tasks and we as they. But if we live nobly, purely or not matters not one whit to any one—save our self.

Because there is a moment of reckoning, all eternity rolled into one moment when we are ourselves as we are, know ourselves for good or bad and automatically regulate our selves for the next step.

All old stuff, I suspect, but brought home to me more clearly than I can tell you.

The fire was dead, the moon far on its westward way and presently the dawn came. I lay comfortably in my blanket awaiting it. Desert dawns are so lovely. A gap in the crags showed where the sun would presently pop up but for just a space the world stood still. I *know* it did. It was as if nature knelt in adoration, waited the blessing of the first golden sunbeam.

The colors hung and wavered. Night drawing her purple robes away—*Some* thing juggling rose, lilac-soft blue, gray-gold curtains that would soon part to reveal the king of day.

A little herald breeze rippled past warning every thing of the moment, just as the accolyte strikes the gong. A holy hush—then the golden day.

I had not slept but was rested. I had been some where, some where out-side of my self. I had given Buck his breakfast and had started down to the river for water when "Out of the dawn came a sunbeam," startled me.

"And a beautiful dream came true—"

It was as if the cliffs had greeted the day. I hurried down the sheep trail toward the water expecting to see the horse hunters' camp but as I rounded the shoulder of my cliff I saw the queerest house boat! I was right at it before I saw it, the singer saw me at the same time. We stood staring at each other, he with a whitefish which he had just taken from a trot line he had set in an open place in the river, (the ice is not *all* gone tho' the channel is clear) I with a rusty old can I had picked up to carry water back to my fire . . . [page missing] . . . had not envited you?"

"Spare ribs."

"Spare ribs!" he looked at me incredulously—"There's not room in the cabin of my Lusitania for but one at a time; you go in and wash up, make yourself at home while I go after them alleged spare ribs."

I could hardly stand upright in the small quarters—a bunk under which stores of groceries were stored an oil stove—a gas lantern, some paper and magazines, a shaving set on a box shelf—I caught sight of my face in the little mirror—of *all* the horrors! Where the skin showed through the dirt it was so wind burned it looked boiled—such a sight.

Water on such a surface was out of the question but a large jar of vaseline and a box of talcum solved the problem. As I wiped off the dirt with bits of shaving paper, I looked about. The small cabin was built on a raft of logs which projected several feet all around—a roofless porch. Let's call the projection a porch. On the front porch was a fire place built of stones and clay, it didn't touch the wall of the cabin at all, the chimney barely as high as the low roof. That seemed to me very odd and I was wondering about that when my host returned.

He had been gone much longer than was necessary. So as to not embarass me I suspect. He came striding along whistling loudly, looking up the river, down the river as if expecting some one.

"See my forge?" he asked as he stepped on the porch, "Dandy place to cook. I can even bake on it. You just wait until I get a fire goin' and see what happens. I'll have some breakfast in a jiffy if you just stay in there out of the way."

I told him that I wanted to help cook and to visit. "You just keep from under foot while I clean this fish and finish these ribs—They *are* spare ribs, are n't they? Do you know—I thought you were just tellin' one—" The fire on his "forge" was roaring. The neat little oven suggested biscuits so, while he was down at the water hole cleaning his fish I mixed some biscuits. He fried the fish and I made coffee, he took some cans of groceries out of the boxes under his bunk, set the boxes out on the porch to serve as table and chairs. We sat down to the very best breakfast in the world—I had the fish, he the ribs. We both ate from the frying pan, I had the only cup, he had a can for his coffee cup—No knives, no forks, spoons, table cloth. Just lots of comfort and appetite.

Between bites—"My name is Stewart."

"Is it? Stewart is a pretty good name. Scotch or Irish?"

"Scotch—spelled Irish though."

"Hm—these ribs are fine. I've been havin' fish all winter—I set lines in air holes and have had all I wanted."

"The fish is a treat. I live on a ranch—"

"I knew you did—or a farm. You look it."

"The reason I look this way is because my horse ran away with me—I came out to be with a friend on a horse chase. Before I found camp my horse got caught in a stampede. The wind is a gale when horses go like that—and the alkali dust, no wonder I look queer."

He threw back his head and laughed. "I believe you are a bootlegger."

"There would be a nice, brisk market on the desert, would n't there? I believe *you* are a moonshiner!"

"I suspect *any* one would think that, my floatin' house and all. But I'm not. I don't mind relievin' your very evident curosity a little. I was over seas and came back with a lot the matter with me. My brother, two years younger than I, enlisted at the same time I did. He might have escaped the draft but I urged him not to wait for it.

I was burnin' up with the holy fire of patriotism—damn foolishness, but I didn't know then. I pointed out to him the fineness, beauty, nobility of offering our selves, a living sacrifice for humanity—Hell! He was sent to one training camp, I to another—It was just accident that I ever saw him again—We had both been shifted around a lot—neither of us much to write. Both in France but neither knew that the other had left America.

Then, one day some replacements were brought up and Clif was the first man I saw. He didn't belong to my outfit but there was a lot of jumble in replacement so he stayed by me. That night we ran into a barrage, we were being shelled like hell. We dug in as fast as we could—We lay side by side in a shell hole, whispering. What do you think we whispered about? Ted, our little old broken legged dog. Of the big Catfish Clif caught years ago, of the time I mashed my thumb and the nail came off—Foolishness. We gripped each other's hands like children. Then, we both thought the same thing at the same time—

We had both found war to be, not the glorious thing we had thought, but a foolish, useless, filthy slaughter. Morals, decency, thrown to the

Winds All our thoughts of high sacrifice a delusion— "We are just like cattle in a slaughter pen, no better, maybe worse." said Clif. "The world will be no better for all this carnage. And it doesn't matter. We had just as well die here as any where. *Nothing* matters."

We talked on awhile and then I said, "If I go first, Clif, I will try my best to get some knowledge back to you of what it is all about, of what comes next." "All right," he said, "And I'll do the same for you. I'll get it across to you some way."

A shell burst—I awoke in the convoy train. A lot of things wrong but I didn't care. Men screaming, swearing, screeching, dying—I didn't care—nothing matters. After it was all over and I back—two years in the hospital—Out and back—Out and back. One day the doctor told me it would be wise to put my affairs in order. None to put—I told him. "How long have I?" I asked him.

The doctor said he didn't know, not long.

Well, that didn't matter. I am the very last of my family. In all my life I have not had time to do *all* I wanted to—now I can. The doctor's news was not so sorrowful—I had become acquainted with another fellow who could talk of nothing but exploring Green River. He planned if he got well to hunt out some spot on Green River where some member of his family with some other fellows spent the Winter placer mining— they were trappers but happened to run onto the gold so they just laid away traps and went to washing gold. They woke up one morning to find them selves surrounded by Indians. They held out all day but by night only one man was left. They had hidden their gold. The last man concluded to take a chance in the river so as soon as it was dark he got away that way. But he had been shot and afterwards died of the wounds.

He made a map of the country, left it with the doctor who attended him, the doctor sent it on to his family—the doctor believed and the family believed the [sic] was delirious—so they paid no attention to the map. My friend and I planned to look it up anyway—My friend died and I came on—not because I want the gold or expect to find it but because it would fill in the time and—if it comes so soon I'd like just to drift off down the stream—"

"But," I said, "you must certainly get out of here—Ledore canyon is a terrible place—even if you were not swamped before you get there you'd be dashed to splinters going through the canyon—And your raft is so tightly frozen in that the high waters will swamp you—may anytime—"

"I know—but it doesn't matter. I keep thinking of Clif—he's on my mind some way. We were orphans, brough up in a little back-water town and had never seen an electric light until we were quite big boys. Then one day we were taken to a town where there was electric lights. We were very anxious to see what they were like so we hung around a post on the street waiting to see how the light got there—strangely enough, I was not looking at the lamp when the light flashed on, but at Clif—That is the picture my memory carries of him, His head tilted a little to one side, a look that at the same time was all of eager happiness, expectancy, satisfaction on his face as the light suddenly flashed on. And that last night—why he stood up I don't know. There was a flare and for just a second I saw him looking at the light exactly as he did when as a boy he saw the first electric light. 'I'll get it across to you *some* way.' His last words—he never broke a promise."

I sat silent, I didn't know what to say. The grease in the pan was cold, the coffee cold. His face was drawn and there was a look in his eyes that frightened me. He lighted a cigarette his hands trembling so he could hardly hold the match. "Brotherhood of man—Hell! *I* offered my life, gave the squarest brother that ever lived to that false idea. He might have stayed out if I had not persuaded him—His life, my ruined life, the blood I shed—the rivers of blood other men shed, the rivers of tears—just waste. Well, it's a closed incident. We dreamed great dreams—we thought we were giving our lives for a holy cause—we *wanted* to, but—I could rejoice in it all, could go back to it all, starve, stand in mud made of blood if I could just believe now what I did when I went into the war. But I can't, I can't ever. So I had this raft built and launched, I started down the river, tied up here one night and got froze in. If the high water catches me, sweeps me, all right. As well that way as any. But—I can't hurry things, I must wait for Clif's message. I know it will come. If there is any where for it to come from."

He looked so hopeless, I was so sorry for him, I wanted to comfort him—I found myself saying, "It *does* matter—every little single thing does—Millions of people have experienced the state of mind that you are now in. You cannot claim that Christ did n't matter, that Lincoln did n't. You can't say that it didn't matter that you felt for a little while the grand desire to *help,* to give yourself, your *all* for humanity—That it seems to you to be a failure is not your affair—What *is* your affair is that you did your part—"

A pounding rumble broke upon my consciousness. At first I thought

it might be the high water which could be expected at any time and I
sprang up to get ashore, but just then a few rocks rattled down the tall
cliff opposite and I stood as if paralized while five dark forms hurtled
over the edge and struck the ice and water three hundred feet below.
Horses! My host paid no attention to them at all, when I could take my
eyes from the dreadful sight he was looking at me queerly.

"Do you know," he said "that I have been trying to account for the
way Clif has been in my mind all morning. It is your face—his face was
powder burned and mud soiled just as yours is wind burned and dirty—
you looked just as he looked that last time when you stood looking at
that animal come over. And—why—the answer to it all is right here! It
is Civilization that is wrong!—"

I could n't wait to hear more. I ran over the ice to where a huge, black
horse was floundering, the others had hit open water and had been
washed under ice—The big black fellow had been captured and had gotten away, the wire that had been used to hobble him still hung to the
poor broken leg—a heavy piece of iron had been tied to his fore lock so
that when he ran it beat him cruelly between the eyes—it was still there,
the flesh beaten off his face by the iron. That is one of the practices of
horse hunters—hobble their catches and tie on the 'pounder'. Then they
can be turned out to shift for themselves until the hunt is over. Then
they are rounded up and taken to the ranch.

The man shot the horse. Merciful. He removed the iron and the wire.

"You have been magnificently free all your life, old boy—Death has
completed that freedom but you shall not carry the shackles of the slav-
ery you fought with you. go on." A cake of ice broke away, the big body
slid into the water and was gone. .

"The hunters must be near, I must be going. Perhaps I can go into
camp with them. You know I am lost." I said—

He helped me to saddle and to tie on my pack. I mounted. He reached
up to shake hands and as I looked down into his blue eyes I was glad to
have met him—It was as if each of us had solved a problem—

"Good by, Madam Bootlegger," he smiled.

"Good by, Mr. Moonshiner. Don't forget—I have found out too, that it
does matter, *every* thing is good if we take it that way."

"Perhaps. Well, so long. If I get through Ladore I'll write you. At
Burntfork did you say? If I get through I'll write you and if I don't—"

"You'll let me know? There will be *some* way I'll know."

"Yes. Good bye." I turned old Buck and rode away with out looking back. After a bit I saw two riders away ahead. I tried to catch up with them but didn't until they reached camp. Dinner was long past but Lillie and Mrs. Lyle had cooked enough for all comers—while we enjoyed the antelope steak the boys told of their disappointment over losing track of the escaped stallion and his band. I told them what had happened.

"It was just suicide," one of them said. "They will do that some times."

Next day Lillie and I rode out and had a small adventure but as it brought us into familiar country I struck out for home. I had a feeling that I had found some thing that satisfied my urge to go on the jaunt and I wanted to get back with it. And I wanted to write this letter to tell you that all this month you have been in mind as you always are in heart. And today (March 29) I found a little violet tucked up under the foundation rock of the house where the sun could reach it but frost could not. The violets were planted in memory of dear Mrs. Coney. Her eyes were so like violets, were n't they? She meant more to me than any one else. She was a perfect friend. I loved her—I love her memory.

Your friend

Elinore P. Stewart

Although Elinore seems to have written this wild horse story expressly for Mr. Zaiss, the last paragraph appears to be addressed to Mrs. Allen, as were the other March story-letters written to commemorate Mrs. Coney's birthday. The following letter suggests Elinore sent copies to Mr. Zaiss as well as to Mrs. Allen, or perhaps the letter was circulated, round robin, among her correspondents.

Nov. 3rd, 1930
Burntfork, Wyo.

My Dear Mr. Zaiss—

If only you knew how glad I was to get your card! You would have thought I would have acknowledged it sooner. Well, after I wrote you about the horse hunt and received no reply I thought I must have outraged your sense of decency. When the lovely card came I thought a letter would come telling me how terrible my escapade seemed to civilized persons. But anyway, what ever is the matter I still have you and "Never shall you ever get away".

Really I should hate to lose you and if I have offended I am sincerely

sorry and beg your pardon, if I *ever* offend it will be unintentional.
Please take my crudities that way.

I was very happy yesterday and quite a lot of the pleasure has trickled
through to this day. I was happy because I was planting tulip bulbs. I
thought of you, it was a pleasure you could have shared if you like the
smell of new turned soil and the feel of warm, friendly sun on your back.

It was lovely. Away to the North the dim bad-land hills shone whitely
in the sun, to the South the Uintah Mountains stood guard. And down
back of the garden there is a hedge of sunflowers, black and dead now
but full of seed heads for the migrating birds. That is what The Stewart
does every year, plant sunflowers for the birds. Autumn is late this year,
no snow yet, so the birds are tardy. But they *are* drifting Southward and
it is so good to see the little travelers feast. Just beyond the sunflowers is
a little brook. The birds took great pleasure in their bath. You could have
heard their happy twittering and there was this fair, fat and fifty-odd
friend of yours kneeling on the terrace, sticking fat, brown little bulbs in
the rich, brown earth.

There will be a long row of sentinels to keep the cabbage from coming up on the terrace among the pansies. And there was so much to
think of, we could have talked as incessantly as did the birds.

Today, looking Northward, I can see a storm gathering. Tomorrow it
will be here, then I cannot dig in my garden.

Did I ever tell you that each plant in my garden means some one? Iris
for my French grandfather, peonies for a sister, forget-me-nots for my
dear Mrs. Coney, daisies for Helen Groves, a sister of Mrs. Coney—lots
and lots of dear ones, lots and lots of flowers. It is such a comfort, almost
like doing something for those we love, to care for the sweet representa-
tives. Pansies and sweet peas both do marvelously here—iris and
gladiolus, too. Roses have not proved much of a success but some kinds
of lilies do well. I have had twenty-two dear years of experimenting with
growing things.

Once I could only have fifty cents each year. I had to choose carefully
and the seed books were *so* alluring. It sometimes happened that a precious dime went for something that wouldn't grow in our high altitude.
Morning glories, for instance. They will only grow to about three feet
and the blooms are sickly looking things. Poppies and snapdragons are a
delight. As the years have gone by I have learned many things about gardening. The knowledge has cost me ten cents a packet and sometimes

the season's work as well as the disappointment. But there are the years of happiness to remember when I get so I can't hoe and dig. I make the vegetable garden, too; I never plant or gather peas but I think of you because you once wrote me about them. This is so much longer a letter than most polite persons write that I must stop. But I want to explain that in this big West women may do things that in the East might be considered queer. That is why we two old gray-heads could join the horse hunt without anyone here thinking anything about it. Then, when I wrote you about it all I didn't stop to think that it might shock you to know that we ride out just as the men do, taking our part of the hardships.

Please forgive me. I will promise you most faithfully that I will not go on any wild horse chase when I come East to see you. I must warn you, though, that I cannot be a *lady*. I'm just me. I cannot put on airs.

· Thank you for writing, please do so again.

Your friend,
Elinore P. Stewart

ᐓ FOUR

The Last Years (1930–1933)

ᐓ The concern for others that Elinore expressed in her letters and
stories manifested itself in many other ways. Besides always having
the welcome mat out for visitors, the Stewart home became a sort of refuge
for people down on their luck and for transients. The Stewarts' hired man,
Ernest Eubanks, had wandered in, homeless, and had become one of the
family. During the dust-bowl era, the Stewarts held out their hands to
many, relatives as well as strangers, fighting the Depression on a one-to-one
basis. A clean bed, warm meals, and heartfelt concern often became the
impetus needed for a new start.

Nov. 28, [1930]
Burntfork
My Darling Woodsey-Person.
You may get your little self ready for a perfectly terrible letter, it will
have to be such a *huge* letter. I have not had time to write a single line
since I wrote you.

Well, I'd best begin at the beginning which was 'way last summer. It
frosted every single night in June and froze hard the second and third
night of July. A most discouraging prospect in a place where the growing
season is so short. But we had to take a chance so we went to work and
replanted all we could. Then the rain set in. It rained some every day for
two months, some days all day. That made it so we could n't get the hay
up before the children had to leave for school. But we worked almost
night and day when we could hay and all the short crop stuff we planted
to supplement the frozen-out alfalfa grew splendidly owing to the rain,
so we had a bumper hay crop.

The day came when there was just the Stewart and I left and much of
the hay still in the field. So the Stewart saddled old Fanny and rode out
to the neighbors who had had hard luck by being flooded over and envited them to come and put the rest of ours up on shares. They were
glad to do it. And all the while we were getting too much water news
kept coming of terrible drouths else where. Not a paper but told of hard
times every where. Mines near us shut down throwing hundreds out of
work. The U.P. railroad layed off hundreds of men—cream prices
reached the lowest level—We could n't sell a beef because of the financial depression. Along in September our dairy paper published a call for
help for drouth victims. We talked a great deal about what we could do
to help. I was for taking two or three children or a couple of old folks
but the Stewart shook his head. "If we take children we may be taking
them from a better chance, education, every thing that a child needs is
so hard for us to get. It is best for *them* that we don't take children—And
old folks couldn't stand the climate—they would be unhappy so far
away from familiar things, church and friends. We are old folks ourselves, we can't give them the care they need, we might not live to see
children through. No. It can't be either children or old folks."

I was too busy to give the matter much thought and so it ran on 'til
the third notice came. We milk twenty cows, I do my part of that and
take all care of the vessels so there was very little time for any thing else.
The Stewart feared the grain would be snowed under so he was cutting
grain all day—then when the night work was done we were filling the
cellar by lantern light. A storm was threatening and we were working
like mad getting in the cabbage—already the bins were full of beets, carrots, parsnips, turnips, onions and salsify. Out in the field was an acre of
fine potatoes to be got in when we could get to it. "So much to eat and
just we two to eat it. We must send for our young people," the Stewart
said. We got so enterested in our argument and work that it was day
light before we knew it. But at breakfast I still held out for children.

"We can only give a *chance*. That's all we *have* to give. We must give it
to some one who can use it. Despair is just terrible in a young man's
heart as it is any where else. We will hold out a helping hand to some
young married man, let him bring his wife and little ones here where
they can have a home and plenty to eat. They can help us and next
spring we can rent them some land, let them have seed and get them
started."

Well, I gave in. I had to if they were to be helped before they starved to death. That very day a letter was sent and two weeks later we had our young couple with their almost two year old baby boy.

Poor, poor things! It would wring your heart to see them, to hear of their hardships. Almost at once the baby came down ill. Then the little mother. The father kept up but he should have gone to bed with the rest. They are all well now and I almost have the house back to normal again. For awhile it was hardly safe to sit down in any chair, there was sure to be a mustard plaster, a saucer of lard and turpentine or something of the sort. I am so glad that we have them, the boy is a dear and the young parents are so anxious to please us, they needed the help *so* badly. They are lots of help and company. We expect to fix up a cabin for them in the spring, let them farm for us a year so they will have seed and some thing to go on and then help them to home stead. That is all there is to tell about them just now.

Jerrine didn't come home this summer, she was a practice teacher in the Summer school at U.C. [University of Colorado]. Also she had a job in the office of the registerar. She is well and happy—Just now she is tormented by the wish to finish at the American School of Art in Rome and she wants a year at Heidelburg—*I* don't know how she will get all that— Junior is a Sophomore at U.C. He is taking journalism and is doing very well. He is making his own way, he clerks and delivers for a grocery man in all his spare time. He boarded at the same place last year. Calvin went to Oklahoma with my sister who [remainder of letter is from typed and edited transcription of the original] visited me last summer. And Robert is on his own, too. He is in Boulder. He milks for a dairyman and goes to preparatory. They will all be back next summer unless Jerrine has to work. She has such a yen for foreign places that it may be she will stay in Boulder and teach. She will have to work hard and save like everything to go where she wants to go. . . .

[*Elinore Stewart*]

During the following winter of 1930–31, Jerrine fell ill and was hospitalized for six weeks. When finally released from the hospital, she still was not strong enough for the journey home. On her arrival at Burntfork in the spring, she could hardly walk, and Elinore nursed her through the remainder of the year. Jerrine lost her scholarship, and the elder Stewarts were unable to help financially. Yet in this trying period, as in earlier ones,

Elinore maintained her strength through the simple pleasures of nature and fought her own depression by helping others whose misfortunes loomed even larger than hers.

Jan. 26th, 1931
Burntfork
My Dear Mr. Zaiss.

You must please forgive me for being so slow to tell you of my great happiness in the vase. It is lovely, the vase, and shall be my own especial joy as long as I live. Our first flowers to bloom in the spring are purple Siberian iris. They are very sweet. There will be three of them in my vase every day for a month, then the tulips, three of them each day. Then the tall iris, purple, blue, white, yellow and a mauve-pink. Then the lemon lillies, then the peonies. After the peonies sweet peas and baby breath. Every single day the vase shall have all of beauty it can hold. I am so glad to owe to you all the happiness the vase gives me. I *wanted* just that vase though I didn't know what it was I wanted. Please believe that I thank you.

And now I must tell you that I have been quite ill. Through the Christmas holidays I was helping to care for an old neighbor who was very ill with pneumonia. Perhaps I overdid myself or was exposed too much by my long walks across the ice that has spread over all the rocky flat between our homes.

Whatever the cause, I suddenly went to pieces one day and have had to stay in bed for two weeks. That is why you have not heard from me.

We are having very little snow this winter but the shallow stream that runs past my door is frozen tight to its bed. But that doesn't stop the water coming from the warm springs at the head of the little creek.

It just flows down and spreads in a great lake of ice which grows larger every day. Any thing that gets on this ice is perfectly visible these moonlit nights. Last night I sat by a window and saw two jack rabbits playing in the moonlight on the ice. From the tall, dark pines across the ice and in the swamp beyond came the call of the big white owls. Then, from the bare, dun hills came the quivering wall of a coyote. Soon the rabbits stopped playing and sat up. They seemed to be listening. They darted away and a coyote came trotting across the ice. He sniffed about where the rabbits had been playing. Then he sat down with his nose pointed toward the moon and howled. In just a moment the hills resounded with yelping echoes. This stopped but in a short time there were three more coyotes out on the ice. I could see shadowy shapes coming from every direction. I counted twelve and there may have been more.

The coyotes sniffed about when they first came up but soon sat on their haunches as the first one did. Pretty soon the first old fellow gave a long, quivering howl and the rest yelped a few times and followed, trotting after him toward the swamp.

This morning our neighbor came over to tell us that last night the coyotes killed twenty-six of his sheep in his pasture last night. I feel sure that it was the same pack that gathered on the ice that did the killing.

Mr. Hicks says that they killed more than they could eat at one time just so as to have other meals when the killing is not so good. I had often wondered why, when a coyote gets into a flock of sheep, they kill so many.

Today is baking day. I have eight loaves of bread, two coffee cakes and three dozen doughnuts. I feel a little like the coyotes, getting eats ready ahead of time. Tomorrow I shall begin braiding a rug—it takes me three years to save up enough rags for a rug but at last I have quite a respectable box of rags so tomorrow I begin on what will be a pleasure.

Last year I made quilts—pieced together all the new scraps I had— that was fun and the quilts came in very handy when a family of drouth refugees came to us. There are so many hungry people in the drouth stricken states. We felt that we should do something so we took a family of three to care for until times mend. I must stop before I tire you but I cannot stop until I tell you again that my vase is the loveliest thing I have and I thank you.

Most Sincerely your friend,
Elinore P. Stewart

P.S. Have you ever read "Death Comes for the Archbishop", by Willa Cather? Please let me know.

World War I had first brought the outside world with its political manueverings into the isolated Burntfork Valley, causing Elinore to look with a skeptical eye at the devastating effects of war on its veterans. But the Great Depression created problems closer to home. In her last letters, Elinore inquired firsthand into the consequences of the depression on the community.

The ironic juxtaposition of the balance of nature described in the first part of the following story-letter with the imbalance of society in the second part accentuates Elinore's fundamental belief that society, like nature, should take care of its own.

Oct. 8th, 1931
Burntfork
Dear Mr. Zaiss—

All summer long I have thought of you every day, the flower holders have seen to that, but even if they had not been here you would have been in my summer anyway for there has been much that I should have liked you to know. This for one thing—The very last of June I went with my boys about seven miles up into the mountains to an old deserted saw mill.

The boys went to get a load of slabs to use in building a rough shelter; they had to work the slabs out of a huge pile that had lain there for years. It was hard work and took a long time. That gave me time to ramble over the mountains and up the shady canons. It was very, very lovely. Columbines were in full bloom. Here they are ivory white in color—just once in a while is there one of the blue and white ones. They are much larger in this altitude than they are elsewhere. And they were just as thick as they can possibly grow under the great pines. I walked through miles of them. Up that high the mornings and evenings are so cold that a heavy sweater is very comfortable, necessary. But at ten o'clock it is too warm for comfort out in the sun.

So I was keeping in the shade. I had been climbing and walking rather vigorously so I sat down on a log to rest. What I had not seen when I chose my place to rest was two little fawns curled up almost like a dog, lying against the log, almost concealed by the columbines. They were very young, their speckles blended with the white flowers and the tan of their coats could hardly be told from the but little darker browns of the dead twigs and sticks about.

A grouse with her seven little ones came by, not at all afraid. The grouse very leisurely strolled on. About that time a small black squirrel began to bark and chatter. A jay bird took offense and began to scold. Here the jays are not the bright blue they are elsewhere, they are so dark they appear black. And there's a bird called a camp-robber, a dark gray, melancholy kind of bird. Miners in Colorado say the camp-robbers are

the old prospectors who died without finding gold returned to the
mountains. It may be. Of course, I don't know. But I do know that they
manage to warn everything in the forest when there is a stranger about.
The chattering and scolding soon had the effect of bringing the doe, the
mother of the two little fawns, to see what it was all about.

She stamped and snorted repeatedly but would not come near. You
would have liked the walk, I know.

Here there are no snakes, scorpions, tarantulas or poisonous spiders.
Nothing in the world to hurt one. There are, of course, bobcats, wolves,
coyotes and some bear, lots of porcupines, but all the wild things will
leave man alone. They ask only to be left alone. So, except for the in-
equalities of the ground you could walk in perfect safety.

Oct. 16th

Dear Mr. Zaiss:

You can tell how I have to stop writing and get sidetracked. But this
time I went for a visit. I visited just for you and so you cannot scold if it
so happens you would rather stay in the green shadows of the forest and
know what the deer did. To begin with, the thing I found hardest to get
used to when I came West was the rough way Western women talk. It
was startling to hear one say, "Gee, it's as hot as hell today" or "It's cold
as the devil outside", "The damned old wagon is about to fall down." It
was kind of shocking but I soon learned that the women were good
women, good neighbors, kind, good mothers. One of them told me
shortly after I came that I was just like the rest of the damned tenderfeet,
thought I could remake the country overnight. I didn't fool myself quite
that much but I have often wondered what my beloved Mrs. Coney
would have thought if she could have heard.

I am trying to prepare you for a shock. Are you prepared? The little
old woman I am taking you to see is seventy-six years old and she swears
like a trooper or a parrot "or sumpin". Her name is Mary Alice Gillis, she
lives with her son Dave who runs sheep on the desert.

'Ma' Gillis homesteaded and she lives alone all the time that Dave is
gone with the sheep.

I knew that she was alone so I rode down to see her. She is a small
woman, kind of square in build. She wears Dave's old shoes and she has
very thin little legs. The big shoes give her a very splay-footed appearance. She has a round, rosy face framed in a fringe of silvery bobbed

hair. She has big blue eyes and she doesn't wear glasses. I rode along slowly, enjoying the glorious color spread everywhere. The wind was friendly, just merely hinted at future blizzards, the sun seemed to smile even at the hint. Riding slowly down the path, I made no noise as I approached the Gillis cabin.

I could see Ma's silvery head shining in the sunlight and I could hear her busily talking as she worked at something on the ground. She spied me.

"Well, I'll be damned! *You've* come. This is the best thing that's happened since Cornwallis surrendered in 1781. Get down. I've been washing wool and I'm puttin' it out to dry on this here tarpaulin that some durned fool left hangin' on my fence."

I dismounted and knelt down to help spread the wet wool to dry in the pleasant sun.

We talked of the great drouth that has worked such havoc to Wyoming stockmen.

"I was just tellin' God what I thought about it as you rid up. Damn poor management, *I* call it, floodin' out some, burnin' out others."

"Did He answer you? What did He say?" I asked.

"I have to think the answers when I talk to God, the first thing that pops into my mind is the answer. This time the answer was the world is God's. He has a right to do what He likes with what's his own. He made it all. Can't anybody dispute that. Dave bein' gone so much and nobody here to talk to, I kind of got into the habit of talkin' to God. He never tattles." It sounded weird, unbalanced.

"How much wool do you think you have here?" I asked her just to change the subject.

"Sixty pounds in this lot. I pulled every damned stinkin' hair of it off sheep that died last winter. It's a rotten job. You got to wait til the sheep have been dead so long they are about to fall to pieces so the wool loosens up and can be pulled off, just like you pick a chicken. I have washed this through nineteen waters. It sure was lots of work, packin' the water from the creek. But it is nice and clean now, ain't it?"

It was. Soft and fluffy, light cream color.

"I am goin' to make quilts and comfortables with this wool, that's what I saved it for. That gives me something to do while I'm alone and maybe I can raffle them off and make a little money. The price of sheep is just beggery for the sheepmen but I guess Dave and me will pull through."

We patted and spread wool til it seemed my back would break but at last it was all spread to dry and we went into the cabin to get a bite to eat. Ma is a good cook as you will say when I take you to visit her. Today she had barbecued mutton. It wasn't quite done when we went in for dinner and while we waited we looked at her quilts, so many of them, so beautiful, The Lost Ship, The Blazing Star, Friendship, Irish Chain.

The history of each quilt as interesting as the quilt is lovely. "Now this quilt is a Christmas quilt and a kind of a tombstone together. It's a Lone Star. One day I got to thinkin' of my girlhood and of a beau I had. I thought a lot of him. He's been dead a long, long time. I just happened to remember he was from Texas and was always talkin' about the Lone Star State. I hadn't seen him for years before I married Dave's pa, but I knew he was dead. I have never even seen his grave, never laid a flower on it or nothin'. I don't even know whether he has a tombstone. So I just went at it and pieced a Lone Star.

"Every time I got a little fretted or tired I just set down and sewed a little on my Bobby Drake quilt. It rested me. I'd mighty near think I was back in Missouri, barefooted, drivin' the cows up the lane in the twilight. I could almost smell the four o'clocks that used to grow along the walk from the cow pen to the well house where we kept the milk. It sure was like goin' back. Well, I vowed I would get the quilt done by Christmas and give it to the first person from Texas that came to see me. But no one came and so I still have the quilt.

"And as I worked on the Star and thought of getting it done by Christmas somehow the Star of Bethlehem kept coming to my mind. I sat up til midnight Christmas Eve to finish it. I sure *am* goin' to give it to the first Texan I see and I hope it's for Christmas."

We hadn't got the quilts put back into their numerous boxes when a car drew up before the cabin and two men got out. They stayed to eat with us and while we were enjoying the mutton they told us of the efforts being made at Rock Springs to relieve the pressing want of the unemployed. One of the men said, "It's not our *own* unemployed that are in such distress, it's the poor drifters. They come through our little town literally by thousands, a constant stream going both ways. East and West. A constant stream of misery and want. Since the sheep industry is bankrupt there is no wool to store, so we are turning the wool storehouses into places for the down and outers to eat and sleep in. We are out soliciting help. We need potatoes, beef, mutton, anything to eat and anything we can get for clothes and bedding."

Ma was all enthusiasm. She asked dozens of questions. The men left after dinner. We stood watching their big car roll away when a whirlwind dropped down over the rim, whirled into Ma's drying wool and strung it high up in the tall pines and all over the neighboring willows and cottonwoods.

Ma was appalled. With almost unbelieving eyes she looked at the havoc, then she said, "Now God, what the hell did you do *that* for? That's *sinful* waste and all them poor folks got to be fed and bedded. I sure can't make you out at all, God, ruinin' all I *had* to give."

But she was only talking. Next day a truck came to gather the donated supplies. I helped Ma wrap the quilts she sent in. Among them was the Lone Star.

"Surely you won't send that!" I said.

"Sure I am," she replied. "That's why God scattered my wool, so I would have to give my best. After all, it's right. Why offer a poor gift in His name?"

"But the people who will use your lovely quilts are just hoboes."

"What of it? Jesus Christ was a hobo once. And God and hard times made these hoboes."

"But your Lone Star is a memorial."

"I guess it is but Bob Drake might have been a hobo himself if he had lived. He would be older than I am, too. But he would have been a good one. He was hard to beat at anything."

So the Lone Star went with the rest. Later I went into town and visited the old wool houses to see what was being done. To me it was inspiring to see the friendly earnestness of people bringing order out of chaos.

Laundries had washed the contributed clothes free. Men with trucks had given their service free and had gathered food all over the country. Women of all ages and descriptions were just as busy as could be sorting and mending overalls, shirts, great piles of hopeless looking socks, underclothes, coats. As fast as they were ready they were placed neatly in piles, ready to be passed out.

I couldn't begin to tell you all I saw but I must tell you this. A long, cheerless-looking warehouse was being converted into a flop house. As I stepped in I heard a very familiar voice saying "That's a hell of a mess you've made of that paste, Minnie. You might as well paste the papers on straight, the men will read what's on the walls. I never see it fail. Put the papers on straight. It's damn hard on the eyes to try to read something on slaunch ways."

Ma Gillis supervising the work!

A dozen women were busy pasting newspapers over the dirty walls. That made the great barnlike place cleaner and warmer. At either end of the place were great old box heaters and coal was being supplied by the Rock Springs coal miners. Rows of bunks were built along both sides of the room and these were filled with wool sacks and covered with quilts and blankets.

One bunk, very neatly made up, had Ma's Lone Star for a cover. She came up to me. "Get busy, get busy! What are you standin' around gawkin' like a kid at a circus for? You look like the Devil sued for murder in that damn outfit. Did you bring beddin' or what?"

I left her there bossing and sweating while she worked far beyond her strength. I visited the cook shack and saw the arrangements made to feed the hungry. They are going to let the needy do their own cooking mostly. Some one will be in charge of provisions all the time and will pass them out as needed.

Ma is at home now, still bewailing the loss of her wool. She would die if she couldn't work. Just now she is cleaning and stretching sheep pelts to be used as rugs on the flop house floor.

I must stop now before you get so tired that you will never write me again. But you will write me again sometime, won't you? *Please.*

Your friend

Elinore P. Stewart

This is finished Nov. 13th

Illness plagued the Stewarts. Jerrine, recovering at home from the illness for which she had been hospitalized, still had not regained her strength when Clyde became seriously ill. Clyde, Jr., and Robert left school and returned home to take over the ranching duties. Then, in December 1931, illness struck Elinore too, and the doctor prescribed complete bed rest through the holidays. Although she professed to enjoy lounging abed, Elinore lamented that she had to severely curtail her writing. By the time spring calving and planting began and a new influx of guests arrived, the rest of the family had sufficiently recovered to tend to the chores. Elinore did not regain her former health and stamina, although she slowly resumed her flow of letters.

January 26, [1932]
Burntfork
My Darling Woodsey-Person.

Your friend Elinore has been quite ill—quite ill—All through Christmas time, couldn't send even a card. I think I could have written before this but they would n't let me. I was just tired—lazy I believe.

What ever the reason a very gruff old doctor said it was the bed for me so I said my prayers and went to bed. And I went to sleep. Just like a big, fat old bear, hibernating for the winter. Seems like I slept for weeks and was never fully awake tho' I was often aware of hushed sounds, of the smell of medicine and of the great comfort of clean, smooth sheets and of everybody's being so kind, so kind.

But I was horrified when I found I had fooled away a lovely Christmas—the first I can remember when I was completely out. But I am all right now, dear Woodsey—I know you have been worried about me but I am all right. Dr. Lawser says I have worked too hard and must now rest. That doesn't sound so badly—I've long wanted to lie abed and let some one else wash the separator and sweep under the beds. I can do so now. It is a little disconcerting to find that I am not so important as I had supposed, that the world rocks on just as well when I do none of the agitating but it is comforting, too. I don't need to feel all the responsibility. But my writing period is up—just a little while each day.

I have a lovely box of chocolates on a stand near my bed—lovely, lovely to have one piece now and then and to have them to offer friends who call. Thank you for them Woodsey—you have been a joy every minute of the time since you have been my own dear friend. With much love

Your friend
Elinore P. Stewart

Burntfork
August 10, [1932]
My Dear Woodsey-Person.

You have been neglected because there has been such a rush of company all summer, some that were expected, some that just came. I haven't been very well and so much company made so much extra work that I just *had* to let something go.

But I am sorry if you have been worried, you ought to cast me off, if you did I would come crawling back. One of my visitors was a Chicago woman whose husband had eloped with another woman. That put her . . . [?] . . . entertain. Then, one influx was an Indian family and it was a little difficult to get them adjusted. About the time I would get every thing running pleasantly a new bunch arrived and there had to be another shifting around. All this sounds as if I didn't enjoy my visitors. I did, tremdiously. One visitor is a Theosophist—four are Catholic six Presbyterian, two Baptist, three didn't declare themselves but all talked politics. It was all a little confusing but enteresting, I know a lot more than I used to about What's What.

One thing cheering about the times is that all the visitors went back to jobs, some of them had not had work for months and had not expected to get to work, They were all helpful to each othe. in getting jobs. The Chicago woman works in a bank; she got jobs for two men in the bank where she worked—the woman from Seattle placed a whole family with a lumber company. My ink has run out, a hint that I have said enough but I can't stop until I tell you about the family. I am not so very well but every one else is better than they have been for a long time, Jerrine weighs more than she has ever weighed. But the depression has put a stop to our educational program. We have to do our work whether there is any money in it or not. But living on a ranch is a joy now because there is always plenty to eat and some to spare—It is so beautiful this year, an abundance of flowers and a wonderful garden—I must begin to can . . . [?] . . . beans next week—corn after that. Dear Woodsey-Person, please write me when you can and please remember that I love you.

> Your friend
> *Elinore P. Stewart*

Burntfork, Wyo.
Nov. 26th, 1932
Dear Mr. Zaiss.

Many times this last summer have you been in my thoughts. When I have been picking peas I would catch myself thinking, "Mr. Zaiss would enjoy helping me, he would like the warmth of the sun and the cool little breeze right off the snow. He would enjoy the lark's song and the scent of the pines, the sagebrush and of the wild roses. Perhaps even more would he enjoy these peas for dinner." Many things brought you to mind but peas particularly because you once wrote me something about peas.

You might not have enjoyed the canning activities that went on all summer long. Each day was a very busy one for each member of the family. We are a very valiant army. We fought the depression with hoes, plows, rakes, mowers, hayrakes, pitchforks, milk pails and Mason jars. We kept up our morale with sweet peas, pansies, lilies, iris, tulips, gladiolus, delphiniums, poppies, baby breath and peonies.

A few annuals scattered through the vegetables in the garden lend interest to the dull tasks of weeding, thinning and cultivating.

Jerrine and I do as much of our work as we can out doors. We sat out on the porch to shell peas, cut corn from the cob, string beans for canning, *all* such work. That way we saw the flowers and the butterflies all day long.

We could see the buttes and the badlands in the marvelous color changes. We planned trips and trips that we shall never have time to take. It was all very pleasant.

And there was the very real satisfaction of seeing the store room shelves fill with shining jars of food for ourselves and others less fortunate.

Our local Red Cross is sixty miles away. We ranch women found it hard to work with the Chapter because of the distance and our own work. We were not satisfied, either, with the way some of the relief work was being done.

For instance, the outing flannel issued by the government was made into pyjamas and these were given out to the youths and men beating their way from coast to coast.

Sleeping garments meant nothing to men who had to sleep in freight cars or any place they could. We ranch women felt that the cloth should have been kept for needy families both in town and in rural districts. Town members felt that rural women should have nothing to say since they were not there to sew on the days set for work and never got their garments in on time to be checked and distributed. It was hard for us to get the garments into town even when we found time to sew. So we decided to do our relief work our own way. Early in the Spring we checked up the families in our own community who would probably need help this winter. There was so little money to be had that seeds for garden planting were hard to get. We tithed our own supply and gave to the families who needed help. Then we took turns at calling on the ones being helped to see that the gardens were properly planted and cared for, so on through the canning and drying season. Those who have cars went to the needy homes and took the mothers to all the demonstrations put on by the Extension Service of our University to teach rural women the preparation and care of foods, Cheese Making, canning and preserving. Next we tithed ourselves to accumulate a surplus to help out our town sisters. But we wouldn't take our town sisters' word for any thing. We sent our own investigator who was instructed to visit around "casual like" and find out the truth of the situation and get the names of families needing neighborly help, *not* charity. It has been fun and has given much satisfaction, even though the work has been hard. I think we helped ourselves as much as anyone else. We know what we *can* do when under stress.

We were "all het up" about the campaign, too. Of course, local politics interested us most because we know the candidates. I think you might have found many laughs in the various situations which arose. For instance, Daggett County, Utah, is a new little county, it is just a slice off big Uintah County and was organized because all the persons who live north of the Uintah Mountains were practically disfranchised, seventy five miles over the mountains to vote and to attend Court. In winter the roads, where there *is* a road, is very often impassable. So, a few years back Daggett was formed for the convenience of the few who live on this side of the Mountains. They had a very limited choice in electing officers. The prosecuting attorney never saw a law book, the sixth grade was his limit in school. Yet, he was duly elected and must have qualified over night. He announced the opening of court this way. He rang a little bell used at the school to summon children from the playground. Ringing the bell vigorously he shouted, "Hey! You bob tailed Sons of Wild Jack asses. Get yourselves in here. This here court is open for business and no foolin'. The first case goin' to be called to docket is Jabe Bennett, accused of killin' deer out of season. All the witnesses for Jabe stay on the south side of this here court house, all agin on the north."

"All that's been examined will be locked up in jail to be helt for rebuttal and so they can't get together to swap no lies."

This little county is in Utah, about thirty miles away from my home. I hope some day to be able to attend court there. It will be great fun. Our own Sweetwater County has afforded me a great deal of amusement and instruction on several occasions.

I think people of the Eastern states would hardly believe some of the things our courts do. Of course, it may be the same everywhere but it seems to me that the Solomons on our Western benches interpret the law peculiarly to our country. A horse thief may be given a life sentence. A murderer be found not guilty, the Jury holding that "The durned galoot got what he had comin'" or "He ought 'a been killed a long time afore, any body that 'd steal another man's cattle!"

But anyway, leaving the Courts and coming back to the elections, this state is jubilant over the outcome. It seems to me foolish to blame the present administration for the depression. But Wyoming does just that.

Sheepmen who were millionaires when they voted for Hoover are now penniless. Thousands of flocks were turned loose to starve on the range.

Cattle men cannot sell their cattle for enough to pay freight charges to market.

All business is at a standstill. Oil and coal in which the state abounds, in many cases are just another liability since taxes must be paid. But the population is not suffering much because it is mostly rural and there is plenty to eat on the ranches, plenty of work to keep us out of mischief, plenty of fuel and shelter. But no money.

At that, there are many to help. They are the miners and oil workers and the people who depend upon Railroad work.

And, of course, there is the constant stream of transients, down and outers, forever hunting for the promised land.

We of the ranches are more secure, *we* could vote as we pleased. We had no grouch to nurse and no boss to placate.

Dear Mr. Zaiss, please write me when you can.

Your Friend
Elinore P. Stewart

Finally, nine years after Elinore's last known publication in the *Atlantic Monthly,* B. A. Botkin, a folklorist at the University of Oklahoma and editor of several books of Americana, invited her to submit a story for the fourth volume of *Folk-Say,* a collection of stories published by the University of Oklahoma Press. He accepted "Sagebrush Wedding," a story about Ma Dallas, a widow who travels to a neighbor's isolated ranch to tell her about the government's "seed loan" program. The widow soon discovers that the neighbor is in the process of marrying Ma's son. Ma Dallas, much like the other sheep-herding characters Mrs. O'Shaughnessy, Mollie-Jane Patton, and Mrs. Pond, is based on Elinore's neighbor Ma Gillis.[1]

Burntfork, Wyoming
March 30, 1932
Dear Friend,

The seed loan has caused a great stir in our community. Many who had never thought of farming will try it this year. Two weeks ago Ma Dallas rode up on her pinto pony, a frisky little outlaw that Ma rides very easily.

If there is such a thing as a white sparrow, that is what Ma is like. Seventy-three years have only added to her enjoyment of life, allowed her to acquire a wide, picturesque vocabulary, and given her a keen insight into human affairs. This is what she is like: small and beaming; full of energy, fun, and fight. Blue-eyed; silvery bobbed white hair; round, rosy face. Workworn, knobby hands too large for the slender wrists. Slender little legs that terminate in huge old shoes that have been cast off by her son, giving her a peculiarly elfin appearance. She is as quick to bless, curse, or praise as she is to help, as she says, "in any other way."

I was delighted to see her. Left the bread I was putting into loaves to run out to offer her help that was not needed.

"Hello! I hear that Stewart is on the committee 'bout this here seed loan business. I came up to find out all about it."

She beamed as she divested herself of a ragged old mackinaw, more ragged old sweater, and her son's old arctics.

"Is Dave going to apply for a loan?" I asked.

"No, Dave is too tied up with them dam' sheep. He can't get in off the range long enough to shave. I'll bet when the shearers come they can't tell Dave from the sheep until they clip a piece of his hide and hear him blat. But I want to know all about the loan. I want to go down to Melvina's and tell her about it."

"That's a long ride, thirty-five miles, snow just going out and no roads most of the way. Every one will be notified through the mail anyway," I reminded her.

---

1. "Sagebrush Wedding" was published in *Folk-Say IV: The Land Is Ours,* edited by B. A. Botkin. Copyright © 1932 by B. A. Botkin. Published by the University of Oklahoma Press. Reprinted by permission.

"Melvina don't send to the post office once a month and she ain't got no telephone. She shore does need a lift. Bein' a widow ain't so darned funny, no one to do a thing like that for you. *I* know. You can hibernate like a damn fat old bear but I am goin'. I did hope you would want to go, I hate to go by myself."

Next morning was clear and bright, no sign of a storm anywhere, the pinto and old Fanny saddled and waiting at the gate for us when we came out after breakfast. The ground was rutted and frozen where the snow was off. Our horses stumbled and minced along in a most provoking way. Riding was not an unmixed pleasure but the sky was so blue, the buttes so white in their snowy wraps, and the mountains back of us were so majestic that it was good just to be out.

We headed northeast, crossed the creek, wound our way up a long dugway where fossil oysters and snails showed in the rock all the way up. Arrived at the top, we crossed a sagebrush flat and left the road to strike out across the badland country. What a time we had! As the sun warmed the earth, the ground thawed and the slippery badland mud all but mired our horses; the gulches were filled with snow and trickling water. When we needed to cross one, we were never sure of how deep we were going to go into snow. We tried to keep out of the gulches as much as we could but we had to cross occasionally and when we did our poor horses went slipping, plunging, and panting into snow.

We stopped on a warm, dry hillside to rest our weary horses while they enjoyed a few oats we had brought for them and we ate some sandwiches. While we rested Ma told me her story. I have known her for years, but this was the first time I had heard it.

"The Bonneys were a notch higher up in life than the Carsons, my maiden name was Carson, so my mother just about threw a fit when she found out that Hugh Bonney wanted me. Clem Dallas and me had kind of made up our minds to get married as soon as we could get a few things together to housekeep with. We were as pore as Job's turkey, so Clem went down to St. Louis to drive a dray. He was makin' good money, twenty-five dollars a month. We 'lowed we wouldn't have to wait long and could set up housekeepin' right. But as soon as Ma found out about Hugh she just wouldn't let up till I married him.

"Well, I married him and run a hotel twenty years to support him. Finally he drank himself to death. I was afraid Dave would follow in his father's footsteps so I persuaded him to come with me to Wyoming where we could both homestead, I wanted to get him away from his drinkin', carousin' friends. So we came. We were poorer than the devil. Dave got a job from the cattle men's association, ridin' the deadline to keep the sheep and sheepherders back off the cattle range. Sometimes the sheep-herders got pretty sassy. Dave's boss told him not to hurt them in any way but to smoke 'em up a little and scare the sass out of 'em.

"We had taken homesteads adjoinin'. Dave built two cabins right close together, not joinin', so they would be separate residences. One for him and one for me. They were the same as a two-roomed house. The law requires a homesteader to establish residence on his land for seven months a year. You have to eat and sleep on your own land. Dave and me solved that problem by each sleepin' in his own cabin but movin' the cook stove time about. Each got the benefit of that one little stove. Dave could hold down his job and his claim at the same time. I was nearest to bein' happy that I'd ever been. We had been here nearly two years, our place had begun to look rale homelike and cosy. I was so glad I had Dave away from temptation.

"Of course folks drink here, same as any place but they are so far apart they can't do it so often. I was feelin' mighty satisfied and pretty well set up. But one day just afore sundown, I heard a wagon comin' like hell beatin' tanbark. I'd just gone out to shut the chickens in and to gather the eggs. I had my apron full of eggs. I stood peerin' up the trail through the brush when here come Dave, drivin' and lashin' a gallopin' team, a sheep campwagon rockin' and reelin' behind 'em. As soon as he got to where he could see me he began to holler, 'Ma, I shot a man! Ma, come help, hurry! He's shot, he's dyin'.' 'Dave,' I said, 'git down out of that sheepcamp and come here. I want to smell you.' He wouldn't come to me but he didn't need to. He smelled like one of these here moon-shine stills after a federal raid. I just stood paralyzed while hope kicked off. At last I looked in the wagon. You could have knocked me down with a feather from one of my hens. It was Clem in the wagon.

"I hadn't seen nor heard of him since he left when I married Hugh, here he was all smeared up with mud and blood and the eggs I had let drop when I saw him. Well, there's no use to go into it all. It seemed kind o' queer to be takin' care o' Clem but I felt I had to, Dave had been too hasty with his gun; he didn't know it was Clem and Clem didn't know Dave was on earth. He'd been in Wyoming all these years workin' with sheep. That's how come Dave and me are in sheep now.

"Guess a man borned to be drowned can't be hung. Clem was borned to marry me and I was borned to take care of booze fighters. We were as happy as a left-handed sheep shearer the three years he lived. I ain't goin' to marry any more."

The recital over, we rode on. We crossed the badlands and came out upon the trackless desert. A cold wind came hurrying to meet us and seemed to be trying to push us back to safety. Much of the ground was bare, but huge drifts of snow, piled high by the restless winds, remained. We saw flocks of lost, abandoned sheep. Discouraged flockmasters had turned their sheep loose when no more money was to be had to pay herders. Often a flock of sage chickens was scared up and took flight through the hazy air. For it was nearing sundown and things were beginning to settle for the night. A coyote sent up a quivering wail and was answered from a dozen sand dunes. A drove of antelope, like gray shadows, flitted silently past, between ourselves and the reddening sun. I became frightened. Our horses were fagged, we were miles from any house and it is no joke to be out on a Wyoming desert in March. Ma rode ahead, kicking and slapping her tired horse with her bridle reins. Spur and slap as I might, I couldn't induce Fanny to keep up with the pinto. Ma drew rein.

"Well, I guess we are in for a cold night. We can't possibly make it to Melvina's to-night. Let's stop and hunt a sheltered spot, gather up some sagebrush, build us up a big fire, and do the best we can till morning."

I had unpleasant visions of sudden, sweeping storms, of being snowed under, frozen to death, of our poor horses' discomfort. *Why, oh, why had I not stayed safely at home!*

We slowly made our way round a small butte, seeking an overjutting rock or a wash deep enough to shelter us. No such place presented itself until we rounded a shoulder of the butte and came full upon a sheep camp, two wagons drawn closely together. A light glowed in one. An astonished young Mexican stopped cooking to stare at us as we came up to the door. We explained our predicament, he smiled, bowed, waved his arm in a sweeping gesture toward a band of sheep bedded down a little way off. The young herder, also Mexican, came up smiling and bowing. Without a word he began to unsaddle our horses.

Stiffly we climbed the step into the lighted camp. Almost too tired to move, we clambered upon the bed to be out of the way. Blessed rest! Can you fancy an apartment about the size of a kitchenette? Kitchen, dining room, sitting room, store room, bedroom all in one? That is just the way a sheep wagon is built. A full-sized bed is built across the back end, beneath it are drawers and cupboards, and a sliding table pulls out for meals and is pushed back when not in use. A small cook stove is bolted fast on one side of the door. Benches are built along the sides of the wagon bed, these have lids to be raised when something is wanted from the compartment underneath. Several thicknesses of canvas and oil cloth make the roof, the floor is covered with linoleum.

From a tiny window we could see our horses being cared for, fed, blanketed. Hot, delicious odors of cooking filled the camp. We wondered a little that we were not sent to the other wagon; that was soon explained by the thick smoke arising from the stovepipe. There had been no fire there, it was cold. Here was warmth and comfort. We dozed. The young men ate their supper; half asleep, we could hear their soft voices and the soft clatter of carefully moved dishes. Presently the voices were louder and we realized that they wanted us to arise.

White, clean towels clothed the table, a most tempting supper was served on the best dishes. A basin of warm water awaited our hands, some condensed milk was offered us to apply to our wind-burned faces. We ate alone. Both boys were out somewhere with the sheep or they were thoughtful and considerate.

Presently one of them came to the door and said something. We couldn't understand his words but we could see that he was very embarrassed. He jabbered and bowed, we could only shake our hands uncomprehendingly. Finally he beckoned. We followed him to the other shep [sic] wagon. A bright fire glowed in a tiny heater. There were no pots or dishes. A clean, comfortable bed awaited us. The young Mexican murmured, "*Buenas noches,*" closed the door for us, and left us to our rest.

"This is the boss' camp. He sleeps here when he comes out," said Ma drowsily.

We were up in time to see the sun take its first cautious peep over the rim of the distant mountains next morning but there was no one at camp but ourselves. Breakfast was left where it would keep warm, a lunch was packed and left on our hats. Our horses were saddled and waiting for us.

"Well," remarked Ma, "it looks like we got our dismissal. No women allowed."

As we rode away, we could see the sheep spreading out over the sand dunes but no herder was in sight. We reached Melvina's at noon. I had met Melvina only a few times, but her daughter 'Lisa I know quite well.

Little as I know Melvina, her behavior seemed a little odd as she met us at the door. She seemed embarrassed and surprised. Some way I got the impression that our welcome was not so cordial.

"Well! How did *you* happen to come?" she asked Ma.

"I came because I wanted to," said Ma serenely. "Have you heard about the seed loan? I came to tell you so you could get in on it."

"No, I haven't heard anything about a loan. What's it all about?" We removed our wraps and Ma began to tell her about the loan. I went out to help 'Lisa and Fallon, the two children, take care of the horses. There was an air of suppressed excitement about the place, signs of recent housecleaning, untimely in March.

"What is it all about, 'Lisa?" I asked.

"Don't you know? Honest?"

"No, I don't. Is it anything I shouldn't know? Is it a secret?"

"Mama is going to be married to-day, as soon as they get here from Green River. I do hope Mrs. Dallas is not going to butt in. If she does, that will knock my plans all to kingdom come. You see, if Mama married I could. Carmon wants me to."

"But why should you fear Mrs. Dallas?"

"Because—well, you see—I must hurry to the house, there is so much to do."

And indeed there was. I told Ma that we had stumbled in on a wedding, but instead of making any move to go home she rolled up her sleeves and went to cooking.

" 'Tain't no weddin' without a cake. I see you have lots of eggs, Melviny. I'm going to make you a cake you will be proud of. Just like I would make for Dave if it was him gettin' married." Melvina looked at her curiously but said nothing. I felt extremely out of place and would have left had there been any place to go that I could reach before night. As it was, we all worked furiously. 'Lisa seemed bubbling over with some secret joke of her own. Even Fallon, the twelve-year old boy, seemed to find much to smile about.

"Are you so glad to have a new father?" I asked him.

"No! I don't give a damn about no new dad but I *am* glad I am going to have a new saddle and a gun and maybe get to go to Mexico on 'Lisa's wedding tour."

"But I thought it was your mother getting married."

"It is, but 'Lisa will too soon as Mama gets off of hand."

I was busy helping 'Lisa hang curtains, Ma in the kitchen was having the time of her life, the bride-to-be was flitting about from task to task, a worried, questioning look on her face. The little log cabin took on a festive appearance, even the table was being set for the wedding supper. Ma, sweating and beaming, came out of the kitchen to speak to us:

"Melviny, you go lie down and take a rest. We'll have everything spick and span in a jiffy. How many's comin'? How many must we set the table for?"

"I don't know. I didn't envite anybody but I guess they'll bring somebody for witness from town."

She retired to her room and the rest of us worked on until four o'clock, then 'Lisa said:

"They should be here pretty soon. I do hope they didn't strike any drifts. He went in a car to bring the minister and to get the license. He had to go clear around by Manilla to get on the mail road, the only road that was open."

"Who is "'He'?"

'Lisa giggled. "Why—Carmon—went." Mystery! At five they began to dress for the wedding. 'Lisa looked sweet in a blue dress and Melvina was almost beautiful in gray. Ma and I were scarecrows in our old travel-stained things. We planned to stay in the kitchen and not show ourselves. It was growing dark when we heard a car roll up to the front door. We peeked and saw some men getting out, we just could hear them speaking.

"It is a blamed mess to be in but I'm glad we are here and not out tryin' to find shelter on the desert. But if I had knowed about all this I would have stayed home. Melviny don't need no seed loan now."

Soon we heard a scraping of chairs, some one threw open a door, a laugh. We crept into a little adjoining room where we could see the ceremony. There was no light in the little room, we made our way carefully. The bridal pair had just risen to take their places before the minister. Ma gasped and clutched my hand till it hurt.

"Dave! Oh, Dave!" she whispered.

She stood trembling for a moment, she leaned against my shoulder and clutched me fiercely while she tried to get command of herself.

"I'm a fifth wheel now but I guess I can stand it as well as the next one. After all, Dave's forty years old, he's got a right to marry if he wants to, only I hoped he would wait until I was gone. He's all I've got."

We slipped in as quietly as we could. No one noticed us.

'Lisa stood just back of her mother with some one by her side. When the minister pronounced the couple man and wife, they turned and saw us for the first time.

"Ma! Why, Ma! I—I—didn't know you were coming," stammered Dave.

'Lisa and her young man had quietly taken the place the other couple had held a second before. Before the confusion was over between Ma and Dave, the minister was pronouncing a second benediction. Surprise number two! Carmon, our polite young host of the night before. More surprise, Melvina didn't know it was going to happen. A surprised, baffled look came into her face. She turned to Ma.

"I know just how you feel, Mother Dallas. I don't blame you a bit now. I didn't want 'Lisa to marry Carmon Oryes. I know how you feel."

A tear trembled on her lash, one rolled down Ma's cheek. In another moment they were in each other's arms. After all it was a happy time. Lots of tears but mutual forgiveness all around.

"I'm glad you came, Ma. I hated like the devil to keep my wedding a secret from you but I was afraid you wouldn't like it and I thought you would take it better if it was past helpin' before you knew."

"If I have been the kind of mother that would make you think that-a-way, then I guess I had a come-uppance comin' to me. Anyhow it is all right, son. Melviny and me understand each other."

We were at supper. I sat next to 'Lisa. "How do you manage to talk to your Carmon?" I asked her.

"Listen with my eyes," she replied.

They are still laughing at Ma and me for occupying the bridal sheep-camp before the bride had even seen it. Carmon Oryes is "the boss."

Very sincerely,
Elinore Pruitt Stewart

Although Elinore had doubts about the caliber of the *Folk-Say* collection, she felt a new impetus to write for publication, so in the spring of 1933, the family took Elinore up into the mountains to camp in "the Cedars," the land Grandma Stewart had homesteaded. She wanted to recover her health, refresh her spirits, and renew her writing career. They helped her set up camp, erecting a large tent and hauling in a stove. She began a diary-letter to her longtime correspondent Josephine Harrison.

May 16, [1933]
Burntfork
Dear Josephine Harrison:

For a long time you have been in my mind as you are always in my heart. In mind because I am having an adventure which I wish to share with you as much as I can. To do that I shall set down the happenings of each day, But first I must tell you why I am having an adventure at all. My health has begun to fail. I arose in the morning just as tired as when I went to bed, everything any one said hurt me, even their very kindness enraged me. I had to watch myself every minute to keep from doing or saying something regrettable. It has been a terribly cold, hard winter, hard on stock and hard on people. Then, when it normally warms up and pleasanter days come, came great snows. Everything was *so* miserable, thousands of sheep lying snowed under—smothered and crushed under the terrible weight of snow. Thousands of cattle with no feed left after the long winter standing in snow, midsides deep; starving. Nowhere to lie down, no shelter from the driving snow laden gales. And our own long struggle looked so useless then.

When Jerrine came home so weak and ill my heart was joyful because I had a big, airy, sunny room, a big clean bed and plenty of wholesome food for her. I was glad that she could sleep and rest the clock around if she wanted to, as often as she wanted to. I was glad that the flowers she loved grew right up to the door and nodded in at the windows. My garden has always been a thing of joy to me, never failing, and many kinds of joy. The kind of work I like out in the sunshine with the birds and bees, the great mountains to admire and speculate about while I worked—deepest enjoyment, but not idle enjoyment, quiet time to mentally digest bits I had read, knowing all the while that the generous earth would supply in plenty my own table and have some left from my own garden for those less fortunate. Then, when the Red Cross trucks began coming we *all* had the great pleasure of having bags of food to help out with.

I have had more than half a century of such happiness. A great deal of worry and sorrow, too, but never a worry or sorrow that was not offset by a purple iris, a lark, a bluebird, or a dewy morning glory.

Until this spring.

I suddenly lost courage. It all seemed so futile, just treadmill routine, nothing really settled.

One day I overheard Jerrine saying "Dad, what is the matter with Mama? She never talks with us as she used to, goes around as silent as a clam."

Something was wrong—they had guessed, but they did n't know how wrong. They decided that a long rest away from every thing was what I needed. I could think of no place so restful as this spot—up in the juniper hills. I have always liked the fragrant quiet and the silence of this remote spot. It is a part of Mother Stewart's land and, except that it is fenced, nothing has ever been done to it. Around by the road, as we have to go it is five miles from home, but it is not so far straight across. Twice each week they will come to see how I am.

I have a rusty old stove, salvaged from our junk pile which serves my purpose, I have a large tent, and a very comfortable bed, plenty of home-grown food. This is my third night there, last night my first alone. I am not afraid, there is nothing to fear, but I could n't sleep at all last night. The wind blew and a tent can make so many queer noises. Many times it sounded as if some one was crawling in. But at last morning came, and I heard a lark as soon as I stepped outside.

May 17—I shall write to dear defenseless you each day as long as the pad lasts. Whether it ever gets mailed is another matter. As you see, I am safely through another night, rested and nerves quieted. I forgot to tell you in the general summing up of misery that a cough has fastened itself upon me, been my unwelcome guest all winter. I am better of that already. No cough at all last night and just one spell this morning. The wind roared last night but it did not annoy me at all. I raised the tent wall so I could see the stars and the tardy, sullen moon, so late in coming up. I saw the very first streaks of dawn this morning and arose in time to see all the wild life this place affords going about their affairs. I saw a badger mincing along a hillside, presently a tawny beauty of a coyote came loping along and stopped to pass the discourtesies of the day with the badger. Presently the coyote concluded he didn't want badger for breakfast, went on after a rabbit—which outran him going up hill. Did you know that a rabbit can outrun anything going uphill, but is easily overtaken going down hill? The front legs are shorter and weaker. He hurls himself with his powerful back legs so that in going down hill he is clumsy and falls; that's why rabbits always make for the high ground. That is—Jack rabbits, the little cotton tail seeks a hole in which to hide.

My spring is about four blocks from my tent, it is down in a steep wash. I was surprised this morning when I went for water to see a crane stalking along the branch. I stood up on the bank watching him getting his breakfast of luckless waterbugs. On my way back, a sage hen fluttered across the path, uttering the most piteous cries. That means she has a nest somewhere near. Perhaps I'll find it. Now I've had a cup of coffee, a scrambled egg and a biscuit so I am going out to burn off some sage brush so I can plant a garden.

May 18—Jerrine came yesterday. I wonder if you will forgive me if I tell you that I admire my girl's character? She's sterling. She has her own code of morals and manners and she acts accordingly. She annoys me many times, enrages me because she is accepting life as she finds it and, as far as I can see, is not trying to direct its course. She has had many chances to make friends with influential people. She treats them exactly as she does anyone else. She says she won't be a wire puller, that friendship to her is a beautiful thing, a pansy, a spring morning, but never a rung in a ladder. All that is lovely in theory, but foolish in practice, it seems to me. Any way, she is a fine girl. In *any* emergency I know exactly what she will do. It will be right.

Now that I have that sentimental spasm off my chest and I ask you to forgive me and for doing what you would do, I can tell you that Jerrine is as brown as a berry, has rounded out until she is almost fat. She enjoys life. She can do any kind of ranch work. Recently she bought for herself a vaccination needle so that she can claim for herself the pleasure of vaccinating the calves against blackleg. But that is not what I wanted for her, I have big strong boys for that. I wanted her to develop her talent so that she could give to the world the beauty she sees so readily. I told her so. She said—"I don't see any beauty in a swollen dead calf. I do see beauty in this shining clean needle filled with life-saving serum, thrust into the shoulder of a calf that would surely die an agonizing death otherwise."

May 18—I've been thinking of you all this morning, wishing you could share the quiet, the sunshine, the blue, blue sky and the breeze right off the snow capped mountains. I went for a long walk yesterday, not a flower, hardly a blade of grass hardly to be seen. In the gorge below my spring is a great ice bed, it must be six feet thick, ten feet wide and more than two hundred feet long. There will certainly be ice there throughout June, so that I can have ice for my needs that long.

When Jerrine was here we went to the spring. We both were wearing men's shoes, we made broad tracks. Yesterday when I went down for water I was surprised to see deer tracks in *our* tracks. Deer for neighbors! That will be fine for everything but my garden. Yesterday I put a cup of salt on a rock by the spring. This morning the salt is gone, so it is really a deer.

I have some very pleasant neighbors. A bluebird lives in a hole in a big juniper right out in front of my tent. A robin inspects every bit of soil I spade; two cedar wax wings dine near enough to my door so that I can see they are eating juniper berries. Two birds, known as camp robbers, passed over. They stopped only long enough to find a few scraps the chipmunks had failed to gobble. I have heard the camp robbers are reincarnated prospectors. It is said they are never found except in mineral bearing regions. No gold on cedar crest.

May 20—I went to work this morning before breakfast. I became so interested in gardening that I did n't think of even coffee until the sun turned. I have a fine oval bed planted to mixed flowers and I have a row of sweet peas. In my little vegetable garden I have four rows each of radishes, lettace, cress, cabbage, celery, beets, turnips, rut-abagas, onions, peas, tomatoes and salsify. Later I shall plant beans, corn, cucumber, squash, pumpkin. Also I am going to try a few peanuts, watermelon, muskmelon and okra. I am experimenting on a number of things they claim will not grow here. The land is not irrigated and is even higher than the ranch. It is something over 7,000 feet down there.

May 21—I think I am keeping this sort of diary to keep track of time. Anyway, this being Sunday I went for a long walk. The wind is blowing so that it is impossible to stay in the tent in any comfort—so I have brought this little pad way over here among the thickest cedars and am enjoying the wonderful view. There is so much snow in the mountains that it looks pretty desolate. I had more than one reason for coming up here. I really needed the rest, but the real reason was that I hoped to work on a long contemplated piece of writing. About a year ago a Dr. B.A. Botkin of the Oklahoma U. asked me for a contribution to his book, "Folks Say." It seems he puts out one such book each year from the University Press. I had never seen a copy of "Folks Say," but I sent him what he asked for, and when my copy reached me I regretted contributing, for to me "Folks Say" is trash. However, next came a letter from the head of the journalism department saying that they print books twice yearly and asked me to get to work on some Oklahoma subject, as they are confined to Oklahoma. So I came up here with the intention of working on white childhood in the Indian Territory. I very much doubt that I can do it. For such a recital should be the truth and no one would believe the actual truth of my own childhood fifty years ago.

Here is a test for your credulity. I was ten years old before I knew any one could die without being shot. That is absolutely true. I saw my father and two other white men barricade themselves and shoot all day long in a bloody fight to the end with thirty drunken men of mixed Indian-Negro blood. My first teacher was taken from our little log school house and hanged for horse stealing. Every family had a feud or was in some way mixed with them. I came up in turbulent times and there were hundreds just like me. It was a state of affairs peculiar to the place and not to any one family. So when I look back and reflect on the every day happenings I wonder what I *can* write of that won't be shocking.

June 10—It is a long time since I have scribbled a line. Weather conditions ran me out. I had to go home for a while. The wind was so strong that I was unable to keep my tent walls down; the snow came down so fast and so heavily that a roof had its appeal. I was needed at home, too; Jerrine wasn't feeling well, the work *is* heavy for her. So I stayed to help plant the garden, and to cut the potato seed for the boys to plant. Jerrine got over her "period of depression" and so here I am—back again. I have a little garden and some flowers up here. The Picket Pins [a type of squirrel] and the chipmunks are determined to dig out every seed and plant.

June 11—Camping out is n't *all* a joy. Big flies come in and ruin any food exposed for a moment. It is so cool in the mornings that the flies do not stir much before sunrise, so I outwit them by doing all of my cooking for the day as soon as it is light enough to get about. All the world is very beautiful then, too. My camp is on a high hill. I can see for miles down the valley. It is a wonderful picture in the early dawn. Irrigating water has been turned on, so that all the ranches look like large lakes when the sun first comes from behind the twin buttes. All the country around is piled and left in terraces, palisades and buttes just as it must have been when the ice age broke up. In the hush of early morning it does n't take too much imagination to picture the scene here when God divided the waters. These clear, moonlight nights have been revealing.

For some reason I have been unable to sleep. In my wakeful hours I look out upon a night panorama of the world in its first animal life. The picture is large. Miles and miles of a long mountain with juniper over the sides but no timber on top. That makes a fine back ground for the presentation of the huge creatures whose bones today are buried in the [badlands] that form this mountain. In the moon light the junipers take the forms of mammoths, dinosaurs and many others whose names I am unable to spell. I never tire of looking at the picture, the great beasts seem to be feeding peacefully, not with the snarls and screams I have always associated with them in reading of them.

This mountain has an entirely different aspect by day.

I happen to know that this mountain is a regular hangout for moonshiners. Many times I see camp fires gleaming—not moonshiner's fires, but the fires of sheep herders. They kindle fires to frighten prowling coyotes.

Here, Elinore's journal ends abruptly. Clyde, Jr., who had been riding after cattle in the Bald Mountain range beyond Cedar Crest, stopped by to check on his mother. Finding her delirious in the tent, he raced home for his father and a wagon to bring Elinore back to the ranch. Two weeks later, too weak to finish her diary, she wrote one last letter.

June 26, [1933]
Dear Josephine Harrison,

All day I have been thinking of you, wishing you could lie on my couch by the open window and look out at my beloved flowers—lillies aflame, iris clean and erect—pansies and clove pinks—

You could see the mountains and you would know that on their cool slopes columbines are nodding, that higher up, under the edge of the snow, anemones are still blooming. You would like the friendly little robins that are out in my garden pulling worms out of the wet soil. I have been camping up in the juniper hills where it is so high and dry that this irrigated spot looks beautiful to me. While I was in camp I kept a kind of diary which I meant to send to you. Shall I? Look at the I s. Conceited person—

The Fort Bridger Memorial is being dedicated today—Mrs. Roosevelt and all our state dignitaries there—Jerrine went over to enjoy it all, that is why I came down from camp—to attend to things while she is gone. You would beam if you could see how sturdy and strong Jerrine is— almost fat much to her disgust. Times are slowly mending they say— Perhaps my youngsters may get back to school yet.

I have four books which I think you would like—'The Road Mender,'

'Wak'Kon Tah', 'A Victorian Village' and 'Reminnices'. This last is a book
of travel by a sister of Bayard Taylor.[2] If you haven't seen these books
may I send them? Hoping you are enjoying this fine weather.

Your friend,

Elinore P. Stewart

By mid-September, Elinore had become so ill that she had to be taken to
the Rock Springs hospital, where she underwent a gallbladder operation.
Although the doctors termed the surgery successful, on October 8, at age
fifty-seven, she died from a blood clot in the brain. She leaned back on her
pillow, turned toward Clyde, and said, "Night, night." Josephine Harrison
received the diary-letter twenty-two days after Elinore's death.

Several newspapers published obituaries or news items on Elinore's
death. On November 8, 1933, the *Rocky Mountain News* ran an article
under the headline "Ex-Denverite Dies: Mrs. Elinore Pruitt Stewart Noted
for Published Letters."

> Mrs. Elinore Pruitt Stewart, formerly of Denver, who became widely
> known about 15 years ago thru her published "Letters of a Woman Home-
> steader," died Friday at Burnt Fork, Wyo., friends here learned yesterday.
>
> Mrs. Stewart lived in Denver for several years prior to going to a home-
> stead near Burnt Fork 20 years ago. As a result of her experiences on the
> homestead she wrote a number of letters which friends induced her to
> publish. They first appeared in the Atlantic Monthly and later in book form.
>
> Surviving her are her husband, Clyde Stewart; a daughter by a former
> marriage, Jerrine Rupert, and three sons, Clyde, Robert and Calvin Stewart.

2. *The Roadmender* is by Margaret Fairless Barber (1869–1901), who also wrote
under the pseudonym of Michael Fairless. First appearing in the *Pilot,* the stories
include "The Roadmender," "Out of the Shadow," and "At the White Gate." The first
editions are not dated, but subsequent publications date from 1902 to 1925. Barber
also wrote *Stories Told to Children* (1915). The University of Oklahoma Press
published *Wah'kon-tah,* subtitled *The Osage and the White Man's Road,* by John
Joseph Mathews in 1932. *A Victorian Village* (1929), by Lizette Woodworth Reese,
contains accounts of daily life in a small English village, and *Reminiscences* is
supposedly a book of travel by a sister of Bayard Taylor. The sister mentioned could
be Annie Carey; however, no travel book exists in her bibliography. An annotated
bibliography of books mentioned by Stewart in her letters and books can be found
in Lindau [George], "*My Blue and Gold Wyoming,*" 360–75.

The family buried Elinore in the Burntfork Pioneer Cemetery, a site as sparsely populated as her "blue and gold Wyoming." Meadow grass and wild flowers blanket the field, and a spring-fed creek trickles over stones nearby. A sandstone slab, once the front steps of her homestead, now serves as her monument, and nameplates hand cast in bronze by Clyde, Jr., mark her grave and those of other family members.

In the years after Elinore's death, all four of the children periodically lived at the homestead, helping their father with the ranch work. During the school term, Robert attended high school in Cheyenne until his graduation in 1934. In 1935, Clyde, Jr., attended the University of Wyoming at Laramie; he married in 1937 and moved to Yellowstone Park and then to Missoula, Montana. Robert found work on the Coulee Dam project in Washington, and by 1942, Calvin, Robert, and Jerrine had all moved east. The children settled into their careers and began families of their own. Clyde, Jr., worked in construction, Calvin became a machinist, Robert began a career in steel erection and founded American Steel Erectors, Inc., and Jerrine married Frank Wire, a Philadelphia millwright, and had four children.

From 1940 through 1943, Clyde leased the ranch. The next year, Calvin and his wife moved back to Wyoming and began ranching again. The family decided to sell the land in 1945, and Clyde moved with Calvin and his family to Whitefish, Montana. There, in 1948, at age eighty, Clyde died and was buried beside his wife in their Wyoming valley. An era had ended; the world of The Woman Homesteader had passed.

A new generation of readers is now beginning to learn about the life of Elinore Pruitt Stewart and enjoy the adventures of The Woman Homesteader. The University of Nebraska Press published a paperback edition of Letters of a Woman Homesteader, with a foreword by the novelist Jessamyn West, in 1961 and one of Letters on an Elk Hunt in 1979. In the latter year, the movie Heartland premiered and gained worldwide acclaim. An independent film financed in part by a grant from the National Endowment for the Humanities, it was inspired by Letters of a Woman Homesteader.[3] In

3. A Wilderness Women/Filmhaus Production directed by Richard Pearce, produced by Annick Smith, and written by Beth Ferris, Heartland has been awarded the Best Independent Film at the U.S. Film Festival, the Grand Prix Golden Bear Award at the Berlin International Film Festival, and the prestigious American Playhouse Neil Simon Award for 1983–1984, among other honors.

1982, Houghton Mifflin reissued *Letters of a Woman Homesteader* in paper-back, including original illustrations by N. C. Wyeth.[4] The University of Nebraska Press reprinted its edition in 1989.

Elinore often lamented that she had little money to buy gifts for her friends. As she wrote to Miss Wood on February 19, 1925, she had only one quarrel with life: "It will not be long enough to get my loving done up. I just love people, I just love to love them." Her life and her writings have become her eternal gifts of love in ways she could never have imagined.

4. Since 1982, *Letters of a Woman Homesteader* has sold an average of more than nine thousand copies a year. The success of Stewart's work prompted Houghton Mifflin to issue a new edition of the *Homesteader* letters in April 1988.

The Literary Flowering of
Elinore Pruitt Stewart

🌿 Literary scholars and historians have generally believed that Elinore
Pruitt Stewart's two published books, *Letters of a Woman Homesteader,*
1914, and *Letters on an Elk Hunt,* 1915, are merely lively autobiographical
accounts of the settling of the West as seen through the female eye. This
interpretation is accurate, for the most part, because Stewart describes in
detail the joys and hardships of homesteading and raising a family in
pioneer Wyoming, and readers can glean much about our frontier heritage
from her writing. But Stewart's writings, important historically, not only
should be read as reports of frontier life for social documentation but also
should be appreciated for their contribution to American literature. Although Elinore did base her letters on her own experiences, I believe that
she deliberately wrote for publication, embroidering her facts with fiction,
and that she firmly and self-consciously relied on literary tradition when
composing her works, publishing under the guise of "found literature."

Though Stewart's formal schooling was brief, she spent her entire life on
a quest for knowledge through reading. Her first real contact with the
literary world probably came from Mrs. Coney, the widow who employed
her as a nurse during her stay in Denver. The wealthy lady not only chose
books for Stewart to read but also introduced her to a genteel Victorian
culture she had never before experienced. Later, after Stewart moved to
Wyoming, she continued to receive books from Mrs. Coney, as well as from
her ever growing circle of correspondents.

Stewart referred to several works in *Letters of a Woman Homesteader* and
Letters on an Elk Hunt, giving some clues to her literary background. In
addition, her unpublished letters mentioned books and poems she had
read, as well as names of newspapers, magazines, articles, and writers

appealing to her. In my research of her unpublished letters and manu-scripts, I also discovered—on the back of a page of the handwritten manuscript of her novel *Sand and Sage,* composed in the early 1920s—a typewritten list of book titles. Apparently, Jerrine had been playing with her mother's typewriter, for after a few lines of experimentation, Jerrine began typing the titles of books stacked nearby, simply to have something to copy. Stewart, always short of paper, must have needed extra pages and used the scrap pieces to continue her novel in progress.[1] Along with her acquisitions of newspapers, magazines, and government pamphlets, these books formed a diversified literary milieu for the Wyoming author. By analyzing Stewart's reading background, one can begin to establish her literary heritage.

Influences evident in Stewart's work include a sense of nature and the individual in nature, a tradition that echoes the transcendentalists and earlier-nineteenth-century romantics. From late-nineteenth- and early-twentieth-century realists she inherited an interest in dialect and local color, and from her acquaintances and her reading she developed an eclectic religious philosophy. In addition, classic and popular children's literature, with its sentimentalism and strong didactic element, influenced her choice of subjects and themes. However, the most important literary heritage to affect her writing came from the epistolary tradition.

During the eighteenth and nineteenth centuries, the "familiar letter" of the genteel class flowered into a literary genre of major importance and popularity.[2] Letters, especially those the reader believed had not been intended for publication, satisfied the public's taste for verisimilitude. This form, one Stewart may not have realized she was employing in the begin-ning, linked her to an outside world and an audience with whom she could share her experiences and talent. In addition, the letter genre, with its aura of authenticity, its journey patterns, its use of the familiar style, its struc-tural unity, and its stylized Victorian conventions, easily encompassed the type and variety of subjects she wished to record.[3]

---

1. For an annotated listing, see Lindau [George], "My Blue and Gold Wyo-ming," 360–89.

2. According to Godfrey Frank Singer, in *The Epistolary Novel,* the revival of novels of letters in the later nineteenth to early twentieth centuries in America paralleled their renaissance in England.

3. Ruth Perry, in *Women, Letters, and the Novel,* explains that "the letter, as form,

The claim of authenticity was central to the epistolary mode.[4] Houghton-Mifflin, the original publisher of *Homesteader,* chose to emphasize the accuracy of the letters in a special note, claiming they were "genuine letters" that were "printed as written, except for occasional omissions and the alteration of some of the names." However, the reader can only theorize why the editors deemed this notation necessary. Perhaps because Stewart wrote so vividly about situations many readers would have trouble believing, they considered it important to underline the veracity of the narratives. Or possibly they added the characteristic claim to comply with the conventions of epistolary fiction.[5] Whatever the publisher's reason for the assertion, one wonders whether Stewart was simply writing to a friend or whether she meant the letters for publication.

Stewart herself admitted in a letter to Miss Wood on February 19, 1914: "Publication was no part of my thoughts when I was writing them, I was just trying to enterest Mrs. Coney. . . . No one could know her and not love her and I used to think she was lonely so that is how the 'Letters' came to be." Her insistence on the veracity of the letters raises many questions. Were the letters really written to entertain one housebound lady? When Stewart later gave up all hope of ever having any of her stories published again, she continued writing letters and stories to her friends, mainly lonely old people, to bring some joy to their lives. She repeated over and over again in her letters how much she loved helping elderly people.

Or did Mrs. Coney, an avid reader and devotee of the *Atlantic Monthly,* suggest to Stewart that she too should attempt the type of writing being published at that time and that her adventures as a homesteader would be a worthwhile subject? Partway through the correspondence, either Stewart or Mrs. Coney may have realized that the letters contained material inter-

was a perfect frame for travel reports or essays of any length in this new age which so valued collecting information" (7).

4. As Robert Adam Day states in *Told in Letters,* "The use of letters afforded a writer many advantages in meeting the most universal requirement of authenticity" (86).

5. Such assertions fed the public's taste for first-person narratives, for "personally verifiable documents" (xii), notes Perry in *Women, Letters, and the Novel.* Perry adds, "Readers loved best of all, those letters which they believed were not for public scrutiny" (66).

esting enough to be shared with the world. The arrangement and content of *Letters of a Woman Homesteader* promote this argument. Why did Stewart, an intimate friend of Mrs. Coney's, need to explain how she came to homestead in Wyoming? Wouldn't her former employer already know this? And why did Stewart wait until December 2, 1912, to tell Mrs. Coney? Granted, when Stewart dated her letters, she neglected to include the year, and their chronological arrangement becomes a difficult task for any editor. But since this particular letter also mentions her marriage and the death of her first son, it seems odd that she would explain at all unless to give background to a public unaware of her former life.

Perhaps Stewart felt bound to authenticate her own claim of accuracy because of her publisher's desire for firsthand accounts. The *Atlantic Monthly* editor Ellery Sedgwick, who first published Stewart's letters, wrote in his autobiography, *The Happy Profession:*

> Of its nature, Literature is aristocratic, a little deferential to its long line of ancestors, a little lacking in (shall we say?) coziness, and to anyone desirous of building a magazine subscription list, a certain geniality of approach is very useful. I could see that a fringe of informality would be of great advantage to the magazine. . . . I bethought me of the warmest and friend-liest among the satellites of Literature and found them in familiar letters. Very soon I began a definite search for them. What I wanted was an unpremeditated record of interesting happenings by an interesting person. Grammar could be overlooked, spelling could come to heel, punctuation could be peppered and salted at will. If only interest were there, and personality, I could stake out an original *Atlantic* claim in the pleasantest of all the outlying territories of Literature. (197)

Behind Stewart's insistence that her letters were "unpremeditated" may have been a fear that Sedgwick or her readers would discover that her letters were "made-to-order" and that she had an underlying need for a public audience and for financial reward. It is curious, though, that no-where did either Stewart or the publisher of *Homesteader* claim that the letters were *not* fiction. Houghton Mifflin asserted only that the letters were "printed as written" and were "genuine letters," that is, correspondence sent through the mail.[6]

6. "Simple writing that lacked ingenuity" and "direct reporting of lucid experi-ences" were becoming the favored literary styles, states Perry in *Women, Letters, and*

Of these theories, I believe that Stewart began writing to Mrs. Coney simply to entertain her elderly friend, basing her stories on actual incidents but embellishing them to add interest. Then, through the Coney family's acquaintance with Sedgwick, the editor became aware of the letters and, sometime around 1911 or 1912, suggested publication. Whether Stewart consciously or unconsciously intended her first letters for an audience beyond Mrs. Coney, whether her tales were authentic accounts or imaginatively embroidered anecdotes, they worked well and pleased an audience hungry for realistic stories, especially about the West.

Letters on an Elk Hunt was another matter, for Stewart explicitly wrote it for publication. On March 24, 1914, the *Atlantic Monthly* expressed its interest in publishing further adventures of its Wyoming correspondent and arranged for a new series to appear in the magazine that autumn. The entire work was to concentrate on the preparations and events of an elk-hunting expedition. That fall, on September 27, 1914, while in her elk-hunt camp, Stewart again wrote to Miss Wood of her plans. "All that I love most and believe you would like I am trying to put truthfully in the new series soon to appear in the Atlantic," she explained. But she admitted, "If in any letters it seems as if I enjoyed *hunting* you will know that is humbug." This collection has no publisher's note to verify its authenticity, leading the reader again to various speculations. Stewart may, in this volume, have applied even more imagination to her sketches, may have fictionalized more accounts, causing the editors to judge the work more fictional than true. Or the publisher may have banked on her established reputation for authenticity and considered a foreword unnecessary. Authentic or not, the elk-hunt letters too proved popular with the American public, and Houghton Mifflin published them in book form in 1915, the same year that they appeared serially in the *Atlantic Monthly*.

Besides adding authenticity, the epistolary mode enabled Stewart to develop and organize her wide range of subjects, episodes as diverse as the southern feud between the families of Zebulon Pike and his lover Pauline, the death of Stewart's firstborn son, and the sewing bee for Cora Belle. In the *Homesteader* letters, Stewart sustained a single plot line involving the daily events in a woman homesteader's life, from her arrival to her experi-

---

the Novel. The Victorian reader believed that "unvarnished truth could best be found in simple language and direct sentences" (75).

ences while "proving up." Marching in and out of this plot are various characters—Zebbie, Cora Belle, Mrs. Louderer—each with his or her own subplot. These separate narratives, depicting people and events in Stewart's life, could be lifted out of the collection and could stand alone, although some subplots are better developed than others.[7]

Letters on an Elk Hunt also has a single plot, the narrative of a fall hunting expedition, and except for the curious inclusion of the almost autobiographical Connie Willis story that opens the collection, all of the letters describe incidents pertaining to the elk hunt. But *Elk Hunt* progresses more rigidly. The time is chronological with no deviation, and Stewart regulated the unnarrated time more precisely than in *Homesteader,* with letters usually at three-day intervals. Her correspondence served a specific purpose, and Stewart faithfully adhered to her task. Perhaps this accounts for the lack of spontaneity in the *Elk Hunt* letters, the absence of the authentic feeling found in the *Homesteader* collection. Her audience became not simply dear old Mrs. Coney but "The Public," and Stewart evidently felt that she must meet them at the front door in her Sunday best—starched apron, polished shoes, and corset. In her everyday clothes, she moved more easily.

A discernible pattern or theme cannot be as easily discovered in Stewart's previously unpublished letters. The story-letters written to Florence Allen, Mrs. Coney's daughter, seem to be an annual event commemorating the March 9 birthday of Stewart's beloved employer and friend, but the subjects and themes are varied. Friendship seems to be the major concern in the letters to Miss Wood, and Stewart took care to see that the southern lady felt special and loved. The letters to Mr. Zaiss, abounding in sensual description, all seem to be introductions to a foreign existence, appropriately written to one who was blind and lived in a different culture. However, no single plot or theme comparable to that of the *Homesteader* or the *Elk Hunt* collection exists in the letters to Mrs. Allen, Miss Wood, or Mr. Zaiss except for the normal unfolding of life. Only in the Culberson series of children's stories, where a small core of characters dominate the different plots, did Elinore attempt her former continuity.

As Stewart's writing progressed, she drew slightly away from a continu-

7. In *Epistolarity: Approaches to a Form,* Janet Gurkin Altman views this relationship of parts to whole as a well-organized mosaic: "Within the epistolary work the letter has both a dependent and an independent status. Like tesserae, each

ing story embedded within several letters to a more formal short story, only perfunctorily prefaced by her salutation "Dear Friend." After the publication of the Culberson stories in the *Youth's Companion,* the short story itself became her genre. No longer did a plot string itself throughout several letters. Seldom did her chatty intimacies of daily life frame her fictions. Instead, her stories, especially those sent to Mrs. Allen, seem to be appendixes to her personal letters, and the letters themselves, although still intriguing, appear to be more newsy than crafted. Also, Stewart's 1930 story of a wild horse hunt is separate from the letter announcing her intention of writing it and from the following letter apologizing for her seemingly uncivilized behavior.

Only in her 1931 letter to Mr. Zaiss did Stewart revert somewhat to her former carefully crafted method of combining everyday life on the frontier with fictional characters or embroidered episodes. This particular letter began on October 8 with a description of a wood-gathering trip to a deserted sawmill and continued on the sixteenth with the fictionalized adventure of Ma Gillis and her Blazing Star quilt. After a brief apology—"I must stop now before you get so tired that you will never write me again"— Stewart noted in a postscript that she completed the narrative on November 13. However, even the Ma Gillis story was divorced from the personal portion of the letter by a week's lapse of time and a new salutation, showing how Stewart had advanced from short sketches within letters to the more formal short story form.

In her efforts to please the reading public, Stewart kept a wary eye on the popular literary trends of her day. She must have noted that many successful contemporary writers captivated their audiences by borrowing Victorian conventions to add sentimental appeal to their plots. This was especially true of her own favorite writers, Eleanor H. Porter, the author of *Miss Billy* (1911) and *Pollyanna* (1915), and Kate Douglas Wiggin, famous for her Rebecca series, all works Stewart owned.[8] Even the classic works on her kitchen shelf, books by Charles Dickens, Sir Walter Scott, William Makepeace Thackeray, and James Fenimore Cooper, as well as children's

---

individual letter enters into the composition of the whole without losing its identity as a separate entity with recognizable borders" (167).

8. For further explanation of sentimental patterns, see Reed, *Victorian Conventions,* and Kaplan, *Sacred Tears.*

stories by Louisa May Alcott, Robert Louis Stevenson, Horatio Alger, Jr., Sir Arthur Conan Doyle, and Johann Wyss, employed many sentimental techniques. Stewart read them all with a writer's eye.

Unfortunately, Stewart's reliance on sentimentalism thwarted her publication efforts. After the elk-hunt and Culberson series, when editors began rejecting Stewart's stories, she could not understand why. Her insecurities as a writer, stemming from her lack of formal schooling and her isolation from the literary and publishing worlds, increased Stewart's reliance on the once popular Victorian conventions rather than on her own intuition and experience. Desperately needing money to finance the ranch, she tried harder than ever to employ the romantic themes and sentimental conventions that had worked with her public audience in the past, an audience whose tastes were now turning toward realism.[9]

Doubt of her own ability further inhibited Stewart. Throughout her letters, she continually apologized for their length and quality. "I really dont think you've done any thing to merit such punishment as having another letter flung at you," she wrote to Miss Wood on June 12 (ca. 1914), "but that is one of the afflictions that goes with my friendship." To Mr. Zaiss, on April 6, 1929, she declared, "There is much I wish to say but I am such a bungler of words that it is hard for me to express myself without seeming mushy."

Another reason Stewart was unable to find publishers for her stories may have come from her deep respect for both the *Atlantic Monthly* and Ellery Sedgwick. Even the acceptance of her works in the *Youth's Companion* tied in with Sedgwick, a former editor of this family magazine. After being published in such prestigious magazines, Stewart was not impressed by lesser periodicals. Furthermore, she remained faithful in her friendship with Sedgwick. Such fidelity had both positive and negative effects. The readership of the magazine brought Stewart national, even international, fame. But Sedgwick, a busy editor who typically would not have had time to advise each author on how to write and who admitted that he liked the

---

9. "The letter form, with its minute, voluminous, and easy circumstantiality," according to Herbert Ross Brown in *The Sentimental Novel in America, 1789–1860,* presented "ample opportunities for didactic and sentimental appeal, and its comparative formlessness, made it a tempting model for beginners" (52). He adds, "To the Sentimentalist, it provided an unrivaled means of depicting every tremor of the feeling heart" (72).

informality and rusticity of the letter form, did little to nurture Stewart's talent. He warned her in a March 24, 1914, letter, "You will unquestionably get invitations to write elsewhere, but it is my honest opinion that, for the present, it will be best for you not to scatter your seed, and, above all, not to cheapen your material by writing too much." Then, on August 27, 1914, rather than giving her concrete advice on how to improve her writing, he further cautioned her, "You need not try to write regularly, for I have an idea that you are one of the geniuses who write best when the spirit moves them." Moreover, he advised her to increase the story interest, when local color was Stewart's strength. So she did not "scatter her seed" and actively seek other publishers.

In 1919, an interesting change in her writing occurred. Stewart, perhaps influenced by the women's movement, began to draw her female characters with more spirit. Beginning with the publication of "The Return of the Woman Homesteader," Stewart began rejecting the conventions of passive sentimentalism that she had relied on in her earlier efforts to appeal to and enlarge her audience. Instead of descriptions of an orphan strewing pine boughs on her parents' graves, Stewart began to depict strong characters, especially women. In "The Return of the Woman Homesteader," Mrs. Louderer helped Mrs. Lund break free from her submissiveness to her husband by urging her to write a check for war bonds without his permission. Mrs. Louderer declared: "Fife hundert dollars it is, and for the first time in her life she is free. Never before did she spend a dollar without Lund says so." Mollie-Jane too showed independence when she escaped from the stifling conventions of society to live in the sagebrush and raise sheep, always remaining thirty years old. Even The Woman Homesteader began leaving the confines of her cabin on more daring adventures, such as rehabilitating veterans, tracking moonshiners, visiting depression-era flophouses, and witnessing the brutal treatment of wild horses. These concerns signaled an outward movement from Stewart's personal homesteading adventures toward a more active participation in the moral issues of her day. In addition, Stewart returned to realistic descriptions of everyday scenes similar to the ones that had made her first collection so successful— kitchen curtains made from Jerrine's dress, coyotes howling in the moonlight outside the window, mason jars filled with sauerkraut, and as always, flowers everywhere.

Ironically, it was when Stewart relinquished all hope of publication, and again began writing to please her friends and herself, that the "sentimental spasms," as she later termed her emotional outbreaks, began to give way to realism. Still, Stewart published only three stories between 1919 and 1932, two in *Atlantic Monthly* and one solicited by the Oklahoma Folklore Society. In fact, although she mentioned an interest in entering story-writing contests, the only publishers that we know she submitted manuscripts to were Doubleday and *House Beautiful*, a specialized magazine that did not publish fiction.

Perhaps Stewart did not publish more stories after 1919 because her many household and ranching duties, coupled with her own and her family's health problems, permitted little time for the tedious tasks of submitting and revising manuscripts. A series of articles in the *Saturday Evening Post* in 1925 may also have intimidated her. After reading about how publishers handled manuscripts, she wrote to Houghton Mifflin and thanked the company for being her publisher: "Until I read the article in the Post I had no idea of how fortunate I have been to fall into the hands of Houghton-Mifflin." By this time too, she was sending manuscripts to several correspondents, whose enthusiastic responses may have satisfied her need for an audience. Tragically, her death at age fifty-seven stopped short the literary career that she had hoped to revive in the spring of 1933 when she had secluded herself at "the Cedars" to write.

Although Stewart's list of published works is short, with most of her writings in epistolary form, readers would be wrong to assume that Stewart's works merely contain true, but naive, accounts of a pioneer woman. Naive she was not, for her letters were carefully crafted, with a keen awareness of self and of audience. Her simple and straightforward style, her fresh view of the world, and her keen perception of human nature elevate her writing above the commonplace letter; her work thus deserves a place in our American literary heritage. Yet, despite the literary as well as historical and sociological value of her letters, it is the courage and compassion of Elinore Pruitt Stewart herself, and her persona of The Woman Homesteader, that first drew readers to her and accounts for her continued popularity today.

Many interpretations could be made of Stewart's life. She could be viewed as a victim of society's actions and attitudes toward women. Life did, after all, strike blow after blow to Stewart: her childhood poverty and lack of education, the oppressive labor of working for the railroad, the disintegration of her first marriage and the necessary invention of her widowhood to conceal this social impropriety, her inability to support herself and her daughter adequately in Denver, her hasty remarriage that hints of convenience, the overwhelming family debts to finance the children's education, and her frustrated attempts at becoming an accepted writer in the eastern circles of the publishing world dominated by wealthy, well-educated males.

However, Stewart refused to be a victim, and she became the personification of the unconquerable democratic spirit of the times. Her life was a concrete example of the search for the American Dream. Rather than dwelling on her hardships, Stewart considered life an "adventure" and moved resolutely, even joyfully, forward, doing what she had to do, stepping outside the traditional female role if necessary. She faltered only when attempting to give too much to too many or when judging herself too harshly, perhaps doubting that she could match the stride of The Woman Homesteader. It is difficult to separate Stewart from The Woman Homesteader, who embodied Stewart's physical energy and unconquerable spirit. The main difference is that The Woman Homesteader never had to stay home to mend socks, bake bread, or weed the garden. She always had time and good health.

In Stewart's search for her own identity, her persona became her ideal, her means of self-identification. This blend of person and persona becomes most obvious in her personal, unpublished letters, for she emphasized the positive, joyful aspects of her life, living her belief that "the past is past, let's get on with tomorrow." Her May 22, 1920, letter to Miss Wood summarizes her philosophy of life: "But I can tell you my dear, that it is a relief when things get to their worst. You know what the worst is then and can begin to plan for better things. That's what I have done. I have planted flowers evry where."

The seeds Stewart planted are still yielding blooms today.

❧ BIBLIOGRAPHY

WORKS BY ELINORE PRUITT STEWART

Published (first publication)

"A Homesteader's Holiday." *Atlantic Monthly*, October 1913.
"A Wedding and Other Matters." *Atlantic Monthly*, November 1913.
"The Story of Cora Belle." *Atlantic Monthly*, December 1913.
"The Adventure of the Christmas Tree." *Atlantic Monthly*, January 1914.
"Horse Thieves." *Atlantic Monthly*, February 1914.
"Calling on the Mormons." *Atlantic Monthly*, April 1914.
"A Burnt Fork Santa Claus." *Youth's Companion*, December 10, 1914.
Letters of a Woman Homesteader. Boston: Houghton Mifflin, 1914.
"When Culberson Lost the Sheep." *Youth's Companion*, January 7, 1915.
"Bread upon Waters." *Youth's Companion*, January 21, 1915.
"How the 'Young Uns' Got Their Chance." *Youth's Companion*, February 4, 1915.
"Letters on an Elk Hunt, I." *Atlantic Monthly*, February 1915.
"The Adventure of Crazy Olaf, II." *Atlantic Monthly*, March 1915.
"The Adventure of Danyol and His Mother, III." *Atlantic Monthly*, April 1915.
"Mrs. O'Shaughnessy's Elk, IV." *Atlantic Monthly*, May 1915.
Letters on an Elk Hunt. Boston: Houghton Mifflin, 1915.
"The Return of the Woman Homesteader." *Atlantic Monthly*, May 1919.
"Snow: An Adventure of the Woman Homesteader." *Atlantic Monthly*, December 1923.
"Sagebrush Wedding." In *Folk-Say IV: The Land Is Ours*, edited by B. A. Botkin,
    263–69. Norman: University of Oklahoma Press, 1932.

Unpublished (in the collection of the Elinore Pruitt Stewart estate)

Culberson Series (ca. 1914–15)

"Battles and Victories"
"Things to Be Thankful For"
"Wakin' Up"

Story-Letters to Mrs. Allen (included in this volume)

"Mollie-Jane." 1925.
"Some Where on the Road." August 26, 1925.
"Goof." March 15, 1926.
"Moonshine Cache." August 29, 1926.
"Moonshiners." May 15, 1928.
"Wild Horse Hunt." March 29, 1930.

Other Stories

"A Prospector Who Made Good." Ca. 1924–25.
"As It Happened." Ca. 1910–15?
"Sand and Sage." 1921.

OTHER SOURCES

Letters, Interviews, and Manuscripts

Anderton, Lois. Carnegie Library for Local History. Letter to the Author.
    October 19, 1987.
Basore, B. Oklahoma Historical Society. Letter to the Author. February 3, 1987.
———. Oklahoma Historical Society. Letter to the Author. November 25, 1987.
Bullard, Bess. Telephone Interview. October 21, 1987.
Genres, Eleanor M. Denver Public Library. Letter to the Author. October 31,
    1987.
Knecht, Bob. Kansas State Historical Society. Letter to the Author. December 17,
    1985.
Lee, Elizabeth D. Letter to the Author. December 15, 1987.
Nine, Rhea. Ellis County Historical Society. Letter to the Author. May 10, 1987.
Oliner, Stan. Colorado Historical Society. Letter to the Author. October 16, 1987.
Rice, Mrs. Sam. Telephone Interview. March 3, 1991.
Samuels, Buddy. Lafayette County Historical Society. Letter to the Author.
    November 16, 1987.
Sides, Gail. Roger Mills Deputy County Clerk. Letter to the Author. June 11,
    1987.
Smyers, Kathleen K. Letter to the Author. August 26, 1991.
———. Personal Interview. July 29, 1991.
Stewart, Clyde. Personal Interview. October 17–20, 1985.
———. Telephone Interview. March 24, 1985.
Stewart, Robert. Personal Interview. September 21, 1986.
Stewart, Robert, Clyde Stewart, and Jerrine Wire. Taped Interviews with Beth
    Ferris and Annick Smith. Wilderness Women Project. November 1978.
Wallace, John Ryland. Telephone Interview. January 26, 1988.

Wire, Jerrine. Personal Interview. September 19–22, 1986.

Wright, Mae. Sweetwater County Historical Society. Letter to the Author. November 25, 1985.

Published Sources and Dissertations

Altman, Janet Gurkin. *Epistolarity: Approaches to a Form.* Columbus: Ohio UP, 1982.

Armitage, Susan. "Through Women's Eyes: A New View of the West." In *The Women's West.* Ed. Susan Armitage and Elizabeth Jameson, 9–18. Norman: U of Oklahoma P.

Blavatsky, H. P. *The Key to Theosophy: Being a Clear Exposition, in the Form of Question and Answer, of the Ethics, Science, and Philosophy for the Study of Which the Theosophical Society Has Been Formed.* Pasadena: Theosophical UP, 1889.

Brown, Herbert Ross. *The Sentimental Novel in America, 1789–1860.* New York: Pageant, 1959.

Brown, Opal Hartsell. *Murray County, Oklahoma: In the Heart of Eden.* Wichita Falls, Tex.: Nortex P, 1977.

Brumley, Shelley, and Ricky Manning. "Whitebead School Remembered, Community's History Recounted." *Pauls Valley Democrat* January 18, 1987.

Cronley, Connie. "Hell on Wheels." *Oklahoma Monthly* October 1979: 55–63.

Day, Robert Adam. *Told in Letters: Epistolary Fiction before Richardson.* Ann Arbor: U of Michigan P, 1966.

Dorsett, Lyle W., and Michael McCarty. *The Queen City: A History of Denver.* Boulder: Pruett, 1986.

Frost, Donald McKay. *Notes on General Ashley: The Overland Trail and South Pass.* Worcester, Mass.: Am. Antiquarian Soc., 1945.

Hazlitt, J. M. *From Bluestem to Golden Trend: A Pictorial History of Garvin County, Covering Both the Old and the New.* Fort Worth, Tex.: University Supply and Equipment, 1957.

"The Joys of Homesteading." *Dial* July 1, 1914: 21–22.

Kaplan, Fred. *Sacred Tears: Sentimentality in Victorian Literature.* Princeton: Princeton UP, 1987.

Krishnamurti, J. *At the Feet of the Master.* Chicago: Theosophical Press, n.d.

Larson, T. A. "Wyoming's Contribution to the Regional and National Women's Rights Movement." *Annals of Wyoming* 52.1 (Spring 1980): 2–15.

"Letters on an Elk Hunt," *Boston Transcript,* October 13, 1915.

Lindau [George], Susanne Kathryn. "My Blue and Gold Wyoming: The Life and Letters of Elinore Pruit Stewart." Diss., U of Nebraska, 1988.

Luchetti, Cathy, and Carol Olwell. *Women of the West.* St. George, Utah: Antelope P, 1982.

Meigs, Cornelia, et al., eds. *A Critical History of Children's Literature*. Rev. ed. London: Macmillan, 1953.

"One Hundred Years to History . . . and the Race to Purcell." *Garvin County Advocate* October 14, 1987.

Perry, Ruth. *Women, Letters, and the Novel*. New York: AMS P, 1980.

Powell, Alvin. *The Whitebead Church History and Early Methodism in Chickasaw Nation*. N.p., n.d.

Reed, John R. *Victorian Conventions*. Miami: Ohio UP, 1975.

Sedgwick, Ellery. *The Happy Profession*. Boston: Little, 1946.

Shirk, George H. *Oklahoma Place Names*. Norman: U of Oklahoma P, 1974.

Singer, Godfrey Frank. *The Epistolary Novel: Its Origin, Development, Decline, and Residuary Influence*. 1933. New York: Russell, 1963.

Smith, Sherry L. "Single Women Homesteaders: The Perplexing Case of Elinore Pruitt Stewart." *Western Historical Quarterly* 22 (May 1991): 163–83.

Speer, Bonnie. "Grand: The County Seat That Died." In *Our Ellis County Heritage: 1885–1979*. Vol. 2. Oklahoma City: Bark Curtis, 1979.

"A Woman Homesteader." *New York Times Book Review* June 7, 1914: 259.

Other titles in the series Women in the West *are:*

Martha Maxwell, Rocky Mountain Naturalist
By Maxine Benson

The Art of the Woman: The Life and Work of Elisabet Ney
By Emily Fourmy Cutrer

Emily: The Diary of a Hard-Worked Woman
By Emily French
Edited by Janet Lecompte

The Colonel's Lady on the Western Frontier:
The Correspondence of Alice Kirk Grierson
Edited by Shirley A. Leckie

A Stranger in Her Native Land: Alice
Fletcher and the American Indians
By Joan Mark

So Much to Be Done: Women Settlers
on the Mining and Ranching Frontier
Edited by Ruth B. Moynihan, Susan Armitage,
and Christiane Fischer Dichamp